DISCOVERING PAST LANDSCAPES

Discovering Past Landscapes

edited by
Michael Reed

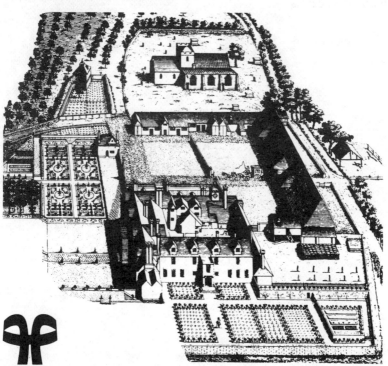

CROOM HELM
London & Canberra

© 1984 Ch. 1. S.T. Coppock, Ch. 2. R.J.P. Kain, Ch. 3. M. Palmer, Ch. 4.
M. Turner, Ch. 5. M. Overton, Ch. 6. C.F. Slade, Ch. 7. B.K. Roberts,
Ch. 8. and all remaining items M. Reed

Croom Helm Ltd, Provident House, Burrell Row,
Beckenham, Kent BR3 1AT

Croom Helm Australia Pty Ltd, 28 Kembla St,
Fyshwick, ACT 2609, Australia

British Library Cataloguing in Publication Data

Discovering past landscapes
   1. England – Historical geography
   I. Reed, Michael, 1930-
   911'.42   DA6000

   ISBN 0-7099-2265-5

Printed and bound in Great Britain

CONTENTS

FIGURES AND TABLES

Figures

Tables

INTRODUCTION

Michael Reed

The word 'landscape' was introduced into English
from Dutch at the end of the sixteenth century as a
technical term employed by painters to describe a
picture of inland scenery as opposed to a sea
picture, a portrait or some other topic. The development of the word in the way in which W.G. Hoskins
used it in the title of his seminal work, The Making
of the English Landscape, first published in 1955,
is nowhere recorded in The Oxford English Dictionary,
its nearest approach being 'inland natural scenery,
or its representation in painting'. The absence of
a dictionary definition of landscape has not hinder-
ed the rapid development of landscape history and
archaeology in the years since 1955, although the
subject matter of this new discipline is difficult
to define briefly and concisely. Nevertheless such
a definition must be attempted.
    The landscape historian takes for his theme the
external physical world that he sees before him,
giving no more than a moment's glance towards those
of a more speculative turn of mind who would call
into question the very existence of this external
physical world. He is interested in every feature
of the most ordinary of landscapes: the mean back
streets of some gritty industrial town, the pattern
of fields and farms in some dull village of the
Midland Plain, the suburban sprawl that surrounds
our larger cities. Thus he is concerned with much
more than scenic beauty, although the aesthetics
that support our appreciation of natural scenery will
be of significance to him since they have been important in the shaping of the external world, whether
it has been at the hands of landscape gardeners in
the eighteenth century or in the administration of
specially designated Areas of Outstanding Natural
Beauty in the twentieth.

1

Introduction

Curious as he must be about the origins and
purposes of everything that he sees, the landscape
historian very quickly becomes aware that the external physical world is a palimpsest - a word that
occurs again and again in any writing on landscape
history - upon which, unselfconsciously, succeeding
generations of men and women, at work and at play,
have written their social autobiography, and that
each generation has been only partially successful
in erasing the script of its ancestors. This means
that, if the landscape historian is to do more than
simply count, record, measure and map then he has to
take account of the social processes that lie behind
the observable reality.(1) The analysis of these
social processes will call for all the skill, learning and empathy that he can muster since he must em-
bark upon a long and difficult voyage of discovery
before he can be satisfied that his analyses are
complete. It is not too much of an exaggeration to
claim that a full explanation of the hedgerow that
forms Fig.57 calls for the exploration of much of
the history of the western world.
    For the study of the landscape of his particul-
ar region the landscape historian must for nine ten-
ths of the time rely upon some vicarious substitute,
since not even the most dedicated student can visit
every corner of his chosen plot, and neither can he
be everywhere at once. No matter how many times he
visits a region, its landscape will appear to him to
be slightly different each time. Each visit is a
unique experience, even if only because of the slow
passage of time and the often imperceptible changes
that each succeeding day must bring.
    The best substitute for being everywhere at
once all of the time is a map. The publication of
the Ordnance Survey one inch to the mile maps began
in the first years of the nineteenth century, and it
was towards the end of that century that one of the
greatest of English historians recognised them for
what they are: historical documents of unique importance. For Maitland 'the ordnance map was a marvel-
lous palimpsest, more eloquent than many paragraphs
of written discourse'.(2)
    Only very rarely however does the Ordnance
Survey map attempt to date, and never to explain,
what it records. Here, as the interpreter of even
the most prosaic of landscapes, lies the role of the
landscape historian. A legitimate part of the process of explanation is the mapping of features, such
as windmills, which have all but disappeared from
the present landscape, or its substitute the modern

2

Introduction

Ordnance Survey map, features which are still to be
found but have changed radically their form and
function, such as parish boundaries, and even features which find no place at all on the map, such as
the uses of those fields whose boundaries are so
carefully recorded on the larger scale maps.

The essays collected together in this book are
primarily concerned with the making of maps. Half
of them, namely Chapters 1, 2, 5 and 8, discuss the
making of maps from certain narrowly defined kinds
of documents - agricultural statistics, tithe files,
probate inventories and Anglo-Saxon estate boundary
surveys. The other four Chapters are concerned with
the very wide range of sources of every kind that
can be used to compile maps illustrative of certain
themes or processes - industrialisation, Parliamentary enclosure, the topography of the early modern
town and medieval settlement patterns. All eight
Chapters discuss documents and themes which are well
known to historians and geographers alike, but in
every case their proper and comprehensive exploitation has scarcely begun, and one of the justifica-
tions of this book must be the fact that the authors
of each essay show the way forward into areas of
research for the future.

As Professor Coppock points out in the first
Chapter, the presentation of maps requires an understanding of the accuracy and reliability of the data.
This applies as much to the exploitation of almost
contemporary statistical data such as that provided
by the agricultural returns which have been collected every year since 1866 as it does to the fragmented and disjointed information to be squeezed from
Anglo-Saxon charter boundary surveys. Indeed as
much of Professor Coppock's essay is taken up with
analysing the changes in the methods of collection,
the questions asked, the definitions of the various
categories of information required and of the areas
from which it is to be collected, as in my own essay
is given to the problems of authenticity, textual
transmission and the territories to which the boundary surveys relate. The significance of boundaries,
whether of farms or fields, townships or parishes,
estates or burgage plots, is one of the most important themes running through this collection of essays.
That the problems encountered in the interpretation
of documents differ in kind rather than in scale is
another.

Accuracy and reliability can only be tested
when the form, function and purposes of the document
have been fully grasped. Only by placing documents

in their contemporary context can the historian
avoid anachronisms of the worst kind. Hence Dr.
Overton's excursus into the niceties of the administration and jurisdiction of ecclesiastical courts
in the seventeenth century, since it is here that the
reasons for the social bias to be observed in a collection of probate inventories are to be found, and
only when this social bias has been provided for can
the proper interpretation of the information to be
found in the documents begin.

Some kinds of documents, from their sheer quantity, or from the nature of the information which
they contain, lend themselves to quantification, and
it is here that the computer can relieve the human
hand and eye of the drudgery involved in the compilation and analysis of the data. Three of the essays
in this book, those by Professor Coppock, Dr. Kain
and Dr. Overton, are concerned with documents of
this kind, and for all three the computer can also
be used in the preparation of the resulting maps.

For other kinds of documents however, especially those discussed by Dr. Palmer, Dr. Slade and Dr.
Roberts, the maps can only be compiled by the patient
addition of minute crumbs of fact gathered in from a
very wide range of sources. Agricultural statistics
and tithe files are a finite store of documents, the
archive is known and fixed. For the study of the
early stages of industrialisation or the topography
of the town in the sixteenth and seventeenth centuries, the range of documents is almost infinite, and
embraces forms of evidence well beyond the conventional range of archives. It can include maps,
drawings and illustrations, surviving artefacts,
whether overgrown drainage leats or disused mine
shafts, structural evidence revealed only as an
ancient building is being demolished, and that to be
obtained from archaeological excavation. The range
of evidence of this kind is infinite, the problems
of its assemblage compounded by the dispersal of
archives over much of the western world. The code
in which the message of this evidence is couched,(3)
and it would probably be better to speak of codes
and messages, is complex, difficult to decipher, and
calls for a wide range of skills and breadth of sym-
pathy on the part of the historian.

The compilation of maps is a technique, however
sophisticated that technique may be. It is a means
to an end. This technique can often, as Dr. Slade
points out, become an all-absorbing passion, an end
in itself, as the topographer, immersed in the infinite, microscopic detail of a single parish, street

4

or row of houses, seeks to know what is in the end unknowable, namely the totality of the past. The student must at some stage call a halt to the endless, fascinating search for yet more detail, recognise that he will never recover all the pieces of the jigsaw puzzle, and turn instead to interpretation and explanation.

Maps are probably the best method of presenting spatial patterns in a way in which synchronic relationships can be easily and readily grasped. They are less than satisfactory for the presentation of change and the processes of change, since all maps are of necessity a 'snapshot', a transect through a moment in time. All of the essays in this book are concerned chiefly with the handling and interpretation of data in preparation for the compilation of maps, but they also all give some attention to the interpretation of the maps once drawn, even if it is only the representation of the processes of change by means of a series of maps.

The maps which illustrate these essays are static abstractions of human activity in the landscape. They do not themselves reveal the motives, ideals and aspirations of human beings who, in the course of their everyday lives, brought change into the landscape, however slowly or however dramatically. An awareness of change over time and of the processes of change as reflected in the documents and in the landscape itself, is another of the themes to be found in all the essays in this book, and it is at this point that they cease to be concerned with technique and instead turn to integration and interpretation. It is now that the men and women who lie behind the maps and the documents come to the fore. In Dr. Palmer's essay we can see a wealthy landlord, the Earl of Moira, in his search for methods by which he could exploit the mineral wealth, real or imagined, beneath his Leicestershire estates, serving, almost certainly unselfconsciously, as the agent of landscape change. His activities are documented through a wide range of sources, including private letters, estate accounts and maps, as well as the surviving artefacts still to be seen in the landscape today. From these it will be possible for the patient and sensitive historian to reconstruct at least something, not only of the thought behind history,(4) but of the emotions, prejudices and assumptions that also lie behind it. At the other extreme it may not be inappropriate to mention the thegn Wulfric, who, in the middle years of the tenth century, obtained two portions of an

estate called Aescesbyrig, in Berkshire. In due
course he gave his name to this new territorial unit,
and it became known as Woolstone, Wulfric's estate.
Almost nothing further is known about him but his
contribution to the landscape was no less unself-
conscious than that of the Earl of Moira, and no
less permanent.

But perhaps the most astonishing illustration
of man as an agent of landscape change, change
brought about almost inadvertently during the course
of a busy life, is Fig. 40, to be found in Dr.
Turner's essay on Parliamentary enclosure. This
map shows the distribution of those enclosures on
which John Davis of Bloxham served as a commissioner.
Altogether he was involved to a greater or lesser
extent during the course of his working life in the
remoulding of the rural landscape of about 180,000
acres, that is 281 square miles, of central southern
England. His impact upon so wide an area in so
brief a span of time was little short of revolutionary, and yet almost nothing is known of his life and
career, his early training, his hopes and ambitions,
whilst those prejudices and values which were held
so close to his heart and mind as to remain unstated
by him, lie beyond our knowledge today. He and his
like, and there were many of them, lie behind the
other maps in Dr. Turner's essay, and, mutatis
mutandi, behind all the other maps and illustrations
in this book.

These essays are primarily concerned with mapping techniques as an aid to the study of the processes of change in the landscape. They have been
arranged in reverse chronological order, with those
dealing with contemporary and nineteenth century
documents coming first and those concerned with
medieval ones coming last, because to begin with a
landscape which can be known in considerable detail
and then to work back into landscapes which can be
less and less well-known seems to be a surer method
of approach than to begin in an almost totally
unknown and alien world and then work forward.
Retrogressive analysis has its pitfalls, as Dr.
Roberts points out, but for the reading of a
palimpsest on which the most recent script is the
most legible it would appear to be the most satisfactory approach.

W.G. Hoskins was undoubtedly right when he
wrote: 'the English landscape itself, to those who
know how to read it aright, is the richest historical record we possess'.(5) But the reading of the
landscape is an immensely complex task, calling for

Introduction

a subtle blend of documents and field work if it is
not to be a mishmash of gush and prejudice. It
involves the rigorous testing of evidence of every
kind together with a close examination, not only of
the forms and functions of buildings and boundaries,
hedges and railway lines, but also of the ideas,
assumptions and priorities of those who made and
used them. It is at this point that the milieu
externe and the milieu interne come together to give
to every feature of even the most mundane and un-
assuming parts of the English landscape its in-
credibly rich historical density.

REFERENCES

     1. R. Geipel, 'The Landscape Indicators School
in German Geography', in D. Ley and M.S. Samuels,
(eds.), Humanistic Geography: Prospects and Problems
(1978), p.158.
     2. F.W. Maitland, Domesday Book and Beyond
(1897, 1960 reprint), pp.38-39.
     3. See J.B. Harley, 'Historical Geography and
its Evidence: Reflections on Modelling Sources', in
A.R.H. Baker and M. Billinge, (eds.), Period and
Place: Research Methods in Historical Geography
(1982), esp. pp.266-273.
     4. R.G. Collingwood, The Idea of History (1946,
1961 reprint), pp.213-217.
     5. Quoted by Dr. Turner, see below, p.145.

Chapter One

MAPPING THE AGRICULTURAL RETURNS: A NEGLECTED TOOL
OF HISTORICAL GEOGRAPHY(1)
J.T. Coppock

The agricultural censuses of Great Britain, which
have been undertaken annually since 1866, represent
the largest single source of data for the reconstruction of British agriculture and for the analysis
of agricultural change throughout this period. They
are available, not only for the constituent countries
and counties, but also for some 15,000 parishes (a
number gradually reduced to about 13,000 today), so
that mapping is an essential procedure if they are
to be used effectively to illustrate the rich
variety of British agriculture. The choice of
method will depend not only on the aims of the
inquiry, but also on an appreciation of the characteristics of the census data and the extent to which
they have changed over these 116 years; failure to
understand their strengths and weaknesses may lead
to erroneous conclusions being drawn, even about
trends at a national level. This chapter is devoted
to an examination of the returns as source material,
with particular reference to the period between 1866
and the Second World War, and to those characteristics that affect the way in which they should be
mapped. It is based both on documentary sources and
on extensive experience of mapping the census data
in national and regional studies, the latter with
particular reference to some 400 parishes in six
counties covering the Chilterns and their surrounding
lowlands.

ORIGINS AND DEVELOPMENT OF THE AGRICULTURAL RETURNS

It will be necessary first to consider briefly how
the agricultural returns originated and developed,
as a prelude to examining to what extent their
reliability, coverage and interpretation have

changed over this period. What was achieved in 1866
and subsequently was largely a compromise between
what governments needed to know and what farmers
were able and could be persuaded to divulge.(2)
Thus, although the ultimate objective was to provide
information on agricultural production, the data
collected were largely confined to acreages under
different crops and categories of grassland and to
numbers of different classes of livestock. Even the
inclusion of the latter was, to a large extent,
fortuitous, since the original intention had been to
follow the example of the 1801 returns(3) and of the
various experiments undertaken in the 1840s and
1850s and to collect data only on the principal
crops.(4) The appointment of a Royal Commission in
1865 to investigate severe outbreaks of cattle
plague led, however, to a request for information on
the numbers of livestock and these were, in fact,
collected first, on 5th March 1866, from all owners
of livestock, including those in town dairies.(5)
The acreages under crops and grass were then obtained on 25th June from all occupiers of more than five
acres of agricultural land. In subsequent years,
both numbers of livestock and acreages of crops were
collected on the same day (25th June, a date altered
in 1877 to 4th June, which has been the census day
ever since).

The returns were collected by the Board of
Trade through the agency of the Board of Inland
Revenue, whose excise officers were distributed
throughout Great Britain. Responsibility was transferred to the Board of Agriculture in 1889 and that
for Scotland to the Scottish Board of Agriculture in
1911, since when there has been some tendency for
the censuses for Scotland and for England and Wales
to differ in detail, although they remain broadly
comparable. The mechanism was (and remains) a
postal census, completion of which was voluntary
until 1925 (apart from the years 1918-21). Excise
officers prepared lists of occupiers from the parish
rate books and from income tax assessments, and sent
schedules to each occupier of agricultural land
requesting the required information. These were
then completed by the occupiers in respect of any
land they occupied and of the livestock on it or on
any rough grazing. On receipt by the excise officer,
the returns were checked and were then consolidated
into parish summaries, which were in turn amalgamated to provide county and national totals. For a
number of years data were also summarised by other
areas, viz., collections (administrative areas of

the Board of Excise) and petty sessional districts.
The main cartographic interest,however, lies in the
parish summaries. The original schedules were
apparently destroyed after a lapse of one year and,
although individual returns for some years have been
retained since the Second World War, they are regarded as confidential and cannot normally be used by
researchers. The county and national totals (and
those for petty sessional districts for 1912-15)
were published in the Agricultural Returns of Great
Britain (Agricultural Statistics, from 1902 to 1911,
and in Agricultural Statistics England and Wales
and Agricultural Statistics Scotland from 1912 onwards). The parish summaries are now held in the
Public Record Office (for England and Wales, apart
from the most recent, which are retained by the
Ministry of Agriculture) and the Scottish Record
Office (for Scotland), but all those for 1868, 1871
and 1872 appear to have been destroyed, as have
those for Scotland for 1873 and 1876, for Wales for
1876, 1892 and 1893, for many English counties for
1876, 1878, 1892 and 1893, and for individual
counties for some other years, mainly before 1886.
    Where occupiers declined to make a return, the
excise officers responsible for the returns were
instructed to make estimates, to compare these with
the total acreages given in the rate books and, in
the event of difficulty, to seek help from magis-
trates, land agents and others acquainted with the
locality.(6) These estimates were included in the
summaries and ultimately in the national totals, and
figures given in a Parliamentary debate (probably
relating to the first three years of the census)
show that the proportion of estimates varied greatly
throughout the country. In Scotland, only 0.5 per
cent of farmers declined to make returns, compared
with 5.5 per cent in England, where opposition was
primarily concentrated in eastern and southern
counties, with over 30 per cent of occupiers refus-
ing in Hertfordshire and Huntingdonshire.(7) There
were also many contrasts between adjacent counties
and even adjacent parishes. In 1866, for example,
estimates accounted for 13 per cent of the acreage
returned in Buckinghamshire, compared with 7 and
45 per cent respectively in Oxfordshire and Hertfordshire, and for O, 45 and 74 per cent respectively in the three neighbouring Hertfordshire
parishes of Essendon, Little Berkhamsted and Bayford.
Estimates continued to be made in subsequent years,
but they became less necessary as the fears and
hostility of farmers diminished and probably more

accurate as officers acquired more experience in
making them.

The first schedules were relatively simple
documents (Fig. 1), requiring information on six
categories of livestock (milch cows, other cattle of
two years old and over, other cattle under two,
sheep of one year old and over, sheep under one year
and pigs) and sixteen categories of crops and grass
(wheat, barley, oats, rye, beans, peas, potatoes,
cabbage/kohl rabi/rape, vetches/lucerne/other crops,
rotation grasses, bare fallow and permanent grass).
They have become increasingly complex as new items
have been added and existing items subdivided. For
example, returns of the number of horses were first
made in 1869, and cows and heifers were subdivided
into two categories (those in milk and those in calf)
in 1906 and into three in 1914. Among crops, flax
was added in 1867, sugar beet and orchards in 1871,
market gardens in 1872 and small fruit in 1887, and
there were likewise subdivisions of existing categories. As a result of such additions and subdivisions, the number of items rose from 22 in 1866
to 50 in 1919 and to 146 in 1951. The collection of
numbers of agricultural workers employed on each
holding (but excluding the occupier and his wife)
began in 1921 and between 1887 and 1941 and 1919 and
1927 occupiers were asked to state the acreages they
owned and/or rented, information that continues to
be collected in Scotland. It is not surprising that
one correspondent of the Ministry of Agriculture
should have felt moved to complain 'You forgot to
ask me how many times I went to Church on Sundays'.(8)

There have also been changes in the criteria
for including holdings in the census. Whereas the
qualifying acreage had been over 5 acres in 1866,
returns were obtained from all occupiers of land in
1967 (though in practice cottagers and holders of
small pieces of garden ground were exempted).(9) In
1869 a lower limit of ¼ acre was adopted and this
was retained until 1892 when the present minimum of
over one acre was substituted.(10) Since 1968 in
Scotland and 1970 in England and Wales, statistically insignificant holdings above that minimum have
been excluded, though significant holdings below
the minimum size have been incorporated in the
census for England and Wales since 1973.(11)

In addition to these annual returns of the
acreages of crops and numbers of livestock, other
information has been collected incidentally or by
means of special inquiries. Thus the returns can
provide data on the numbers of holdings of different

Fig. 1 Schedule used on 25th June 1866 to collect acreages under crops and grass

BOARD OF TRADE.—SCHEDULE FOR RETURN OF ACREAGE OF CROPS.

It is particularly requested that this Schedule may be filled up *as soon as received*, and returned *immediately by Post*, as addressed on the other side. The Returns of *Individual Occupiers* will not be published.

EXTENT OF LAND in the OCCUPATION OF the UNDERSIGNED UNDER VARIOUS CROPS, in the YEAR 1866

If separate Farms in two or more Parishes be occupied, separate Returns are to be made for each Farm.

Parish or Township of _____   County of _____

	NUMBER OF STATUTE ACRES AND PARTS OF STATUTE ACRES UNDER—														
	WHEAT	BARLEY or BERE	OATS	RYE	BEANS	PEAS	POTATOES	TURNIPS and SWEDES	MANGOLD	CARROTS	CABBAGE, KOHL RABI, and RAPE	HOPS	VETCHES, LUCERNE, and any other Green Crops (except Clover or Grass)	CLOVER and ARTIFICIAL Grasses under rotation	BARE FALLOW or UNCROPPED ARABLE LAND	PERMANENT PASTURE, MEADOW, or GRASS not broken up in rotation (exclusive of HILL PASTURE)
Please write on this Line, IN FIGURES, No. of Acres and parts of Acres under each Crop																

Signature of Occupier _____

Dated _____ 1866

sizes (though such information has not always been
published or even preserved); on a few occasions,
the acreages under different sizes of holdings have
also been computed. An example of a special inquiry
is the question asked in 1907 whether each holding
was farmed mainly for business or not. Attempts
have been made to conduct more limited censuses at
other times of year, particularly of livestock. The
results of a voluntary winter census of the numbers
of sheep and cattle in 1930 were so satisfactory
that other experiments were tried and the regular
collections of quarterly returns was begun in England
and Wales in 1940.(12) No parish summaries of the
quarterly returns are, however, available and data
have been collected since 1953 by sampling. In
Scotland a winter census has been undertaken since
1940.

The agricultural censuses have continued to
rely on self-completion of schedules sent by post to
individual occupiers, a procedure that depends for
its success on the completeness of records and on
the ability and willingness of farmers to provide
the information sought. Apart from the estimates
made for those holdings for which no return was
forthcoming, other methods of collecting data have
been confined to two categories, common rough grazings in England and Wales (or common pastures in
Scotland), and yields of crops, although the latter
can be mapped only at county level. Estimates of
the former were first made in 1921 by officers of
the Ministry of Agriculture, though the livestock
grazing such land had been (and continue to be)
returned by their owners on the schedules for their
own holdings.(13) Such estimates, which were last
made in 1952, are not part of the parish summaries,
although they have been recorded by parishes. In
Scotland, estimates of common pastures in the crofting counties are made by secretaries of grazing
committees, but (unlike common grazings south of
the Border) such land has been included in the parish totals of rough grazings since 1891.

The collection of agricultural statistics was
at first confined to measurements of areas of land
and numbers of livestock, but one of the principal
arguments that had been advanced in support of their
collection was the light they would throw on production. In 1884, however, when the agricultural
returns were well established, an attempt was made
to obtain estimates of the yields of the principal
crops - wheat, barley, oats, beans, peas, turnips,
mangolds, potatoes and hay. These were made by

specially-appointed crop estimators, who were
generally people experienced in making agricultural
valuations. Each was given a group of approximately
50 parishes and required to make estimates of yields
in the constituent parishes.(14) Other crops have
since been added and crop reporters are now officials of the agricultural departments. No estimates
for parishes are available and only county yields
have been published (though even these were discontinued in 1965 in Scotland).

The agricultural census thus provides a continuous and increasingly detailed record of the
areas devoted to different crops and categories of
grazing and of the numbers of different classes of
livestock and of agricultural labour; it also
provides incidental information on the size of holdings and, for some years, tenure. Because the
original schedules do not survive, the records of
the agricultural census comprise summaries of varying degree of generalisation; but they are also the
only source of any detailed analysis of agriculture
and of agricultural change throughout the country.

INTERPRETATION OF THE AGRICULTURAL RETURNS

The decision to concentrate on collecting information that farmers could easily provide has exacted
a penalty because this approach presents problems
over the interpretation of the resulting data. Some
of these problems would, of course, have existed
even if records for individual holdings had survived,
but the amalgamation of the returns for many holdings into totals for parishes, districts, counties
and countries presents further difficulties. The
census does not provide any data on what is bought
or sold and attempts to obtain information that
implied the keepings of records proved   impract-
icable in the 19th century and were abandoned in the
face of low response rates. Nor is there any direct
information on how different crops and livestock are
combined into enterprises and farming systems, something which can only be inferred from the basic data.

Crops present fewer problems of interpretation
than livestock, although it is not possible to
distinguish cash crops from others (except in
respect of vegetables grown for human consumption
and of those crops which are not used on the farm,
such as flax and hops). The census records the
acreages under crops in the ground at the time of
the census, together with those for which the land

has already been prepared at that date. It therefore excludes early potatoes that have already been
lifted and any crops for which land is prepared
subsequently, such as late vegetables. Minor problems arise in respect of mixtures, which are divided
among their constituent crops.

The choice of a fixed date for the census presents more serious problems for the interpretation
of livestock, since many of these move from farm to
farm and from region to region in the course of
their lives, and events in the agricultural calendar,
such as calving and lambing, may occur at different
times throughout the country. A striking example of
the significance of dates is provided by a comparison of numbers of sheep recorded in the first and
second censuses; in March 1866 many of the lambs
that would have been included in a June census were
not then born and the increase between that March
total and the total for June 1867 of about 7 million
(31%) must largely reflect this later date. Other
difficulties arise over the use of age classes,
which provide a Procrustean bed into which a variety
of agricultural practices must be fitted. Before
1937, the census provided no indication of the
purpose for which different categories of cattle
were kept, e.g., whether cows were suckling beef
calves or producing milk for sale or manufacture,
and assumptions have had to be made that particular
age groups of other cattle can be identified with
different stages of beef production, e.g., that
other cattle two years old and over were being
fattened for beef. Furthermore, whereas acreages
provide an acceptable basis for comparing crops,
numbers cannot do so in respect of different kinds
of livestock, which have to be converted to livestock units. Relating numbers of stock and acreages
of crops similarly requires the conversion of both
to some other common metric.

Further problems arise over other categories
of information that the agricultural census provides. Although the term 'farm' is often used in
discussions about census data, the basic unit is in
fact the agricultural holding, which is any unit
of land over one acre used for agricultural purposes.
Many of the smaller holdings included in the census
may be no more than a couple of fields and cannot be
described as farms. They may be used for a variety
of semi-agricultural purposes, especially if they
are located near towns; in one survey of Hertfordshire, for example, only 53 per cent of a sample of
holdings in 1931 were strictly agricultural.(15)

The attempts to eliminate statistically-insignificant holdings from the census have eased this problem in recent years, but all earlier censuses contain a proportion of such holdings and many other holdings are occupied on a spare- or part-time basis by those who have other occupations. Dividing the total acreage recorded in a parish summary by the number of holdings in that parish may thus give a very misleading impression of the average size of farm.

THE RELIABILITY AND COMPARABILITY OF THE AGRICULTURAL RETURNS

Mapping the agricultural returns requires an understanding of their accuracy and reliability and of the extent to which they are comparable over time and throughout the country. It also requires, as the next section will show, an appreciation of the cartographic suitability of the administrative areas by which the returns are summarised and of the relationship between the summaries and those areas. Their comparability over time depends upon the accuracy with which they have been made, the completeness with which they have been enumerated and the consistency with which individual items have been defined, interpreted and consolidated into parish summaries. Similarly, although the same definitions and practices have been used everywhere, the comparability of the summaries throughout the country depends on the extent to which they have been interpreted in the same way in all areas. For reasons that will become apparent in this and the next section, the returns cannot be compared directly with any other source and no official evaluations have ever been made public (although tests for consistency are now made and the payment of subsidies has provided a further check in recent years). Assessments of their worth must therefore largely depend on what can be learnt about their evolution and the way in which they have been compiled and on the plausibility of the information they provide when they are mapped.

Apart from 1867, when the lower limit of eligible holdings of over 5 acres was abandoned and the total acreage of crops and grass recorded rose by over a million acres, changes in the basis of collection have not greatly affected the comparability of the returns, at least in respect of the area under crops and grass. The adoption of a

16

minimum of $\frac{1}{4}$ acre in 1868 can have had very little
effect and the increase in that minimum to over one
acre in 1892 is estimated to have reduced the
acreage returned as crops and grass by not more than
0.1 per cent.(16) The inclusion of rough grazings
within the census did, of course, add a further 12
million acres in 1891, and although the removal of
statistically insignificant holdings has had little
effect upon the acreage returned as crops and grass,
it did result in a decrease of more than 900,000
acres in the area returned as rough grazing in
Scotland.(17) Other administrative changes in the
total area of agricultural land in Scotland are due
to the changes in the treatment of deer forests,
which overlap rough grazings in the Highlands and
Islands. Before 1932 only those parts of deer
forests which were grazed were enumerated in the
census, but in that year those parts that were capable of being used for grazing were also included, a
change that led to an apparent increase in the agricultural area of c. 900,000 acres. In 1959, the
ruling was again changed to include all deer forests,
whether they were grazed or not, and this resulted
in a further increase of nearly 1½ million acres.(18)
     Although there is no evidence to suggest that
returns that were deliberately falsified have ever
been common, it does seem plausible to expect that
a return will be more reliable than an estimate. It
also seems reasonable to suppose that there would
have been some improvement in accuracy as the returns
became more familiar to both farmers and officials
responsible for their collection and as the proportion of estimates declined. But there may also
have been a contrary tendency, arising from the increasing complexity of the returns and the con-
sequent greater risk of error. As the commentary on
the agricultural statistics for 1936 noted, 'it is
the common experience of those who collect statistics
that the accuracy of the returns varies inversely
with the number and complexity of the questions
asked'.(19) New questions were often overlooked and
it was generally several years before satisfactory
returns were received; only 70 per cent of occupiers
in England and Wales replied in 1943 to new questions
about temporary grass, though the percentage of
acceptable returns had risen to 94 by 1950.(20) It
is therefore wise to avoid drawing conclusions from
any short-term changes that follow the introduction
of new questions or the modification of old.
     A major cause of improvements in the accuracy
of the returns arises from the progressive dis-

covery of holdings that had previously escaped
enumeration. Between 1867 and 1891 the total
acreage returned in Great Britain increased in each
successive year, the cumulative rise over this
period exceeding 3 million acres. How much of this
increase was due to better enumeration and how much
to the enlargement of the cultivated area which was
said to be taking place it is impossible to say. It
seems likely, from the changing emphasis in the
reports that accompany the published returns, that
both greater completeness and land improvement made
major contributions in the first fifteen years and
that land improvement was subsequently the major
factor, though there must also have been a steady
transfer of land out of agricultural use to housing
and industrial development throughout this period.
This view receives some confirmation from trends in
the six counties covering the Chilterns where there
was little scope for enlarging the cultivated area
(which was almost certainly declining as a result
of urban expansion); the total acreages recorded
rose until about 1880 and nearly all this increase
must have been due to more effective enumeration
and greater accuracy. (See Fig.4 for trends in
Hertfordshire.) Such improvements did not, however,
cease in 1880. Best has shown that the recorded
decrease in the total agricultural area between 1900
and 1950 understates the real loss as a result of
more effective enumeration and changes in the interpretation of land which ought properly to be included in the census.(21) By implication, his findings suggest that the total agricultural area was
still being underestimated in 1900 by nearly a
million acres.

     That these changes should have occurred is not
surprising. There are no cadastral registers in
Great Britain to provide a complete and readily-
accessible record of landholding, and the rate books
on which the returning officers originally relied do
not seem to have been very reliable.(22) Many holdings or parts of holdings were at first omitted and
these gradually came to light, often on a change of
occupier, although the frequency of such changes in
the occupation or extent of holdings (which numbered
some 100,000 a year in England and Wales in the
1950s) would have made it difficult to keep track of
all land.(23) The problem of achieving complete
enumeration continued to cause concern and an independent survey of Buckinghamshire in 1936 showed
that 13,302 acres of farmland were still being
omitted from the returns for that county, including

28 farms of 100 acres and over.(24) Further
omissions, totalling c. 270,000 acres for England
and Wales alone, came to light when livestock
rationing was introduced in 1941, and smaller gains
were recorded in the next two years.(25) Many of
the holdings omitted were small and predominantly
under permanent grass, and such holdings are particularly numerous around towns and in the more pastoral parts of the country. Their discovery not only
led to increases in the total area recorded but also
exaggerated the swing to permanent grass that was
occurring in those areas in the late 19th century.
     The inclusion of rough grazings in the census
in 1891 presented even greater problems. Not only
is such land the least well-known of all farmland
and hence easily overlooked; its distribution is
markedly regional, most of it lying in Highland
Britain north and west of the Tees-Exe line. Moreover, although land was reverting to rough grazing
throughout much of this period, it is impossible to
say how much of the increase of nearly 1 million
acres in the extent of such land in England and
Wales between 1892 and 1924 was due to better enumeration, something which almost certainly included
the discovery of holdings entirely under rough grazings. A complicating factor was the existence of
common grazings in England and Wales. These have
never been included in farmers' returns, though the
livestock grazing on them should have been from the
beginning (a fact sometimes overlooked in calculations of stocking densities). Considerable uncertainty has always attached to common grazings and
this has resulted in both under- and over-estimates,
with true common land being included by some
occupiers on their own schedules and some land held
in undivided shares being mistakenly identified as
common land. It was not until 1922 that it was made
clear that occupiers were to include on their own
returns only land over which they had sole grazing
rights. The rise in the estimates of common grazings from 1 to 1.5 million acres between 1922 and
1950 is some indication of these problems since
there can hardly have been a real increase on this
scale. No such difficulties have arisen in Scotland
where common pastures in the crofting counties
appear to have been included on individual schedules
(and hence in parish summaries) from the beginning;
(26) but here the changing interpretation of deer
forests has had a major effect on the total area
returned, particularly in parishes in the Highlands
and in some of the islands.

Changes in the extent of land included in the agricultural census may also be due to improvements in the accuracy of measurements. Occupiers are now supposed to include not only the actual area occupied by a crop but also any associated headlands, hedges and ditches (i.e., the acreages as recorded on the large-scale plans of the Ordnance Survey). It is not known when this practice was adopted, but before the publication of these plans, farmers in many parishes (especially those where there had been no Tithe Survey) may not have known the true extent of their land. Many fields were (and still are) known by a rough approximation of their true area and even an Oxford college found it necessary to amend the recorded acreage of its estates following publication of the first large-scale plans.(27) Errors persisted into the twentieth century and a survey of holdings of over 5 acres in Oxfordshire in 1941/3 showed that their extent had been over-estimated by some 1,500 acres.(28) Unfortunately, the uncultivated areas of the country have never been covered by large-scale plans, so that improvements are less likely to have occurred in the measurement of such land (though there is some evidence to suggest that farmers often estimate its extent by deducting the area under crops and grass from the total area of their holdings). A further factor of some regional significance is the use, in the early years of the census, of local measurements rather than statute acres. Numerous references occur to the use of such measures, particularly Scottish, Cheshire and Lancashire acres, and although these will often have been detected and corrected, their use must inevitably have affected earlier totals for parts of the country where they were commonly used.(29) Thus, the anomalous movements in the arable acreages in Cheshire and Lancashire in the last thirty years of the 19th century may, in part, be due to the use of such local measures.

The completeness of the livestock returns is much more difficult to evaluate, since there is no kind of overall check (such as the total area of the country provides in relation to land). Only sudden changes in the numbers recorded may (in the absence of other explanation, such as natural disaster) suggest that the results are suspect. A further complication arises from uncertainty whether occupiers who had livestock grazing on moorland included such stock on their returns (as they were required to do), since moorland in sole occupation

was not included in the census until 1891 and common
rough grazings in England and Wales not until 1921.
Some observers believed that such stock was being
omitted, a view that receives some support from a
ruling in 1872 that they should properly be included
in the returns.(30) Despite these complications, it
does seem reasonable to suppose that the improvements in the completeness of enumeration of areas
will also have affected numbers of livestock and
that returns for earlier years will underestimate
these and hence exaggerate the scale of any rise and
minimise that of any fall.

Improvements in the completion of enumeration
are not the only cause of apparent changes in the
acreages of crops and numbers of livestock. Alterations in the definitions of the different categories and in the interpretations placed upon them by
farmers have also been important, though they have
generally resulted in transfers between categories.
It is, however, difficult to separate their effects
from those of changing agricultural practices and
economic circumstances and, in the short run, from
changes attributable to adverse weather. As with
improvements in the completeness of enumeration,
such changes are particularly important in the first
decade for which the agricultural returns were collected, though they recurred from time to time, especially when established definitions were changed
and even when a new format or type of print was used.
Indeed, no item in the census is strictly comparable
throughout these 115 years, though some of the
changes are of minor consequence. Furthermore,
because agricultural enterprises are often highly
regionalised, such changes may not only affect
national totals but often have important regional
dimensions. The principal difficulties concerned
the distinctions between rough grazing and other
rough land, between rough grazing and permanent
grass and between permanent and temporary grass, the
measurement of areas under fruit and vegetables and
the identification of bare fallow. All are of considerable importance, particularly the first two,
since these determine respectively the boundaries
between agricultural and non-agricultural land and
between cultivated and uncultivated land.

The effect on the total area of agricultural
land of the introduction in 1891 of a category of
mountain and heath land used for feeding livestock
has already been discussed; but it also had significant consequences for the acreage of land returned
as permanent grass, particularly in upland counties;

for example, the latter declined by 40,671 acres in
Westmorland and by 56,611 acres in Cumberland
between 1891 and 1892. Subsequently, interpretation
was complicated by the fact that, from the end of
the 19th century, improved land was reverting to
rough grazing; in the late 1890s, for example, much
downland in Hampshire, Sussex and Wiltshire was being
reclassified as mountain and heath land.(31) In
1922 this term was replaced by 'rough grazings',
defined as 'mountain, heath, moor or downland and
other rough land used for rough grazing', and this
new definition, together with the use of more prominent type, resulted in the transfer to this category of large areas of land that had formerly been
returned as permanent grass, particularly downland
and rough pasture in enclosed land, neither of which
had appeared to fall into the category of mountain
and heath land.(32)

The difficulty of finding definitions that have
the same meaning throughout the country is well
illustrated by permanent grass. This, as permanent
pasture, had been defined in 1866 as 'permanent
pasture, meadow or grass not broken up in the rotation (exclusive of hill pastures)'. It had been
intended to exclude only 'mountain land with heathy
and scanty pasture', but it was believed that a large
acreage of down and other hilly pasture that ought
to have been included was being omitted. The definition was accordingly changed in 1867 to read
'Permanent Grass as meadow, down or pasture not
broken up in the rotation (exclusive of heath or
mountain land)', a change that was followed by a
considerable increase in the acreage returned as
permanent grass.(33) Difficulties continued, however, and officers were instructed in 1876 that enclosed grassland should be entered as permanent
grass, but that unenclosed mountain land or heaths
not capable of cultivation should be excluded, a
ruling subsequently extended to make clear that such
rough land should be excluded even when it was enclosed by boundary fences.(34) Adjustments were,
however, complex, and an increase in the acreage
under permanent grass in 1890 was attributed in part
to a more liberal use of the term 'cultivated'.(35)
Subsequently, interpretation was made increasingly
difficult by the generally depressed state of agriculture and the reversion of improved land to rough
grazing.

The distinction between permanent and temporary
grass was similarly complicated by the progressive
conversion of arable land to grassland that was

occurring from the 1880s onwards. Temporary grass
had been defined in 1866 as 'Clover and artificial
grasses under rotation', but differences in interpretation led to the adoption of a revised definition in 1869 as 'Clover, sainfoin, 'seeds' and rye
grass under rotation'. This change was followed by
a drop of 510,000 acres in the acreage returned as
permanent grass, though part of this reduction was
attributed to the dry summer of 1868.(36) It was,
however, found that the new definition had led to
leys other than those down for one year being
returned as permanent pasture, so a third definition
was adopted in 1870, as 'Clover, sainfoin, 'seeds',
rye and other grasses under rotation for one or more
years'. This change too was followed by an increase
(well over a million acres) in the acreage returned
as temporary grass, but interpretation of this gain
is complicated by the introduction of questions on
the acreage of grass cut for hay which had led some
farmers to return as temporary grass land supporting
a corn crop undersown with seeds.(37) Although
there was thought to be greater uniformity by 1871,
further difficulties were noted in 1876 and 1883,
and a special inquiry in 1885 found that the acreage
under temporary grass was being overstated. The
introduction of a simplified schedule in 1897, on
the other hand, led to an increase in the acreage
returned as temporary grass.(38)
     Differences of interpretation also arose from
farmers' reactions to agricultural depression, for
there was a tendency both to expand the acreage
under temporary grass, as the easiest way of meeting
the crisis, and to delay reclassifying temporary
grass that had in fact become permanent in the hope
that conditions would improve. One observer reported in 1886 that a large acreage of temporary grass
had 'simply drifted into permanent pasture' and a
similar comment was made in 1893; for an increasing
amount of temporary grass was coming to be regarded,
in name as well as in fact, as permanent.(39)
Problems of interpretation recurred after the Second
World War when the extension of ley farming in
England tended to blur the distinction between temporary and permanent grass, and the introduction of
age classes of temporary grass likewise led to transfers between the two heads.   Indeed, the distinction between them was abandoned in Scotland in 1960
and was replaced by two categories, of grass under
and grass over seven years old respectively. Although it is unfortunate that such changes of definition should have occurred at critical times in the

history of British farming, many of the difficulties
of interpretation were expressions of the changing
fortunes   and practices of the agricultural
industry and would have arisen under any circumstances.
     Problems also arose over recording land under
fruit and vegetables, though these are less important, not only because the acreages involved were
much smaller but also because much of this land was
also being returned as arable or permanent grass, so
that errors did not affect the total acreage of
agricultural land. Orchards were first recorded in
1871, but the enumeration of market gardens in 1872
revealed that some of the latter had erroneously
been returned as orchards; on the other hand, an
increase in the acreage under orchards in 1885 was
attributed to a reclassification of land formerly
returned as permanent grass.(40) A further complication was introduced by the recording of small
fruit from 1887 onwards, first that growing in
orchards and then in 1888 small fruit growing in
market gardens, a move that led to a fall of 3,056
acres in the area under orchards, at least in part
as a result of this reclassification.(41) The new
schedule adopted in 1897 revealed numerous errors in
the recording of small fruit, and the introduction
in 1907 of separate categories of orchards under
grass and those undercropped with small fruit led to
further improvements in the accuracy with which the
acreage under fruit was recorded.(42) Even so, the
census record of orchards was still thought to be
incomplete and three categories, of orchards with
small fruit beneath the trees, orchards with other
crops and orchards with fallow or grass, were therefore introduced in 1923; the subsequent increase in
the acreage under other crops suggests that not all
the land under orchards had previously been enumerated.(43) The decision to include all land under
orchards as part of the area in tillage also, in
effect, transferred some 150,000 acres previously
recorded as permanent grass to this category.
     Market gardens presented peculiar difficulties,
again in part because of agricultural changes, viz.,
the increasing practice of growing vegetables as
field crops on arable farms; in 1883, for example,
it was noted that a large acreage under peas and
potatoes had been erroneously recorded as market
gardens in Essex.(44) Indeed, because of this trend
and increasing difficulties of interpretation, the
collection of the acreage under market gardens was
discontinued in 1897, though the principal crops

24

continued to be recorded separately.(45) It was not until 1941 that a separate item covering all vegetables grown for human consumption was introduced into the census for England and Wales. Field crops caused few problems of interpretation, although part of the changes in the acreages recorded will be illusory, since they result from the progressive improvements in the accuracy and completeness of the returns. One change was the introduction in 1918 of a category of mixed corn, the acreage of which was presumably previously returned under its constituent crops; there will therefore have been some exaggeration of the acreages under those crops before that date, though mixed corn was only a minor crop until 1940 except in southwest England. Some crops have at times been returned separately and at others included with similar crops; thus cabbage was returned with kohl rabi and rape between 1866 and 1868, separately between 1868 and 1918, with savoys and kale between 1918 and 1941, and subsequently with savoys, kale and kohl rabi. Nearly all root crops, pulses and brassicas have been divided at some time since 1918 into those grown for stock feed and those grown for human consumption. Examination of trends in such crops can usually be achieved by adding the acreages of the constituent crops.

The greatest difficulty in recording the area of tillage (i.e., crops and fallow) occurred over bare fallow which, like temporary grass, permanent grass and rough grazing, was affected both by weather conditions and by the depressed state of farming throughout much of this period. Misconceptions of what should be returned as bare fallow were identified in 1867 and 1868, when some land capable of cultivation but lying waste or untilled was believed to have been erroneously returned as bare fallow.(46) The definition was therefore altered from 'Bare Fallow or uncropped Arable Land' to 'Bare Fallow or ploughed land from which a crop will not be taken this year' and this change was followed by a large reduction in the area returned as bare fallow in 1869 and by further falls in 1870 and 1871.(47) It was also debateable whether ploughed land that had been temporarily abandoned during the worst period of the depression in the 1880s and 1890s should be returned as bare fallow and, if it was so recorded, at what point fields that had tumbled down to grass should be reclassified as permanent grass.(48)

Livestock presented fewer problems of interpretation, except in so far as changes in agri-

cultural practices affect the conclusions that can
be drawn about changes in the numbers of different
age-categories, for example, the increasing tendency
to fatten cattle for slaughter at younger ages. Most
alterations to the categories of livestock have been
achieved by subdividing existing categories, so that
comparisons over time are usually possible by addition, at the risk of some loss of detail. The
major exception, and then only in 1866-7, are cows,
defined in 1866 as milch cows and in the following
year as cows and heifers in milk and in calf.

The changes in the interpretation of permanent
grass and rough grazing also have implications for
what can be learnt about changes in the sizes of
agricultural holdings. These were originally classified on the basis of the acreage under crops and
grass, so that any transfers of land between permanent grass and rough grazings will have led to
apparent changes in the sizes of farms. Since the
adoption of a classification based upon the acreage
of all agricultural land, apparent changes in size
may similarly be caused by the inclusion of land
not previously regarded as rough grazing or the
exclusion of land no longer regarded as agricultural.
The discovery of holdings where common rough grazings were wrongly being included or transfers from
the category of common rough grazings to those in
sole occupation will have had similar effects in
England and Wales, as will the inclusion or exclusion of ungrazed deer forest in Scotland. It is
also likely that many of the holdings omitted from
the returns but included in later censuses will have
been small, and their discovery may thus lead to
apparent changes in the average size of holdings.

A further complication arises from changes in
administrative practices relating to the occupation
of more than one holding, whether these were in fact
separate entities or farmed together. The original
intention was that separate holdings should be the
subject of separate returns; but later, in order to
encourage farmers to make returns, every effort was
made 'to save trouble to the occupiers by allowing
them to make one or more Returns as they please'
and in 1892 it was said that much latitude had been
permitted 'with respect to the custom of returning
separate farms or detached portions'.(49) Subsequently, those responsible for the returns have
attempted to ensure that holdings farmed together
and detached portions of holdings were included on
the same return, though there is no legal obligation
on occupiers to comply. Thomas and Elms, in their

survey of Buckinghamshire in 1936, noted that some
occupiers made separate returns where part of their
holding lay in one parish and part in another. They
also found 768 repetitions of names on the Ministry's
list of holdings, of which 238 occurred more than
twice;(50) many of these must have been parts of
multiple holdings, a view supported by Gardner's
discovery in Oxfordshire of 405 holdings relating
to 173 farms.(51) In recent years, stricter interpretation of what should properly be included in
the census has led to the removal of many of the
smaller holdings from the census lists, a practice
which will also affect estimates of average farm
size.

  Although this review of the effects of changes
in completeness, accuracy, interpretation and administrative practice may suggest that the returns are
of little value for mapping agricultural change, such
an impression would be incorrect. It is true that
official opinion that the years 1871 to 1875
provided a sound basis for measuring such changes
now seems over-optimistic, but there can be no doubt
that the returns can throw much light on the changes
that were taking place, provided their limitations
are recognised and they are used with care.(52) As
far as possible, the early years of the census should
be avoided (although they do mark the beginnings of
very significant agricultural changes). It is also
unwise to place too much reliance on absolute values
or on figures relating to a single year, and there
is consequently much to recommend the use of ratios,
densities and proportions and moving means for, say,
three years to minimise the effects both of administrative changes and of short-term responses to
adverse weather.

MAPPING THE RETURNS

Against this background of the changing accuracy,
completeness and interpretation of the agricultural
returns, it is possible to suggest the most appropriate ways of mapping them. Attention is focussed
primarily on the parish summaries, since what is
true of mapping the parish data is broadly true of
mapping county data, though the latter are necessarily more generalised and physical conditions within
counties will usually be much more varied than those
within parishes. The county data have been used
primarily for national studies, most comprehensively
by the agricultural departments in the volume comm-

27

emorating the centenary of the census, and have been
more widely used than the parish summaries, primarily because they are readily available in published
form and the smaller number of units is much more
manageable.(53)

Maps of census data will be required for a
number of purposes. They can be used simply to find
things out, to record the distribution of the components of agriculture (in so far as these are
identified by the census) at particular dates and to
examine changes in those components over a number of
years, since well-conceived maps can be much more
readily comprehended than large, complex tables.
They can also be used to suggest and to test hypo-
theses. In so far as it is possible to use the
census data to identify enterprises, agricultural
systems and agricultural regions, these, too, can be
mapped, although such procedures involve numerous
assumptions and complex calculations and were not
generally attempted before the advent of digital
computers.

THE PARISH AS A MAPPING UNIT(54)

Before the data contained in the parish (or county)
summaries can be mapped, it is necessary to establish both the nature of the parish (county) as a
cartographic unit and the relationship between the
civil parish (county) and the summary bearing the
same name, not least because, as the preceding
analysis has shown, administrative practices have
varied throughout the period for which agricultural
returns have been made.

Whatever that relationship, the administrative
area is the only unit that can be used for mapping
the summaries, since only its boundaries are known.
Unfortunately, parishes and counties in Great Britain
vary greatly in size; parishes in Scotland in 1965,
for example, ranged in area from under 100 acres
(40 hectares) to over 250,000 acres (100,000 hectares).(55) This upper range reflects the mountainous character of much of Scotland, but although upland parishes on poor land tend to be larger than
lowland parishes, the range among the latter is also
surprisingly wide; in the six counties studied in
southeast England, parishes ranged in area from
under 100 acres (40 hectares) to over 12,500 acres
(5,000 hectares). Furthermore, although there is no
simple relationship between the size of a parish and
the number of holdings it contains, which will vary

with the sizes of farms, the larger the parish, the
larger is likely to be the number of holdings. In
Scotland in 1965 this ranged from 4 to 1,354 and,
other things being equal, the bigger the parish, the
greater the degree to which the data from the individual holdings will be generalised in the summary.
Moreover, the smaller parishes are not only likely
to contain fewer holdings, they may also be dominated by the records for individual large farms.
Anomalous values may thus do no more than reflect
differences in the level of generalisation.

It is not possible to know from the parish
summaries whether the data they contain are representative of a type of farming that is common to
most holdings or whether they conceal a number of
widely contrasting types. Farming does show a fairly marked tendency towards regionalisation and the
holdings summarised by parishes are likely to be
very similar where natural conditions strongly
favour a particular type of farming or where they
are adverse and greatly restrict the range. Nevertheless, the greater the range of soils, relief and
climatic conditions within a parish, the greater the
range of types of farming there is likely to be.
This feature is most marked in the narrow scarpland
parishes of eastern England. In the Buckinghamshire
parish of Aston Clinton in 1941, for example, the
proportion of permanent grass on holdings in that
part of the parish on the Chilterns was 58 per cent,
compared with 88 per cent on those holdings located
in the Vale and an average of 70 per cent in the
parish as a whole.(56)

The parish summaries cannot now be reconstituted
to take account of such internal contrasts, but the
cartographic consequences of the different levels of
generalisation can be lessened by reducing the range
of sizes of parish and, in particular, by elimin-
ating the smaller parishes by amalgamating their
summaries with those of adjacent parishes. This
task is complicated by the great range of sizes and
by the juxtaposition of large and small parishes.
It is possible to achieve something approaching
equality of size only by making very large combined
parishes and this will generally lead to an un-
acceptable loss of detail. A more limited objective
would be to amalgamate all those parishes below a
certain minimum size, the choice of which would be
guided by the range of sizes of both parishes and
holdings in the area being investigated. In the
study of the Chilterns, a minimum of 2,000 acres,
(800 hectares) was chosen and, in the very different

conditions of Scotland, one of 15,000 acres (6,000
hectares). In effecting such amalgamations, regard
should be had both to the physical similarity of the
parishes (since there is no point in complicating
analysis by amalgamating unlike parishes) and to the
extent to which amalgamation could be used to eliminate the effects of changes in the boundaries of
the civil parishes during the period of interest.
The selection of appropriate partners for such combined parishes will not only make the resulting maps
easier to read; they will also facilitate comparisons over time. Amalgamations will also have the
effect of reducing the number of units and hence the
calculations required.

It has been assumed in the preceding discussion
that identifying the parishes to which the summaries
refer and the boundaries of the corresponding civil
parishes is straightforward, but this is not always
the case, particularly in the first fifteen years for
which the returns were collected. These early years
of the census coincided with a period both of administrative reform and of the completion of the mapping of the country at large scales. Both of these
events have affected the summaries. Although these
are now made only for civil parishes, whose boundaries can be readily identified, they have been compiled in the past for some smaller areas, such as
hamlets, townships, liberties and extra-parochial
places, and also for some detached parts of parishes.
For example, the township of Little Haseley and the
hamlets of Latchford and Rycote, all lying in the
Oxfordshire parish of Great Haseley, were separately
recorded in the first census in 1866. Such a
situation was particularly common before the present
machinery of local government was established and
before the numerous detached portions of parishes
were eliminated by the Divided Parishes Acts of 1876
to 1882.

The occurrence of such anomalies in the census
records seems to have been quite haphazard and to be
unrelated either to the administrative areas existing
then or to the subdivisions used in the decennial
censuses of population. A separate summary for a
detached part of a parish was often prepared when it
lay in another collection; for example, a part of
the Oxfordshire parish of Lewknor was so treated
because it lay in the Reading Collection, whereas
its parent parish lay in the Oxfordshire Collection.
In 1886 the officers responsible for the agricultural census were instructed that no township
was to be returned as a separate parish if it did

not exceed 2,500 acres and that only parishes
exceeding 5,000 acres which were already sub-divided
for tax, poor rate or other purposes could be
divided into two parts.(57) Nevertheless, separate
summaries continued to be prepared for some small
townships and hamlets (in one instance at least,
Dagnall, in the Buckinghamshire parish of Edlesborough, until 1934). For some civil parishes, no
separate summaries exist; for example, until 1938
only one summary was prepared for the Buckinghamshire parishes of Hardwick and Weedon. There is
frequently no indication that a summary does not
relate to the whole of a parish and it is easy to
overlook parts that occur elsewhere in the summaries
under different names or in different collections.
Great care is therefore necessary in identifying
the civil parishes to which the summaries refer.

This task is made harder, at least in the early
years of the census, by the difficulty of ascertain-
ing the boundaries of the administrative areas.
Although the Ordnance Survey has had a statutory
obligation since 1841 to record public boundaries,
many of its records have been destroyed. The first
maps to show parish boundaries correct to a specific
date are the county indexes at a scale of four
inches to the mile which have been published by the
Ordnance Survey at frequent intervals since 1888.
It is true that earlier records exist, but they are
not readily accessible and do not relate to a
specific date. Moreover, even when the exact date
of a change in administrative area is known, that
change was not necessarily reflected in the parish
summaries; only since 1937 does this appear to have
been the case.

THE RELATIONSHIP OF AGRICULTURAL AND CIVIL PARISHES

The preceding discussion has assumed, implicitly,
that the land to which a parish summary relates,
'the agricultural parish', can be defined by the
boundary of the civil parish that bears the same
name, but this is frequently not the case. Returns
are made for individual holdings and these often lie
in one or more parishes, as Figure 2 shows for the
Suffolk parish of Denston in 1896.(58) Although it
would have been administratively feasible to require
occupiers of such holdings to make a separate return
for each part of their holding lying in each parish,
such a requirement would undoubtedly have increased
hostility to the returns and probably have led to

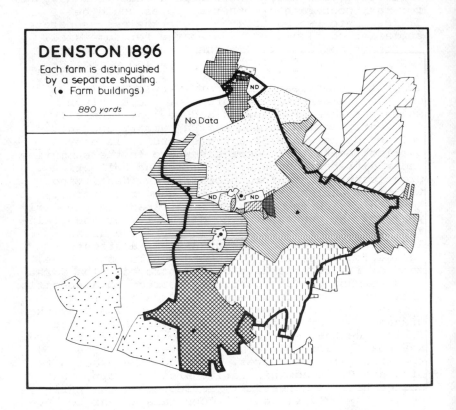

Fig. 2   Farms in the parish of Denston, Suffolk, 1896

less accurate results. Administrative practice
appears to have varied, with holdings being returned
either in the parish in which most of the land was
situated or in that in which the farmstead was
located; but interpretation is further complicated
by the flexibility permitted in respect of multiple
holdings. What is clear is that there is frequently
a discordance between the agricultural parish and
the civil parish.

The nature of the discordance is illustrated in
Figure 3, which shows these relationships in the
Oxfordshire parish of Nuffield in 1941.(59) At that
time, a third of the agricultural land within the

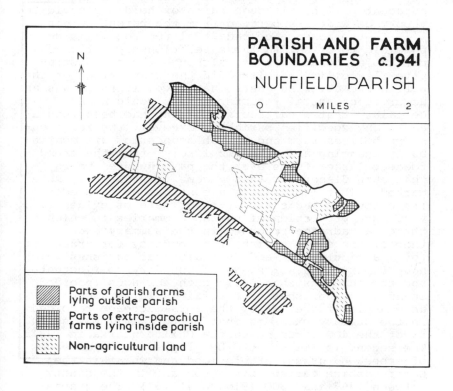

PARISH AND FARM
BOUNDARIES c.1941
NUFFIELD PARISH

N

0   MILES   2

Parts of parish farms
lying outside parish

Parts of extra-parochial
farms lying inside parish

Non-agricultural land

Fig. 3 Civil and agricultural parishes, Nuffield,
Oxon., 1941. The heavily shaded area within the
civil parish (outlined by a heavy line) was returned
in 1941 in the summaries of other parishes; the
lightly shaded areas outside the parish were included in the summary of Nuffield parish. The 'agricultural parish' is therefore the unshaded areas
within the civil parish, together with the shaded
areas outside.

parish was included in the summaries of other
parishes, whereas a third of the land returned under
Nuffield lay outside the boundary of that parish.
On the evidence of other parishes in the Chilterns,

33

this proportion was probably on the high side, but
there was some discordance in nearly all the 400
parishes studied.(60) Furthermore, the great majority of land lying outside the civil parish was in an
adjacent parish, although parts of holdings could in
theory be widely separated from the parent holding.
In the absence of cadastral records it is not
possible to establish these relationships at any
particular point in time, although the administrative flexibility permitted in the compilation of the
parish summaries suggests that, even if there was an
accurate cadastral register, there could be no
certainty that a particular holding had been returned in any specified parish. Moreover, the relationships between farm and parish boundaries are continually changing and it seems likely, from the trend
towards larger farms over the past hundred years,
that such discordance has become progressively more
marked. That it has been a continuing feature of
the census is indicated by three sets of evidence,
viz., the proportion of parish summaries in which
the total acreage recorded in the summary exceeds
that of the civil parish, the tendency for graphs of
total agricultural land in individual parishes which
have experienced no change of boundary to fluctuate,
and the numerous changes in such acreages recorded
in adjacent parishes over a fairly large area. As
an example of the first, the total acreage recorded
in the summary exceeded that of the civil parish in
39 of the 400 parishes in the Chiltern area in 1931.
The second is illustrated by graphs of the acreages
of crops and grass, arable land and wheat in the
Hertfordshire parish of Kimpton and in the county
between 1867 and 1900 (Figure 4).(61) The graphs
for Kimpton show great variations, even though the
parish has experienced no change of boundary. Although some of these fluctuations may be due to the
recording of holdings which have previously escaped
enumeration (which largely account for the rise in
the total in the county), the most probable cause of
these changes is transfers of holdings or parts of
holdings between the summaries of Kimpton and those
of other parishes. Thirdly, comparison of the summaries of 75 parishes in south Oxfordshire in 1931
and 1951 reveals changes which can be explained
only by such book-keeping transfers of agricultural
land between the summary of one parish and that of
another.(62)
This lack of accordance between agricultural
and civil parish must not be exaggerated; it is
likely to be most significant where farms are large

Fig. 4 Trends in acreages of crops and grass and arable land in Hertfordshire and in the parish of Kimpton, Herts., 1867-1900, as recorded in the agricultural returns.

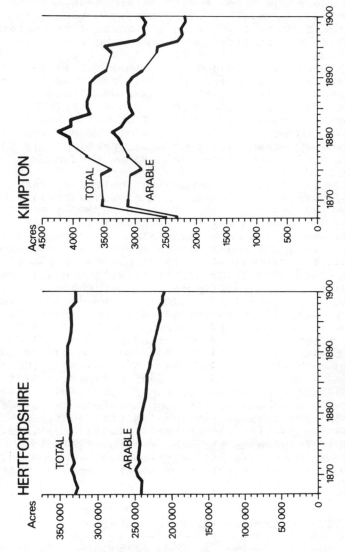

The thin lines in the graph for Kimpton mark years for which the parish summaries have been destroyed or lost.

and where the trend toward enlargement of farms has
been most marked, i.e., in the principal areas of
arable farming in eastern England. Nevertheless, it
clearly has implication for mapping the agricultural
returns, more particularly because the degree of
accordance has changed over time. It is necessary
to use the boundaries for civil parishes, not because they are also the boundaries of agricultural
parishes, but because they are the only boundaries
that are known. The information contained in the
parish summaries cannot therefore be related directly to any other source of data, particularly that
derived from the area enclosed by the boundary of the
civil parish.

Discrepancies between agricultural census and
administrative areas are not confined to parishes.
An apparent diminution of about 16,000 acres in the
acreage returned for the East Riding of Yorkshire in
1885 was explained by land along the county boundary
being recorded sometimes in one county and sometimes
in another, though land lying outside a county but
returned by holdings within it will normally represent only a small proportion of the total area of
that county.(63) A manuscript comment on the summaries for Oxfordshire for 1891 provides an example
of what happened; it recorded that '154 acres had been
transferred from the summaries for Buckinghamshire
to those for Oxfordshire because an occupier holding
land on either side of the county boundary declined
to make two returns'. In 1895 collecting officers
were instructed that returns should always be made
in the same county, although a reference to occupiers making their returns 'in the county in which
they resided instead of that in which the land is
situate' suggests that the return of a holding in
another county is unlikely to have been common,
since it would hardly have merited special mention.
(64)

CHOICE OF CARTOGRAPHIC METHODS(65)

The three principal methods of mapping the data
contained in the parish summaries employ dots,
proportional symbols and shading, examples of which
are shown in Figure 5 for the Chilterns and surrounding lowlands. It is true that isopleth maps
could be constructed and that their use would minimise the problems of identifying the true locations
of agricultural parishes, since the data for each
parish could be treated as a point located at the

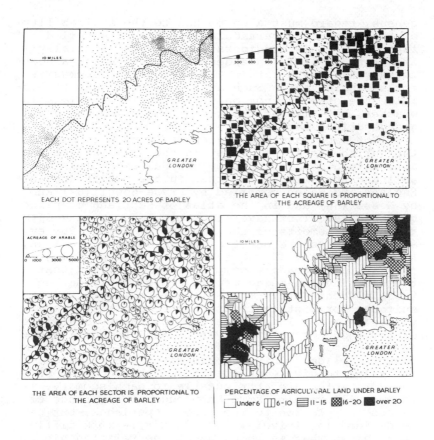

EACH DOT REPRESENTS 20 ACRES OF BARLEY

THE AREA OF EACH SQUARE IS PROPORTIONAL TO
THE ACREAGE OF BARLEY

THE AREA OF EACH SECTOR IS PROPORTIONAL TO
THE ACREAGE OF BARLEY

PERCENTAGE OF AGRICULTURAL LAND UNDER BARLEY
Under 6   6-10   11-15   16-20   over 20

Fig. 5   Various representations of the acreage under barley in the Chilterns, 1951.

centroid of the civil parish; but the method is generally unsuitable for mapping discontinuous variables of the kind represented by the agricultural census. Each of the three methods has advantages and disadvantages which have been explored elsewhere, and their relative importance in part depends on whether the aim of the investigation is to reconstruct the agriculture of a past period or to examine changes over time.

RECONSTRUCTING THE AGRICULTURE OF PAST PERIODS

Although the choice of dates will be influenced by considerations that are external to the agricultural

37

census, regard must also be had to the availability
of the summaries, particularly during the period
1866-1900. This consideration will be especially
important if it is intended to compute mean values
for several years rather than to use the summaries
for a single year. Such averaging will help to minimise the effects, not only of annual variations in
weather, but also of the kind of book-keeping changes described earlier.

Dot maps have been extensively used in mapping
the parish summaries, first in the study of the
agriculture of Kent, Surrey and Sussex in 1911 by
Hall and Russell(66) and then in the two atlases of
England and Wales compiled by Pryse-Howell(67) and
by Messer(68) and in the atlas of Scotland compiled
by Wood.(69) They have also been used in many of
the county memoirs of the Land Utilisation Survey.
Such maps have the merit of being easy, if tedious,
to construct and of requiring little computation;
they are also readily comprehended, provided that
the distribution being mapped shows fairly marked
regional contrasts. They are not, however, very
suitable for distributions that record very high
values in a few localities and low values elsewhere
or for those crops and livestock which occur widely
and show small, but significant differences from
place to place. Only two decisions are required, on
the value to give each dot and on the location of
the dots which are attributable to each summary. The
former will require some knowledge of the range of
values in relation to the size of parishes, but can
be decided intuitively. The latter is more difficult, given what is known about the relationship
between agricultural and civil parishes. In general,
it is not permissable to place dots according to
some assumed relationship, such as type of soil,
though they may properly be excluded from areas
shown on contemporary Ordnance Survey maps as woodland or buildings (except in the early years when
there were numerous dairy cattle in town dairies).
It also seems reasonable to exclude dots represent-
ing crops or those livestock that do not use rough
grazings from large tracts of such grazings and to
locate some dots outside the boundary of a civil
parish when the area recorded in the summary exceeds
that of the parish.

Symbols may be used to represent qualitative
data, e.g., the leading crop in each parish; they
can also represent acreages and numbers by being
constructed proportional to the square or cube roots
of these values. They have the merit of avoiding

any assumption that agricultural and civil parish
are identical since each symbol can be located at
the centroid of the latter and will bear no obvious
relationship to parish boundaries. Such symbols
can be subdivided to show proportions and can also
portray more than one relationship simultaneously,
e.g., the proportions of the tillage area occupied
by different crops. Although divided circles have
been used effectively by Juillard to map French
agricultural statistics, they have not often been
used to map the parish summaries, perhaps because
they are laborious to construct and more difficult
to interpret.(70)

For most purposes, choropleth maps appear to be
the most suitable method of portraying the data
recorded in the parish summaries. They were first
used to show data for counties in the published
volume in 1895(71), but the first occasion on which
the parish summaries have been mapped in this way
appears to be Orr's study in 1916 of the agriculture
of Oxfordshire.(72) They, too, have been extensively used in the county memoirs of the Land Utilisation Survey. Such maps can show both qualitative
(e.g., rank) and quantitative (e.g., ratios, densities) relationships and, since only a limited range
of classes is used, groups of adjacent parishes tend
to fall into the same class, a characteristic that
facilitates comprehension of the resulting maps.
Their compilation does, however, require numerous
calculations (especially for the early years when
subtotals are frequently not given in the summaries)
and they necessarily emphasise the boundaries of
civil parishes when these coincide with class boundaries.

The construction of choropleth maps requires
three principal decisions, on the number of classes,
on the class intervals and on the base to be used in
calculating densities of livestock and proportions
of land. The human eye can discriminate between
only a relatively small number of shades of grey
(twelve according to Mackay, although for most
purposes six represents the upper limit).(73) Class
intervals can be determined arbitrarily or computed
statistically, e.g., quartiles or standard devia-
tions; the choice can also be guided by inspection
of frequency graphs, although some regard should be
had for ease of interpretation and for comparability
with other maps (Fig. 6). Problems over the choice
of bases for computation arise chiefly for the years
before 1921, since only the acreage of crops and
grass was recorded between 1866 and 1891 and (in

England and Wales) only rough grazings in sole
occupation between 1891 and 1921. In upland parishes the omission of either rough grazings in sole
occupation or common rough grazings will have a
marked effect on densities of stocking which has not
always been appreciated by those constructing such
maps. The most satisfactory solution seems to be to
calculate densities of total area for fairly large
groups of parishes, although this procedure results
in loss of detail and will understate densities, not
only because of the inclusion of non-agricultural
land but also because of the omission of holdings,
especially during the early years. For crops and
for livestock in the lowlands the area under crops
and grass can generally be used as a surrogate for
total agricultural area. In view of the difficulty
of interpreting the various categories of grassland,
there is much to be said for computing crops as a
proportion of tillage rather than of arable land.

In the future, ease of construction is likely
to cease to be an obstacle, since computer programs
are now available for the construction of dot maps,
proportional symbols and choropleth maps. The
choice of method will accordingly be determined much
more by considerations of suitability in relation
to the known characteristics of the summaries, the
purpose of the map and ease of comprehension.

Fig. 6 Representation of the proportions of the
acreage of crops and grass under the major crops in
the Chilterns, 1877. The values for the individual
crops are as percentages of areas under crops and
grass:

	A, over	B,	C,	D, under
Wheat:	19	15-19	10-14	10
Barley:	15	11-15	6-10	6
Oats:	14	10-14	5- 9	5
T.Grass:	14	10-14	5- 9	5
Turnips:	12	9-12	5- 8	5
Beans:	6	5- 6	3- 4	3

The area in the centre of the map enclosed by a
heavy line on each map in Figures 6, 7 and 8 is the
Chilterns, which is flanked to the west by the Berkshire Downs and to the east by the Hertfordshire
boulder-clay plateau. Key to shading:

A. B. C. D.

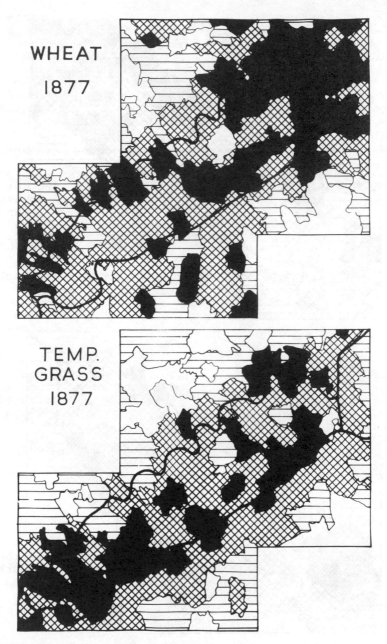

WHEAT
1877

TEMP.
GRASS
1877

Fig. 6

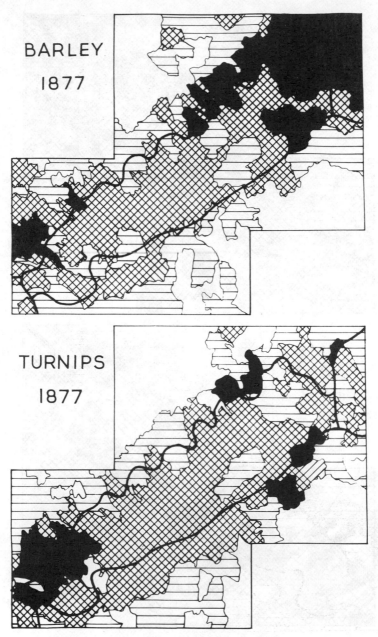

BARLEY
1877

TURNIPS
1877

Fig. 6 continued

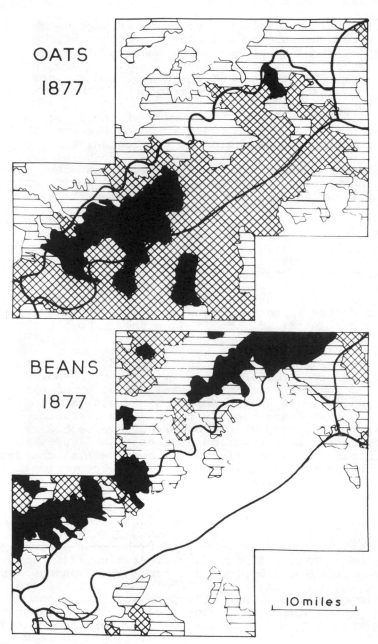

OATS 1877

BEANS 1877

10 miles

Fig. 6 continued

MAPPING CHANGES OVER TIME

Particular care will be necessary in mapping changes over time because of the possible effect of book-keeping changes between the summaries of adjacent parishes, the steady improvements in the accuracy and comprehensiveness of the census and any changes in definition and interpretation that have occurred in the period under discussion.
There are two possible ways of mapping such changes. Maps can be constructed on the same basis to describe the situation at the beginning and end of the period, e.g., by using the same value for each dot or the same class intervals, and then comparing visually, an approach that can provide only a qualitative impression and one that is feasible only if the scale of change over the period is marked (Fig. 7). Alternatively, the net differences between the values recorded in two sets of summaries can be mapped (Fig. 8). Such comparison can be either qualitative (e.g., changes in crop rank) or quantitative. For the reasons already discussed, it will not normally be permissible to map absolute differences in acreages or numbers. Even mapping differences in ratios, densities and the like is not strictly justified, but it does seem probable that a substantial proportion of the land in the summaries for each parish will be the same at the beginning and end of the period of interest and that, in so far as agricultural distributions tend to show a marked regionalisation, comparisons of proportions are unlikely to provide misleading results.
Dot maps are clearly the least satisfactory method of mapping change by either approach since they cannot show relationships and the figures for each parish may be affected by book-keeping changes and by improvements in enumeration. Proportional symbols have similar weaknesses, although the fact that it is a power of the value that is being mapped is likely to limit the significance of such weakness. It would also be possible to use divided circles to show proportional change. In general, however, choropleth maps will again offer the most suitable method in the great majority of studies.(74) They are particularly appropriate for mapping changes in rank and the small number of classes is likely to minimise the influence of the known limitations of the parish summaries. The chief weakness is that the resulting maps are likely to be more fragmented than the period maps and hence difficult to read,

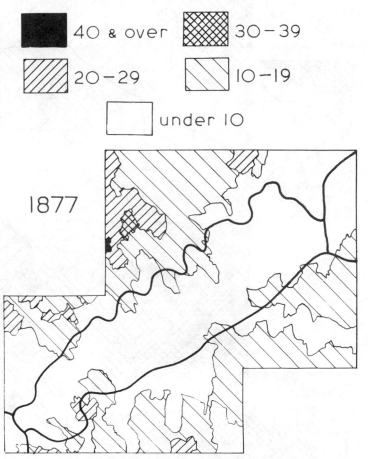

CATTLE 1877—1951

Number of cattle per 100 acres of crops and grass

■ 40 & over   ▧ 30—39

▨ 20—29   ◿ 10—19

☐ under 10

1877

Fig. 7   Representation of the numbers of cattle and sheep in the Chilterns in 1877, 1931 and 1951.

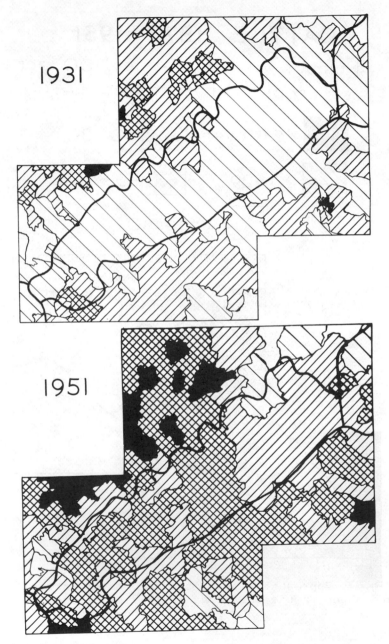

1931

1951

Fig. 7 continued

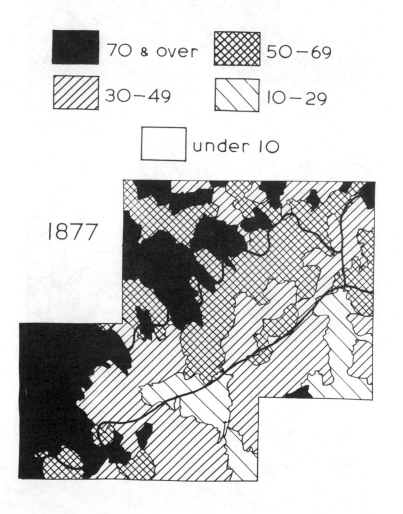

SHEEP 1877–1951
Number of sheep per 100 acres
of crops and grass

70 & over   50–69
30–49   10–29
under 10

1877

Fig. 7 continued

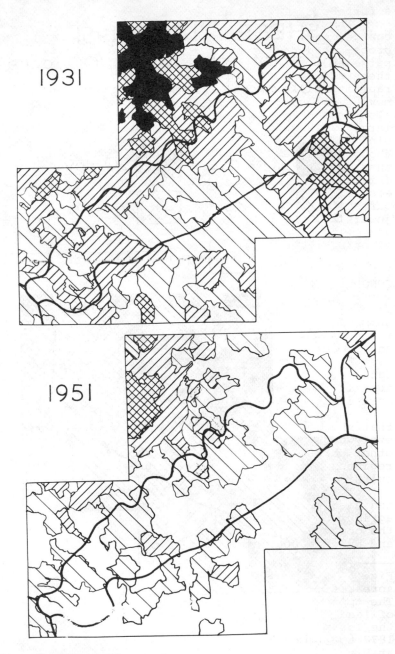

1931

1951

Fig. 7 continued

a further justification for grouping parishes.
In view of the difficulties inherent in mapping
change, there is much to be said for combining
cross-sectional maps with graphs for selected
parishes to show changes in the interval.(75) Unless
there are good reasons for not doing so, such as the
rapidity of change, it is again desirable to use
moving means in constructing such graphs; there are
also strong arguments in favour of using either
large parishes or groups of parishes in order to
minimise the effects of book-keeping changes, although this may run counter to a second criterion,
that such samples should be physically homogeneous
(Fig. 9). Of course, it must be recognised that, in
a strict sense, even graphing data for a single
parish or for a small group of parishes may not be
justified; but calculating proportions and densities
as moving means will again help to minimise the
effects of the known limitations of the summaries.

CONCLUSION

In evaluating the contribution that mapping the
summaries of the agricultural returns can make to
reconstructing the geography of British agriculture
and to analysing the changing pattern of farming, it
must be appreciated that it is the very wealth of
data they contain that has made it possible to
identify weaknesses that would not be apparent in a
more limited source. At the same time, it is this
very comprehensiveness and continuity and the fact
that the returns are collected on the same basis
everywhere that make them so important. For no
other period is it possible to say so much about the
regional components of agriculture or of agricultural change.
The 115 years for which they have been collected also include periods of major change in British
agriculture. In retrospect, it is unfortunate that
the opposition of farmers and landowners in England
and Wales to the census should have frustrated

Fig. 8 Representation of the changes in the
acreages of arable land in the Chilterns 1877-1897.
The upper map shows differences in the percentages
of land under arable in each parish in 1877 and 1897;
the lower map shows the differences in acreages in
1877 and 1897 as percentages of the acreage under
arable in each parish in 1877.

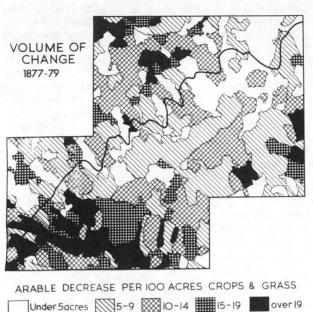

VOLUME OF
CHANGE
1877-79

ARABLE DECREASE PER 100 ACRES CROPS & GRASS.

☐ Under 5 acres ▨ 5-9 ▧ 10-14 ▦ 15-19 ■ over 19

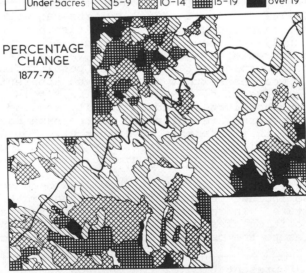

PERCENTAGE
CHANGE
1877-79

PERCENTAGE DECREASE IN ARABLE ACREAGE.

☐ Under 10 ▨ 10-19 ▧ 20-34 ▦ 35-49 ■ over 49

Fig. 8

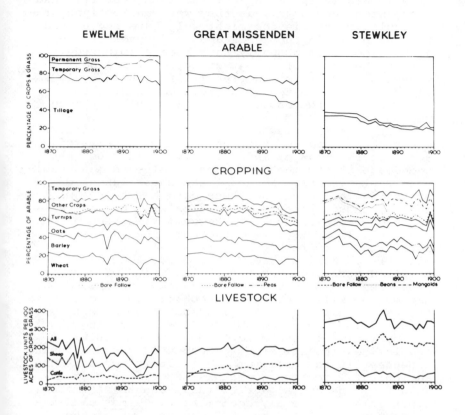

Fig.9 Trends in land use, crops and livestock in the
parishes of Ewelme, Oxon., Great Missenden, Bucks.,
and Stewkley, Bucks., 1870-1900. The three parishes
portray differences within the Chiltern area; Ewelme
lies on the belt of easily-worked loam at the foot
of the chalk escarpment, Great Missenden astride one
of the major valleys that dissect the Chilterns and
Stewkley in the clay vale of mid-Bucks. The acreages
under tillage, temporary grass and permanent grass
are calculated as a proportion of the acreages under
crops and grass recorded in the parish summaries and
those under each crop are calculated as a proportion
of the acreages under tillage. Numbers of cattle
and sheep and of all livestock have been computed
as livestock units and are represented as densities
per hundred acres of crops and grass.

experiments in the middle of the 19th century. Had
these been successful, as they were in Scotland, the
agricultural statistics might well have begun on a
regular basis in the 1850s and their grosser in-
accuracies would probably have been eliminated
before the onset of the great agricultural depression. As it is, the results for those early
years must be treated with great caution, though
they can nevertheless throw considerable light on
regional changes.

It is also somewhat surprising that so little
use has been made of the summaries in studies of
agricultural change; indeed, only limited use has
been made of the much more accessible and manageable
county statistics. No doubt the sheer labour of
extracting and handling these data has been a major
factor, though these difficulties will be increasingly overcome as more of the summaries become
available in machine-readable form and as systems of
automated cartography are more widely used. The
Ministry of Agriculture, Fisheries and Food has itself
acquired such a system and the adoption of such
processes of automated data handling and automated
map making will enable more emphasis to be placed on
the use of maps to find things out and to test hypo-
theses. The use of automated data processing and
map making will also make it much more feasible to
examine how the different components recorded in the
censuses fit together into agricultural systems and
agricultural regions. What is certain is that the
advent of the annual agricultural census has made it
impossible ever to say again, as the Times did in a
leader on the 18th June 1867, on the eve of the
second census (in reality, the first complete
census): 'Nobody knows, even in the most summary way,
what is doing on the thousands of acres spread
before his eyes in any landscape of ordinary extent,
much less in the county or in the country at large'.

REFERENCES

1. This chapter is based largely on a number
of articles by the author and on his unpublished
Ph.D. thesis, The Agricultural Geography of the
Chilterns 1870-1951 (1960), University of London.
2. J.T. Coppock, 'The Statistical Assessment
of British Agriculture', Agricultural History Review,
4(1956), pp.4-21 and 66-79.
3. H.O. Henderson, 'Agriculture in England
and Wales in 1801', Geographical Journal, 118(1952),
338-45, and W.E. Minchinton, 'Agricultural Returns

and the Government during the Napoleonic Wars',
Agricultural History Review, 1(1953), pp.29-43.
    4. J.T. Coppock (1956), 5-16.
    5. Returns Relating to Livestock in the United
Kingdom, House of Commons, Sessional Papers (1866),
59, C.528.
    6. Circular to Collectors, Excise General
Order, 31st May 1866, and Excise General Order,
30th May 1868.
    7. Parliamentary Debates, 117(1869), p.834.
    8. F.L.C. Floud, The Ministry of Agriculture
and Fisheries (1927), p.32.
    9. Excise General Order, 29th May 1867.
    10. Agricultural Returns of Great Britain 1869
(hereafter Agricultural Returns), C.4200, p.4, and
1892, C.6743, p.vi.
    11. J.T. Coppock, 'Agriculture', Reviews of UK
Statistical Sources, edited by W.F. Maunder, 8(1978),
Ch.5, p.17.
    12. J.T. Coppock (1978), p.16.
    13. Anon., A Century of Agricultural Statistics.
Great Britain 1866-1966 (1968), Ministry of Agriculture, Fisheries and Food, and Department of Agriculture and Fisheries for Scotland.
    14. Circular to Collectors, 28th July 1884.
    15. An Economic Survey of Hertfordshire Agri-
culture (1931), Report No.18, Department of Agriculture, University of Cambridge.
    16. Agricultural Returns 1877, C.1878, p.3 and
1892, C.6743, p.vii.
    17. Agricultural Statistics Scotland 1970, p.15.
    18. A Century of Agricultural Statistics (1968)
p.11.
    19. Agricultural Statistics. England and Wales
1936, Part 2, p.139.
    20. Personal Communication, Agricultural Census
Branch.
    21. R.H. Best, The Major Uses of Land in Great
Britain (1959), Studies in Rural Land Use, Report
No.4, Wye College, p.78.
    22. Excise General Order, 8th May 1876.
    23. Report of the Committee Appointed to Review
the Provincial and Local Organisation and Procedure
of the Ministry of Agriculture, Fisheries and Food
(1956), C.9732, p.62.
    24. E. Thomas and C.E. Elms, An Economic
Survey of Buckinghamshire Agriculture (1938), Part I,
p.11.
    25. A Century of Agricultural Statistics (1968),
p.10.
    26. A Century of Agricultural Statistics (1968),

p.11.

27. L.L. Price, 'The Recent Depression in Agriculture, as Shown in the Accounts of an Oxford College 1876-1890', Journal of the Royal Statistical Society, 55(1892), p.7.

28. T.W. Gardner, An Economic Study of the Ownership and Tenure of Agricultural Land in Oxfordshire (1950), unpublished Ph.D. thesis, University of Reading, p.9.

29. See, among others, Agricultural Returns 1878, C.2133, p.3, and 1889, C.5856, p.4.

30. Parliamentary Debates (1869), 197, p.830, and Excise General Letter, 244, 5th July 1872.

31. Agricultural Returns 1897, C.8897, p.xi; 1898, C. 9304, p.viii; 1901, C.1121, p.ix.

32. Agricultural Statistics England and Wales 1922, Part 1, p.7.

33. Agricultural Returns 1867, C.3941, p.3.

34. Excise General Order, 8th May 1876 and 20th March 1895.

35. Agricultural Returns 1890, C.6143, p.xi

36. Agricultural Returns 1869, C.4200, pp.4,8.

37. Agricultural Returns 1870, C.223, p.10.

38. Agricultural Returns 1871, C.460, p.13, 1876, C.1635, p.7, 1883, C.3907, p.5, 1886, C.4847, p.13 and 1897, C.8897, pp.x-xi.

39. Agricultural Returns 1880, C.2727, p.5, 1885, C.4537, p.9, 1886, C.4847, p.14, 1893, C.7256, p.ix and 1896, C.8502, p.xvi.

40. Agricultural Returns 1872, C.675, p.10 and 1885, C.4537, p.11.

41. Agricultural Returns 1887, C.5187, p.13 and 1888, C.5493, p.11.

42. Agricultural Returns 1897, C.8897, p.xv and Agricultural Statistics 1907, C.3870, p.15.

43. Agricultural Statistics England and Wales 1923, Part I, p.10.

44. Agricultural Returns 1884, C.4142, p.7.

45. Agricultural Returns 1897, C.8897, p.xvi.

46. Agricultural Returns 1867, C.3941, p.4 and 1868, C.4057, p.3.

47. Agricultural Returns 1869, C.4200, pp.4, 8 and 1870, C.223, p.9.

48. Agricultural Returns 1881, C.3078, p.14 and 1887, C.5187, p.4.

49 Agricultural Returns 1879, C.2407, p.2 and 1892, C.6743, p.vii.

50. E. Thomas and C.E. Elms (1938), p.11.

51. T.W. Gardner, The Farms and Estates of Oxfordshire (n.d.), Miscellaneous Studies, No.5, Department of Agricultural Economics, University of

Reading, p.13.
52. Agricultural Statistics 1905, C.3061, p.x.
53. A Century of Agricultural Statistics (1968); see also J.T. Coppock, 'The Changing Arable in England and Wales 1870-1956', Tijdschrift voor Economische en Sociale Geografie, 50, (1959), pp.121-30.
54. J.T. Coppock, 'The Parish as a Geographical -Statistical Unit', Tijdschrift voor Economische en Sociale Geografie, 51, (1960), pp.317-26.
55. J.T. Coppock, An Agricultural Atlas of Scotland (1976).
56. J.T. Coppock (1960), p.323.
57. Excise General Order, 12th April 1886.
58. J.T. Coppock, 'The Agricultural Returns as a Source for Local History', Amateur Historian, 4(1958-9).
59. J.T. Coppock, 'The Relationship of Farm and Parish Boundaries - a Study in the Use of Agricultural Statistics', Geographical Studies, 2(1955), p.17.
60. J.T. Coppock, 'The Cartographic Representation of British Agricultural Statistics', Geography, 50 (1965), p.104.
61. J.T. Coppock (1958-9), pp.53-5.
62. J.T. Coppock (1955), pp.19-22.
63. Agricultural Returns 1885, C.4537, p.1.
64. Excise General Order, 20th March 1895.
65. J.T. Coppock (1965).
66. A.D. Hall and E.J. Russell, The Agriculture and Soils of Kent, Surrey and Sussex (1911).
67. J. Pryse-Howell, An Agricultural Atlas of England and Wales (1925).
68. M. Messer, An Agricultural Atlas of England and Wales (1932).
69. H.J. Wood, An Agricultural Atlas of Scotland (1931).
70. E. Juillard, La Vie Rurale dans la Plaine de Basse Alsace (Strasbourg, 1953). Plate 2.
71. Agricultural Returns 1895, C.8073.
72. J. Orr, Agriculture in Oxfordshire (1916)
73. J.R. Mackay, 'An Analysis of Isopleth and Choropleth Class Intervals', Economic Geography, 31 (1955), pp.71-81.
74. J.T. Coppock, 'The Changing Arable in the Chilterns 1875-1900', Agricultural History Review, 9(1961), pp.3,7,10,13.
75. J.T. Coppock (1957), p.225 and (1961), p.11.

Chapter Two

THE TITHE FILES OF MID-NINETEENTH CENTURY ENGLAND
AND WALES
R.J.P. Kain

Although something of a political compromise, the
1836 Tithe Commutation Act can nevertheless be
judged a successful piece of reforming legislation.
(1) It achieved its immediate aim of ending a long
and often bitter period of dispute over tithe payment and obviated an outbreak of the kind of 'tithe
war' experienced in Ireland. In the longer term the
settlement proved permanent. Although the tithe
surveys on which the details of each district's
commutation are recorded did not constitute the
hoped-for 'General Survey' of the nation, they have
proved adequate to settle subsequent confusions
about tithe liability and are accepted in courts of
law.(2)
        Three tithe commissioners were appointed to
superintend the business of commutation and one of
their first tasks was to establish where tithe was
still payable. They addressed enquiries to each of
14,829 tithe districts which were usually townships
in northern England and parishes elsewhere. A minor-
ity were tithings, hamlets, extra-parochial places
and such like, many of which enjoyed separate status
solely for tithe commutation purposes.(3).
        A tithe file was opened for each tithe district
and these are preserved in the Public Record Office
as Class IR 18, having been transferred there from
the Tithe Redemption Commission, the twentieth-
century successor to the original Tithe Commission.
All the tithe files were heavily weeded before the
First World War (most in 1911-12) but they still
contain much useful source material for students of
nineteenth-century rural landscape, economy and
society.
        The tithe files were briefly described in an
article written by the Secretary of the Tithe
Redemption Commission in 1957(4) but their modern

use dates from the years around 1960 when they were
'discovered' by a group of research students from
the Geography Department, University College London
who were working on land use and agrarian change in
parts of England and Wales. Particular attention
was drawn to the value of these documents for agrarian historians by Elwyn Cox and Brian Dittmer in
1965.(5) Work carried out since then has under-
scored the value of the tithe files but has also
brought to light some unsuspected weaknesses. The
main aim of this essay is to discuss the nature of
tithe file source material in the light of information obtained when all the files were searched and
indexed for the compilation of an atlas of agriculture in England and Wales circa 1840.(6)

The 14,829 files can be divided into three
categories on the basis of their general contents.
These are:
1.   Files for 2096 districts where tithe was no
longer payable in 1836 or was redeemed by direct
merger in the land.
2.   Files for 5993 districts where commutation was
effected by the imposition of a compulsory award by
the Tithe Commission (but see category 3). Not all
of these commutations were carried out by apportionment, there were some instances of tithe and land
being merged.
3.   Files for 6740 districts where tithe owners and
tithe payers entered into a voluntary agreement for
commutation by apportionment. These were usually
confirmed by the Tithe Commission but in about 400
places they were replaced by a subsequent compulsory
award.

TITHE FILES OF DISTRICTS WHERE TITHE WAS NO LONGER
PAYABLE

The number of districts in each county exempt from
tithe or where mergers had been made or were about
to be made, varies from county to county. Extinction
of tithe upon parliamentary enclosure was the commonest reason for exemption. As a result, many of the
files of counties such as Nottinghamshire, Lincolnshire, Rutland, Leicestershire and Warwickshire
contain only a copy of the enclosure act as a summary of it, and a note by a representative of the
Tithe Commission confirming that all tithe had been
extinguished. In many urban parishes no tithe was
generated and in a few places tithe owners and tithe
payers were one and the same person and the usual

course of action here was to save the cost of apportionment by merger of tithe in the land. This
commonly happened in Westmorland, for example.

TITHE FILES OF DISTRICTS WHERE TITHE WAS COMMUTED
BY COMPULSORY AWARD

In those parishes and townships where tithe owners
and tithe payers could not reach an agreement, tithe
was commuted by an award drawn up by an assistant
tithe commissioner. Files for these places usually
contain a draft of the award and the minutes of
meetings held in the presence of the assistant
commissioner who called witnesses on behalf of the
various parties, cross-questioned them under oath,
and recorded their statements either verbatim, or in
note form. Some of these files have, however, been
savagely 'weeded'; those for some Shropshire districts are quite empty with just a note on the outside cover to the effect that all the papers were
'valueless' and had been discarded. There seems to
have been little consistency in the weeding process
as the files for some counties have almost entirely
escaped. Those of Somerset are especially rich,
particularly the files of places like Bridgwater
where moduses (nominal money payments in lieu of
certain tithes) were disputed. Charles Pym officia-
ted at many Somerset tithe award meetings and gave
very full accounts of them running to several dozen
pages in which he recorded, often verbatim, debates
about rotations, yields, and farming systems as well
as the history of tithing practices. Those of St.
Cuthbert, Broadway Old and New Enclosures and Chil-
thorne Dorner are particularly illuminating on Men-
dip farming as is that of Winsford on Exmoor agriculture. In Dorset parishes Aneurin Owen usually
set out detailed tables of titheable produce among
his notes on parochial meetings and in those Gloucestershire parishes where Charles Pym encountered
difficulty in reconciling various land valuations he
set out each of them for careful comparison. Many
of these are very detailed, noting acreages of crops
grown and yields obtained by each occupier. John
Johnes' Welsh files are similarly detailed; his
valuations in Pembrokeshire, for example, record
small acreages of potatoes and turnips which were
not noted in the more formal reports on parishes
where tithe was commuted by agreement (discussed in
the section below). R.B. Phillipson was perhaps of
all the local tithe agents the most assiduous in

striving for truth by assembling a mass of detailed information. As well as assessing the acreage of crops and yields for individual holdings, in some Shropshire parishes he increases the scale of enquiry to that of the individual field. It is thus very difficult to generalise about what information might or might not be found in the tithe file of a parish where commutation proceeded as a result of a compulsory award. The reasons for failing to reach an agreement varied considerably. Sometimes tithe payers and tithe owners had been deadlocked in dispute for a number of years. Elsewhere the reason may have been the fact that amounts of tithe remaining were so small that the local community did not accord their commutation a high priority. The more complex the problems, the more likely it was that extensive records would be generated. Other variables which affect the content of these tithe files are the attitudes of individual assistant tithe commissioners. Their interpretation of what they were required to do and the detail with which they were to do it varied greatly. And then there was the pre-World War I weeding which, as noted above, displays little obvious rationale.

TITHE FILES OF DISTRICTS WHERE TITHE WAS COMMUTED BY VOLUNTARY AGREEMENT

When tithe owners and tithe payers entered into a voluntary agreement for commutation and decided to apportion rather than merge the rentcharge, a local tithe agent (sometimes, but not necessarily, an assistant commissioner) was instructed to visit the district and required to write a report advising whether the agreement was fair to all parties and suitable for confirmation prior to apportionment. To help the Tithe Commission's local representatives judge these agreements and to organise and standardise their reports, they were issued from November 1837 with forms on which a number of questions were printed with space provided for answers. These provide much information on the local landscape, farming practices and the output of agriculture. 6,740 reports (including some 450 manuscript reports completed before late 1837) are extant in the tithe files. This represents about 57 per cent of districts where tithe was payable and commuted by apportionment (46 per cent of all English and Welsh tithe districts). As far as can be judged from our inspection of the tithe files, report forms were not

Tithe Files

usually weeded out except where an agreement was
replaced by a compulsory award. Occasionally the
report is the only document which has survived. As
Figure 10 indicates, there are marked variations
in the availability of reports, county by county,
reflecting both the general level of tithe commutation and the ratio of commutation by agreement and
award. Highest percentages occur in Wales where
much tithe remained and was commuted by agreement;
Denbigh heads the list with 88 per cent and seven
other Welsh counties exceed 70 per cent coverage.
The files of East Anglian counties are also particularly rich (Essex 71 per cent, Suffolk 68 per cent,
Norfolk 66 per cent) as are those of a number of
western counties (Somerset 66 per cent, Dorset 62
per cent, Hereford 61 per cent). The smallest
numbers are to be found in those midland counties
where many districts had been exonerated from tithe
payment at enclosure or where only small amounts
remained payable and awaited compulsory award (Leicestershire 12 per cent, Middlesex 17 per cent, Bedfordshire, Northamptonshire and Nottinghamshire 18
per cent). More than 80 per cent of the reports on
agreements (5471) date from the four years 1838-41.
The first one was produced for the parish of West
Grinstead in Sussex by Thomas Smith Woolley in 1836.
The last reports on agreements found in the tithe
files are for three parishes in Anglesey and Leicestershire dated 1848.

Two basic types of printed report form were
used (with minor changes in format over the years)
and these have been described with the aid of speci-
men answers from an Essex and a north-west Wiltshire
parish by Cox and Dittmer.(7) In any one county
only one type of form was in general use. Exceptions to this rule are so rare as to be explained by
the agent or assistant commissioner not having any
of the correct forms to hand and suggest, in the
absence of other evidence (see below), that the Tithe
Commissioners may have organised commutation on a
county-by-county basis.

In the mainly arable farming counties of the
country it was expected that agreed par rentcharges
would be checked by calculating a tenth of the gross
produce of the crops, usually by multiplying estimated crop acreages by average yield. Grassland in
these areas was valued according to the yield of hay
and the agistment value of the pasture. In the
mainly pastoral, livestock rearing counties of the
west, an alternative much shorter form, was used
which put less emphasis on the arable but more on

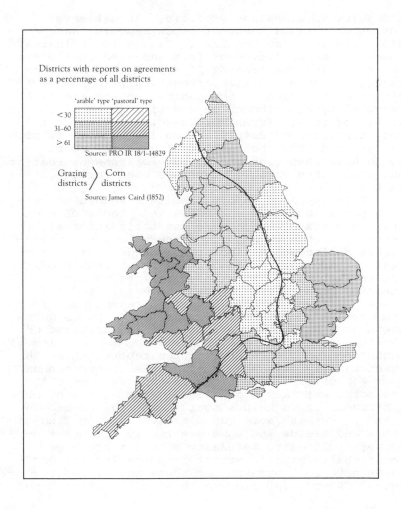

Districts with reports on agreements
as a percentage of all districts

'arable' type 'pastoral' type

< 30

31–60

> 61

Source: PRO IR 18/1–14829

Grazing ⟩ Corn
districts ⟋ districts

Source: James Caird (1852)

Fig.10 Percentage of districts with reports on
tithe commutation agreements and whether of 'arable'
or 'pastoral' type (for definitions see text pp.60-
62). The divisions into corn and grazing counties
made by James Caird in his English Agriculture in
1850-51 is also shown.

the value of grassland products. An estimate of the
number of various sorts of stock kept in these
districts was also required. Figure 10 indicates
that the 'arable' type of form was used in the east
and south and the 'pastoral' type in the west and
in Wales. Some counties, though, are in somewhat
anomalous positions. Shropshire reports are of the
'arable' type, although in counties to the south and
west, 'pastoral' forms were used. In view of the
long tradition of dairy farming in Cheshire it might
be expected that the 'pastoral' type of report
would have been used there, but for reasons that are
not known, the 'arable' type was used throughout
this county.

Both types of report contain a record of certain preliminaries:- the dates and places of meetings, numbers of landowners and their interest, the
quantity of glebe, amount of the rates, the value of
tithes collected in kind or compounded during the
years of average (1829-35), the relationship of this
sum to that of neighbouring districts, whether it
included amounts for personal, mineral or fish
tithes, and whether the agreement reached was fair
and could be confirmed. On 'arable' reports questions on these topics are printed and answered on
the forms; in 'pastoral' reports the information is
found in a supplementary written report which the
agent usually attached to his completed questionnaire.

The critical questions in many ways were 'Is
the agreement fair?' and 'Should the agreement be
confirmed?'. To help answer these, the agents were
asked to furnish some quantitative data on land use,
crops and yields and some descriptive information on
matters related to assessing a fair rentcharge.
Additionally, the 'pastoral' reports include estimates of animal numbers but these apart, their
detail is much inferior to those of 'arable' type.

QUANTITATIVE DATA ON FARMING IN 'ARABLE' REPORTS

The 'arable' reports required local agents to provide either 'a rough valuation of the tithes of the
parish' (1838 forms), or (from late 1838 onwards),
'a description and rough estimate of the amount of
the titheable produce'. Under this heading a great
deal of material useful to historians is provided.
The valuations generally set out the titheable
acreage of the district, and the amounts of meadow
and pasture, woodland, common and specialist land
uses such as orchards, gardens and hops which,

because of the high value per acre of their produce,
were sometimes required to bear an extraordinary
rentcharge. (Figure 11) But only the arable and
meadow and pasture categories are recorded with
consistency and tolerable accuracy over the whole
country (see notes on definitions of arable below).
Woodland is often not recorded because it was exempt
from tithe, as on the Chilterns or in the Weald, and
common land, as will be shown below, was difficult
to define and, because of its low titheable value,
often did not merit careful measurement. 'Gardens'
were sometimes narrowly defined as market gardens
but more usually included cottage gardens where
these were titheable. Hop acreages in those areas
where extraordinary charges did not apply were included in the arable acreage as were gardens when
these were not separately identified. Orchards
were either enumerated separately or included with
pasture.

The total acreage of the tithe district is
usually provided together with the amount of tithe
free land, waste and roads. This enables an immediate check to be made on the proportion of the
district that was titheable. Thus the potential representativeness of the data can be judged. For
example, data in only two of the 51 Cumberland reports on agreements cover the whole of a district,
the remainder have either data for only part of the
district or none at all.

The land use data were usually estimates but
almost invariably the local agents described them as
'accurate', although fewer than about one in four
were taken from an actual survey. Tests comparing
these estimates with acreages obtained by summing
the areas of fields recorded in the tithe apportionments (which were computed from the tithe survey)
show no evidence of systematic bias towards over or
under estimation of particular categories of land,
though some considerable random discrepancies have
been found.(8)

As a general rule, greatest confidence can
probably be put on the ratio of arable to grass. The
value of tithes was frequently assessed at about
one-fifth of the arable rent and at about one-eighth
or one-ninth of the grassland rent. Considerable
sums of money could thus be involved. This in itself helped to ensure that unreasonable estimates
would be challenged. As F.D. Hartley has neatly
put it:(9)

On the one hand the parson and lay impropriator

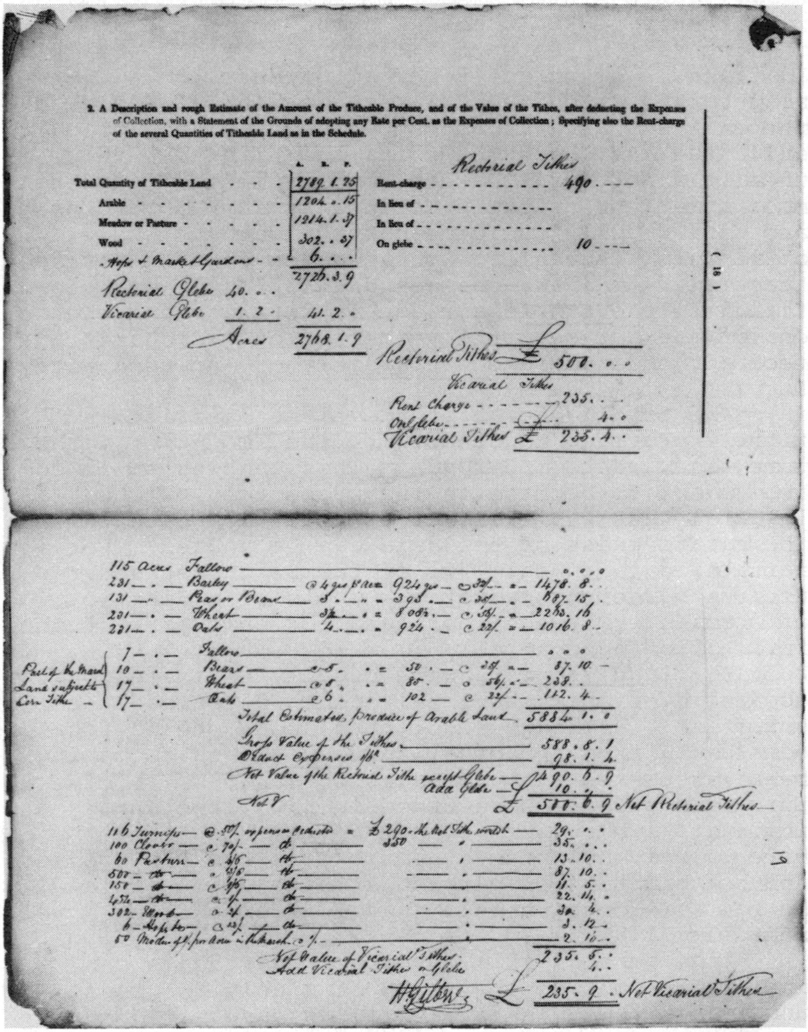

2. A Description and rough Estimate of the Amount of the Titheable Produce, and of the Value of the Tithes, after deducting the Expenses of Collection, with a Statement of the Grounds of adopting any Rate per Cent. as the Expenses of Collection; Specifying also the Rent-charge of the several Quantities of Titheable Land as in the Schedule.

	A. R. P.
Total Quantity of Titheable Land	2789. 1. 25
Arable	1204. . 15
Meadow or Pasture	1914. 1. 37
Wood	302. . 37
Hops & Market Gardens	6. . .
	2726. 3. 9
Rectorial Glebe 40. . .	
Vicarial Glebe 1. 2. .	41. 2. .
Acres	2768. 1. 9

Rectorial Tithes

Rent-charge 490. —
In lieu of
In lieu of
On glebe 10. —

Rectorial Tithes £ 500. . .

Vicarial Tithes
Rent Charge 235. .
On glebe 4. .
Vicarial Tithes £ 235. 4. .

115 Acres Fallow ... . . .
231 — Barley @ 4 qrs p Acre 924 qrs @ 32/ = 1478. 8.
131 — Peas or Beans 3 = 393 @ 30/ = 587. 15
231 — Wheat 3½ = 808½ @ 56/ = 2263. 16
231 — Oats 4 = 924 @ 22/ = 1016. 8

Part of the Marsh Land subject to Corn Tithe:
7 — Fallow . . .
10 — Beans @ 5 = 50 @ 35/ = 87. 10
17 — Wheat @ 5 = 85 @ 56/ = 238.
17 — Oats @ 6 = 102 @ 22/ = 112. 4

Total Estimated produce of Arable Land 5884. 1. 0

Gross Value of the Tithes 588. 8. 1
Deduct Expenses &c 98. 1. 4
Net Value of the Rectorial Tithe except Glebe £ 490. 6. 9
Add Glebe 10. . .
Net V £ 500. 6. 9 Net Rectorial Tithes

116 Turnips @ 50/ expenses deducted = £290 the Net Tithe worth 29. . .
100 Clover @ 70/ do 350 35. . .
60 Pasture @ 4/6 do 13. 10.
500 do @ 3/6 do 87. 10.
150 do @ 1/6 do 11. 5.
456 do @ 1/ do 22. 14.
302 Wood @ 2/ do 30. 4.
6 Hops &c @ 12/ do 3. 12.
50 Modus of 1/- per Acre in the Marsh @ 1/- 2. 10.

Net Value of Vicarial Tithes 235. 5.
Add Vicarial Tithe on Glebe 4.
H Gilbert £ 235. 9. Net Vicarial Tithes

Fig.11 'Description and rough estimate of the tithe-able produce' for Newington, Kent by Henry Gilbert, 1840. PRO IR 18/3728.

would claim their due; on the other hand the
farmers and landowners would attempt to reduce
the claim as much as possible. These two
forces pulling against each other would surely
produce a truthful record.

In practice, however, this truthful record was not
always produced. Errors can frequently be found in
the stated quantities of land of little or no titheable value such as timber woodland (usually only
underwood was titheable), heath, common, mountain,
moor and true 'waste' such as beach, mudflats, roads
and water. In northern counties, where such types
of land were extensive, many schedules are woefully
inaccurate, a fact that was recognised by the local
tithe agents themselves. In Cumberland, many old
enclosures were covered by moduses and only the
recently enclosed commons paid any tithe in kind.
Local agents often remarked on the scale of error
involved with acreages of common in schedules to
tithe agreements in northern counties. Boundaries
were uncertain; at Bootle in Cumberland, for example,
the surveyors included parts of a fell which in fact
lay outside the township. Also, where land was poor,
the difference between arable and pasture rental was
not necessarily very marked so that even this land
use division is less trustworthy than in the areas
of southern England where these tithe file data were
first tested and used by historians. Again at
Bootle, large acreages of common which were just
occasionally ploughed are returned as arable in the
schedule. At Newton in Cumberland, J.J. Rawlinson
considered that a large amount of land which had
been returned as arable was in fact permanent pasture and so he adjusted his own valuation accordingly. Thomas Martin was also aware of this problem
here (as he was in Lancashire and other counties)
and noted that parties had included land which might
be ploughed as well as land that is ploughed, in the
schedules of Ribton, Seaton and Thursby.
    Commons were usually exempt from tithe in north
and west Yorkshire and moorland boundaries were also
uncertain, sometimes only known for the parish as a
whole and not for individual townships. There was
potential here for some double counting and omission.
The tithe files of the several townships of Masham
parish in the North Riding, for example, note moorland in written commentaries but do not enumerate
its acreage. Reference to the tithe apportionments
reveals that there were 6464 acres of common in the
whole parish over which all the townships had rights

of use.

The foregoing comments suggest that little
reliance can be placed on the acreage of those categories of land which, for reasons of local circumstances, generated little titheable produce or were
covered by trifling moduses. Assistant commissioner
Charles Howard's practice in several West Riding
townships can perhaps serve as a final caution. In
his reports he often comments that the schedules are
accurate as far as they relate to enclosed lands but
that there is doubt as to the exact boundaries of
extensive, unenclosed moors. However, he says, that
as he had no intention of apportioning any rent-
charge on the moors, the fact that common acreages
were quite inaccurate was of no material concern.

It was in fact quite rare for a local agent to
challenge an agreement even if his own valuation
departed quite considerably from the agreed rent-
charge. As Eric Evans notes, the Tithe Commission
took a voluntary agreement as prima facie evidence
of reasonableness.(10)

In a separate table after the land use data,
the local agents set out the acreages of crops grown
on the arable, their yields and the prices that were
used to obtain the amount of gross produce. (Figure
11) Rarely are any of these figures taken from an
actual survey, more usually the arable acreage, itself often an estimate, was divided by the number of
courses in the rotation generally followed. Nor
were the yields necessarily those that had actually
been obtained in the previous harvest. For the
purposes of tithe commutation, a fair par rentcharge
over the years of average, 1829-35, was required and
to assess this, average acreages and average yields
were actually better and fairer than those relating
to one particular season. It is important to remember that this generalising filter was applied by the
local agents at the stage when they were compiling
data. For example, in districts of varied soils,
farmers might practise two or three rotations but
yields quoted would be a parish average for each
crop. Sometimes local agents consciously depressed
yields where they were convinced that unusually high
farming with above average investment was being
practised. For example, T.S. Woolley wrote in 1837
at West Stow in Suffolk:

in making my calculations I have taken an
average of crops on the arable land, not taking
the actual produce as now cultivated - but such
as I think could be relied on with ordinary

farms. The present produce would probably be
much greater.

In Warwickshire, on the other hand, the reverse
happened where local agents found that yields were
not as high as they ought to have been because of
the practice of close-cropping. The yields recorded
in the valuations appear much higher than might be
expected from their frequent descriptions of low
farming.
Woodland yields quoted in the files are of
little value as usually only underwood or coppice
was titheable. For example, at Bilsthorpe, Grove
and Thorney in Nottinghamshire, John Pickering
quoted annual values of 9-11 shillings/acre; his 33
shillings at Normanton-on-the-Wolds and 40 shillings
at Ramskill are closer to the full value of woodland
here. Similarly at Cranford in Middlesex, Horace
Meteyard valued wood and plantation at 40 shillings
but at Isleworth the 12 shillings recorded was only
the produce of underwood cut once in 10 years.
There were a number of circumstances that might
persuade a local agent or assistant tithe commissioner that a full valuation of the tithes was unnecessary, as where tithes were covered by a modus
or were about to be merged. In a few instances the
tithe situation might be such as not to require a
visit. Henry Pilkington did not visit Crawley in
Northumberland to value the tithes:

Apprehending you would think my doing so a
waste of time, as there is only one landowner
in it, and only 37 acres of land which are
titheable in kind, and the same individual is
owner both of the land and the tithes which
arise from it.

When for some reason the Tithe Commission's representatives could not recommend an agreement for
confirmation, a visit might be made by a second tithe
agent. For a hundred or so districts there are tithe
valuations made by two people. These often diverge
greatly, something which in itself should caution
against the uncritical acceptance of tithe file data
for any one district. Occasionally these repeat
visits sparked off a lively written debate between
two local agents. At Mavesyn Ridware in Shropshire,
J.M. Mathew reported in 1838 and then T.S. Woolley
visited the parish later in the same year. Mathew
based his valuation on a 6-course rotation while
Woolley considered a 7-course more usual in the

parish. Mathew wrote disputing Woolley's valuation
and the implied slur which it cast on his own abil-
ities. He asserted that the 7-course was not
followed in the county, that Woolley's wheat and
barley yield figures were incorrect and that he himself was much more familiar with Staffordshire farming than 'even the eminent Mr. Woolley' as he had
worked as an auditor on Lord Ferrers' estate. Perhaps
in this case we can side with Mathew as 7-course
rotations are only recorded in the reports on agreements of two places in Staffordshire, the neighbouring Hanstall and Mavesyn Ridware, both of which were
visited by T.S. Woolley! No other local agent reporting on Staffordshire agreements founded his
valuation on such a system of cropping.

QUANTITATIVE DATA FROM 'PASTORAL' REPORTS

Although it is necessary to hedge around 'arable'
report data with qualification, these are relatively
slight compared with the sort of accuracy problems
encountered with 'pastoral' type reports. In these
last, assistant tithe commissioners and local agents
were asked to estimate the acreage of arable defined
as: "land actually ploughed in the present or last
season, whether sown with corn, planted with roots
or fallow, but excluding seeds". Conversely,
question 7 asked for the number of acres of pasture
including seeds. In the tithe apportionments on the
other hand and also in 'arable' reports, 'arable'
usually included land that had been ploughed within the
years of average. For the western counties, however,
the 'pastoral' reports' definition is a realistic
interpretation of arable because seeds were usually
pastured for at least three years and quite often
for ten or more years before being ploughed up again.
Indeed, quite spurious arable acreages will be
obtained if data is taken from the tithe apportionments of this part of the country.(11)
    In 'pastoral' reports, the acreage of crops was
not asked for but rather question 2 said 'What is
the course of crops?' (Figure 12). It is possible,
though, to derive estimates of the acreages of individual crops by dividing the acreage of arable by
the number of courses (excluding the seed courses)
in the rotation. In fact, this is exactly the
method by which most tithe agents produced their
'rough estimate of the amount of titheable produce'
in eastern counties. However, for a number of
reasons it is not possible to derive the acreages of

Parish of *Mamhead* **County of** *Devon*

QUESTIONS.	ANSWERS.

1.—How many Acres of Arable Land (including under that description the Land actually ploughed in the present or last season, whether sown with corn, planted with roots or fallow, but excluding seeds)?

180

2.—What is the course of Crops?

Green Crop - Wheat - Barley & Oats. Seeds Wheat average 14 Bls per acre — Barley and Oats 2.5 Bl. Clover Hay average 15 Cwt per acre - Meadow Hay a ton: about 50 acres of Clover and 40 acres of Meadow are mown every year. No farmer is allowed to plant more than 2 rows of Potatoes in a year about 10 acres are planted in the Parish.

3.—What is the nature of the Soil?

A Red sharp gravel

4.—What is the Sub-soil?

D.°

5.—What description of Timber grown in the Hedge-rows, or otherwise; Oak, Elm, Ash or Beech?

Oak - Ash - Elm

6.—What is the fair average rentable Value per acre of the Arable Land?

18"

7.—What is the number of Acres of Pasture, including seeds?

644.

Fig.12

(2)

QUESTIONS.	ANSWERS.
8.—What is the nature of the Soil ?	*Mostly gravel.*
9.—What is the Sub-soil ?	*Do*
10.—What description of Timber ?	*Elm – Oak.*
11.—What is the number of Acres of Common ?	*30*
12.—Stock : Number of Cows ? _ _ _ - Ditto - Bullocks ? _ _ - Ditto - Horses ? _ _ — Ditto - Sheep ? _ . — ·	*24.* *55* *25* *710* } *From actual Counting.*
13.—What is the fair average rentable Value of the Pasture ?	*27*
14.—Ditto, of the Common ?	*1*
15.—Average Composition on the seven years previous to Christmas 1835 - Add average amount of Rates, if paid by the Occupiers or Landowners for the Tithe-owner - - - -	£. s. d. *136 . 9 . 6* *3 . 9 . 2 2* *139 . 18 . 8 2*

Fig.12

Tithe Files

(3)

VALUATION.

		£.	s.	d.
One-fifth of the Arable, at	18ˢ per Acre -	- 32	8	0
One-eighth of the Pasture, at	27ᵛ per Acre -	-108	13	6
One-eighth of the Common, at	1ˢ per Acre	- 0	3	9

TOTAL - - - £. 141 . 5 . 3

Total Rent-charge, exclusive of Glebe - - -145 . 0 . 0

Difference - - - £. 3 . 14 . 9 .

Remarks, stating the peculiar circumstances of the Parish, which may affect the value of the Tithe.

The Course of Husbandry, which Sir Robert Newman has adopted, tends very much to improve the Parish: but as much of the arable Land is being converted into Pasture - the present value of the Tithe is not likely to be much enhanced -- However the great improvements now carrying into effect in the rough lands of the parish will very probably prevent the Tithes from considerably diminishing in Value.

J. J.

Septʳ 8ᵗʰ 1838.

Fig.12 Report on the tithe agreement at Mamhead, Devon made by James Jerwood in 1838. In his comments he notes crop and grassland yields, covenants restricting the acreage of potatoes grown in a year, that the stock numbers were obtained 'from actual counting' and the improving example set by the principal land owner in the parish. PRO IR 18/1387.

71

all crops in all districts in this way. Firstly,
more than one rotation might be stated without an
indication of the proportion of the district to which
each applied. Secondly, rotations were sometimes
less than explicitly described; at Marma Church in
Cornwall, William Glasson recorded a rotation of:
"wheat, barley or oats - part potatoes and a small
quantity of turnips". With such an imprecise description of the rotation it is not possible to
derive crop acreages. Yield figures are not usually
entered on the printed 'pastoral' forms but are to
be found in manuscript reports which accompany them.
Similar reservations apply to the accuracy of these
yield data as apply to those of 'arable' reports.
     As with 'arable' reports, the acreages of land
of little or no titheable value are most suspect.
'Downland', for example, presented all Dorset local
agents with the problem of whether to record it as
pasture or common. Their practice varied and individuals did not always act consistently.
     Assistant commissioners and local agents varied
much in the assiduity with which they checked for
errors in the data they recorded. George Louis was
one of those most concerned to tighten up procedures.
He decided, for example, to make the Pulham, Dorset,
agreement a test case which he hoped would be pub-
licised and help improve the care with which future
agreements were drawn up. In his words:

          I think this rigid enquiry will have the effect
          of inducing greater precision in the drawing up
          of agreements for I shall have shown in some
          instances that this is done in a slovenly manner.

Further comments on the accuracy of land use and crop
data in 'pastoral' reports are to be found in an
earlier study of Cornish agriculture.(12) A useful
general rule is the one already stated in the discussion of 'arable' reports; the lower the value of
titheable produce, the more 'rough and ready' estimates were likely to be.
     In Monmouthshire and Welsh counties, few reports
contain precise statements about rotations so that
very little crop data can be obtained. But there
are exceptions. John Fenton, who completed all but
two of the Anglesey reports, usually included a
valuation of the parish lands and crops, providing a
source of acreages better than the vague and confused statements on the questionnaires. In Merion-
eth, both of the local agents working in the county
state the acreage in tillage in their reports and

then subdivide it into the acreages of corn, root
and pulse and fallow crops. This practice is, however, exceptional in Wales where even the arable/
pasture distinction is usually very suspect. Acreages in Monmouthshire are usually rounded to 10, 100
or even to 1000 acres. At Goytey, Charles Pym
simply halved the parish to obtain pasture and
arable acreages. At Llanvetherine, the whole
parish was estimated at 2000 acres, of which 1000
were stated to be arable and 1000 pasture. Assistant commissioner Thomas Hoskins suggested that this
total would be found to be less than the true parish area; in fact the 1851 census records a total of
2153 acres so that 'error' is in fact something less
than 10 per cent. In a check on a sample of 12 Monmouthshire parishes for which acreages seem to be
stated precisely to an acre, John Chapman found that
they were not significantly different to the totals
found by adding up the acreages of every field from
the tithe apportionments. (13)
    Local agents were not required to state the
acreage of woodland on printed 'pastoral' forms;
only coppice and underwood were usually titheable
anyway. Sometimes woodland amounts were written in
at the end of the form or included in the covering
manuscript report. This practice varied from agent
to agent and from assistant commissioner to assistant commissioner as well as from county to county;
woodland acreages were infrequently stated in Gloucestershire and Herefordshire, for example. Nor were
the acreages of market gardens or hops required for
'pastoral' forms. This means that consistent data
on hop cultivation in counties such as Worcestershire are unavailable.
    In short, data on land use and crops in
'pastoral' reports are not as comprehensive or as
consistently recorded as in 'arable' reports. On
the credit side, assistant tithe commissioners and
local agents were required to enter the number of
cows, bullocks, horses and sheep kept in the tithe
district in answer to question 12 of the 'pastoral'
questionnaire. On 'arable' reports the produce of
grassland was assessed by the agistment value of
pasture and the yield of hay. Stock numbers were
presented infrequently and incidentally in 'arable'
reports or put, as in Lancashire, not in the form of
numbers but rather as the density of stock which the
pasture could support.
    For a number of reasons, caution must be applied
to the use of tithe file livestock data. Firstly,
and in common with some of the land use data, the

numbers are very often generalised and rounded to
the nearest 10 or 100. Sheep numbers in Devon
appear to be rounded to the nearest 1000! Some
generalisation is understandable and to be expected
in districts with extensive tracts of high, open
moorland; comments on the difficulties of estimating
sheep numbers in such areas are frequent in North
Riding files. But some commissioners in some places
did try to count exact numbers. (Figure 12) Secondly, the time of year when observations were made
clearly influenced the number of animals available
for counting, particularly in the case of sheep. If
tithe data relate to the middle of winter, lambs and
some first year ewes might appear in the enumera-
tions of lowland parishes while if taken in June, as
were the later, official Agricultural Statistics,
this would be the time of maximum sheep numbers in
upland parishes. In some places, particularly in
Gloucestershire where it was the practice to buy in
sheep according to the season, Charles Pym considered
that numbers varied so much that he could not
attempt to put a figure to them. In Monmouthshire,
assistant commissioner John Johnes decided to cir-
cumvent this by producing estimates of the numbers
of stock he considered ought to be kept in the parish rather than taking the number he found at the
time of his visit. Thirdly, any valuation of stock
in a breeding parish was more difficult than in a
grazing parish where simple counting of heads might
suffice. As Frederick Leigh remarked at South
Molton in Devon, to produce a realistic valuation of
stock in a breeding parish:

> A knowledge of the business of rearing cattle,
> with its attendant casualties, varieties of
> seasons, and other risks of local character
> and fluctuations in prices, acquired by much
> observation and practice, is requisite.

Fourthly, while references by assistant tithe
commissioners and local agents to attempts consciously to deceive them about land use and crops
are rare, they frequently indicated that they felt
that they were being intentionally misled by land
owners about the number of stock kept on their farms.
Some farmers in Pembrokeshire refused to cooperate
with assistant commissioner John Johnes by barring
their folds and dairies so he had to base his estimates on what he saw in neighbouring parishes. It
was not only Welsh farmers who were reluctant to
disclose livestock numbers. At Kings Caple, George

Bolls said:

> but with regard to the quantity of stock, I
> will not vouch for its correctness as I find
> it almost impossible to ascertain the exact
> numbers of stock in Hereford.

As with crop statistics, there is undeniably
an element of recording what ought to have been, of
what might have been expected on an average, rather
than of what actually was.

DESCRIPTIONS OF PARISH FARMING IN TITHE FILE
REPORTS ON AGREEMENTS

In 'arable' reports assistant commissioners were
asked to:

> Describe the parish and the quality of the
> lands, the system of farming, and whether
> the quality of the produce has been affected
> by any extraordinary instances of high or low
> farming.

On the relatively small number of report forms used
in 1838, the same request was made but phrased as
two separate questions. The 'pastoral' reports
required: "Remarks, stating the peculiar circumstances of the parish which may affect the value of
the tithe". The differences in breadth of the
questions is reflected in the value of the answers,
though the predilections of a particular assistant
commissioner could greatly influence what was
written. There are those who made do with cryptic
one or two sentence answers on 'arable' forms and
others who filled all available space on 'pastoral'
reports and greatly exceeded their limited brief.
    The papers of the London Tithe Commission have
not yet been found so it is possible only to guess
at the principles which lay behind the assignment
of assistant commissioners and local agents to particular tithe districts (see above). In any one
county, one agent reported on a clear majority of
districts. Therefore, the value of the descriptive
material (as with the quantitative data) can vary
from one part of the country to another in line
with the different approaches of particular
commissioners. Over 80 per cent of the reports on
agreements for Somerset districts were completed by
R. Page who wrote much fuller answers than usual on

'pastoral' forms. On the other hand, John Farncombe, who reported on 158 of the 188 agreements in Sussex, wrote very brief, rather stereotyped accounts, depressing the value of the tithe files as a source in this county despite a good (58 per cent) coverage of reports on agreements. Some of the fullest descriptions were compiled by Henry Gunning who worked extensively in Norfolk, Suffolk and Cambridgeshire. His accounts usually occupy two full sides of closely written foolscap and discuss markets, the quality of different types of land, rotations, summer fallowing and the cultivation of root crops, meadows and pastures, types of stock, and the nature and extent of woodland and waste. He was knowledgeable about high farming, frequently commenting on the types of manures and fertilisers employed, turnip culture, artificial feedstuffs and underdrainage. Nor was he averse to spicing his factual accounts with anecdotes. At one parish he talks about the idleness and drinking habits of the population, at another he speaks of paupers having been recently shipped to North America.

As well as the distinction between 'arable' and 'pastoral' report descriptions and the variability introduced by the knowledge and attitude of the particular local agent, the time available to him to visit the district and the local tithe situation also affected the selection of material for inclusion in his report. The sheer volume of work that some local agents and assistant commissioners accomplished was quite prodigious. Henry Pilkington completed 422 reports in 16 counties between 1837 and 1846 writing 140 in 1838 and 136 in 1839. From 1840, when he was appointed assistant commissioner, he also attended many award appeal meetings. In some individual weeks of 1839 he visited and reported on 10 districts, on the 17th of June he wrote four reports and on the 9/10th July, six. Even this work load pales somewhat, however, in comparison with Thomas Hoskins' 538 reports in 16 counties, written between 1838 and 1844 with no less than 203 completed in 1839 alone. With several townships to report on in a single day it is hardly surprising that accounts are sometimes terse and lack detail.

When time was not pressing and if the man was somewhat romantically inclined, he could look about and describe the scenery. Of Challacombe on Exmoor, James Jerwood said in 1838:

> Most of it is formed of that beautiful open
> sort of country where not a single tree hinders

the wind from blowing upon you - or solitary
bush is wide enough to intercept the sunshine;
... there is plenty of room - you may ride for
miles over the common - your road a sheep's
track, and chance your only guide to find the
right way out of it.

By 1841 the impression had palled somewhat:

I think the parish (Huntshaw) a poor one - its
general appearance and quality are as rough as
the most ardent admirer of moor, bog, and
bramble land could wish to put his foot in.

Most local agents were practical men, well-
versed in the farming and landscapes of the one or
two counties in which they undertook reports for the
Tithe Commission. The more educated and able who
from an early date were appointed assistant commissioners, such as Thomas Smith Woolley of South
Collingham in Nottinghamshire, or those who were
destined for later promotion to that office, such as
Henry Pilkington, a native of Northumberland, conducted work over a larger geographical canvas.
Woolley worked in 23 counties in the east and south
of England from Yorkshire to Kent. Inevitably such
men were confronted with agricultural systems with
which they were less than familiar. They were all,
however, by dint of practice if nothing else, experienced valuers, while observations by a relative
stranger often produced remarks on matters which
might have been commonplace and ignored by a local
man. An extreme example of this is the way that to
John Penny, a southerner, the Lancashire landscape
could verge on the awesome:

The works at Windle are for the preparation of
nitroil and chemical acids which have struck a
deadly blight upon the face of nature for
several miles around so that the aspect in the
brightest summer day is as the cheerless
wilds of Siberia in the most uncongenial season.
Leafless trees with their black trunks and sap-
less branches stand forth as melancholy marks
of the desolation...

Indeed, one of the strengths of tithe file parish
descriptions is that they often contain valuable
comparative or general statements. For example,
both Thomas Martin and Roger Kynaston bemoaned the
general state of fallows in Derbyshire and compared

them with other parts of the county. Kynaston who
had seen tares growing on the heavy soils of the
Kentish Weald said at Longford: "but I did not
observe any tares growing on their fallow; and to my
surprise, the person who accompanied me told me
that they were never grown". Good written descriptions of farming, township by township, parish by
parish, can make up for the lack of quantitative
data in some counties. The excellent accounts of
agriculture by J.J. Rawlinson of Milbeck in Cumberland are some compensation for the lack of reliable
land use, crop and livestock data in that county.

EXPLOITING THE STATISTICAL DATA IN THE TITHE FILES

As far as the use of the tithe files as a source for
agricultural historians and historical geographers
is concerned, this review and other recent studies
have confirmed the main guidelines and underlined
the valuable cautions offered by Cox and Dittmer in
their pioneering paper.(14) In particular the in-
exactitude of the statistics must be borne in mind
when analysing them and it is unwise to place too
much reliance on the precision of data for any one
place. All tithe data gain in strength when those
for one parish are ranged alongside those of its
neighbours and those for one region against those of
another. But when attempting regional comparisons,
it is imperative to ensure that like is being compared with like; arable land, for example, meant
different things to tithe agents in the west and
east of England and even to the compilers of the
tithe apportionment and the tithe file of the same
district in western counties.
    Provided that such cautions are heeded, the
tithe file statistical data can be analysed and
presented cartographically. For many counties,
they are available for a sufficient number of
parishes or townships to enable the delineation
of regional variations in land use, cropping
patterns and yields. Maps of the data for six
counties have already been published and an atlas
of those 33 English counties with 19 per cent or
more parishes with data is being prepared.(15)
Figures 13 and 14 are examples of the computer-
generated maps from the atlas. For these choropleth
maps the data have been reduced to a small number of
classes which is preferable to divided circle or dot
map techniques which demand levels of measurement
more precise than the data possess.

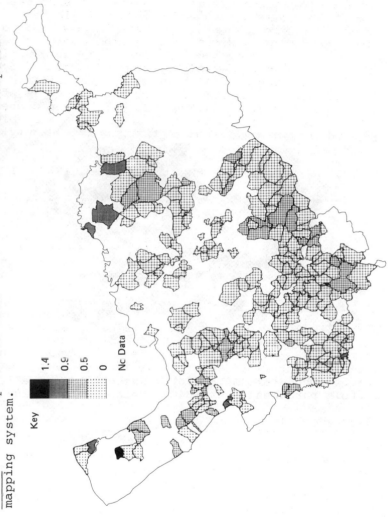

Fig.13 The ratio of arable land to grassland in Cheshire townships circa 1840. Reproduced from microfilm via the GIMMS computer mapping system.

Key

1.4
0.9
0.5
0
No Data

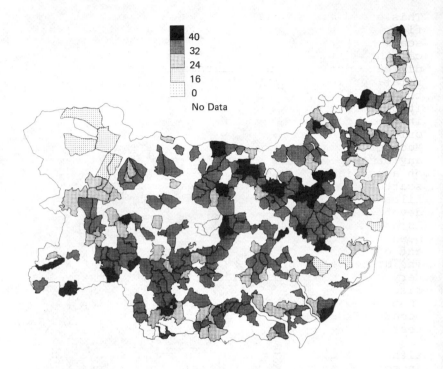

Fig.14 The yield of barley in bushels per acre in Suffolk parishes <u>circa</u> 1840. Method as for Fig.13.

SUMMARY AND CONCLUSIONS

This essay has discussed the value of the tithe
files as a source for agricultural and rural landscape historians. Other topics on which the files
can throw light are church incomes and the condition of the clergy, attitudes of parishioners,
relationships between labourers and farmers, and
the general structure of the community and the way
it organised and administered itself. This is all
information of great value to historians and historical geographers working on the nineteenth century.
Much of it is unequalled in its wealth of detail at
any other period. The problem is that information
on a particular topic is probably to be found
scattered through many dozens or even hundreds of
files so that most researchers have been unable to
devote the time necessary to search through them.
As noted in the introduction, all the files have now
been subject-indexed to enable material on agrarian
and other matters to be more easily retrieved.(16)
The discussion of the files as presented is also
very much an 'inside view' - the method has been to
discuss, test and assess the contents of the files
in terms of internal considerations with only the
occasional allusion to other sources and independent
testing.
        This review has also highlighted the fact that
tithe file data are not as consistently recorded
in some parts of the country, notably Wales, the
west and the north-west, as Cox and Dittmer found in
Essex and north-west Wiltshire respectively. On the
other hand, although relatively little land remained
titheable in the midland counties, those files which
relate to the few commutations made in this part of
the country are quite rich in data.
        It is perhaps appropriate to leave the last
word at this stage with one of the small band of
assistant tithe commissioners and local agents; just
twenty-four were responsible for 82 per cent of
reports on agreements. Their diligence, hard work
and fairness were in no small measure responsible
for ensuring that today we can count the 1836 Tithe
Commutation Act as one of the reforming successes
of the two decades before 1850. As a lasting test-
imony of their endeavours these men have left the
modern historian the benefits of their field experience as agricultural valuers and observers of the
rural scene. Their work load was prodigious and the
privations that they endured just occasionally crept
into their writing. From Plumpton Street in Cumber-

Tithe Files

land, assistant tithe commissioner Henry Pilkington
wrote to William Blamire, chairman of the Tithe
Commission in London and himself a Cumberland man,
to explain how difficult it was to attend meetings
in remote parishes:(17)

> During the night of the 14th, however, such
> fresh snow had fallen, and the coachman of
> The William would not start until a snow plough,
> which he understood the surveyor of the roads
> had promised to send, might have had to some-
> what smooth the passage. He therefore did not
> start till nine o'clock a.m., but bad as I had
> anticipated the state of the road, I found it
> far surpassed by the reality. Notwithstanding
> the snow plough and with six horses, with all
> the speed we could urge them to, and with many
> all-but upsets, we did not reach Newcastle,
> hungry, faint and starved to death (for the
> cold was Siberian) till between six and seven
> at night.

REFERENCES

1.   Tithe and tithe commutation are discussed
in E.J. Evans, The Contentious Tithe: The Tithe
Problem and English Agriculture 1750-1850 (1976) and
E.J. Evans, Tithes and the Tithe Commutation Act
1836 (1978).
2.   R.J.P. Kain, 'R.K. Dawon's Proposals in
1836 for a Cadastral Survey of England and Wales',
Cartographic Journal, 12 (1975), pp.81-88.
3.   The following are among those places
reognised as tithe districts: Boroughs, Chapelries,
Hamlets, Tithings, Liberties, Manors, Parishes,
Lordships, Townships, Villages, and Extra-parochial
places.
4.   The Secretary of the Tithe Redemption
Commission, 'The Records of the Tithe Redemption
Office', Journal of the Society of Archivists, 1
(1957), p.136.
5.   E.A. Cox and B.R. Dittmer, 'The Tithe
Files of the Mid-Nineteenth Century', The Agricultural History Review, 13 (1965), pp.1-16.
6.   R.J.P. Kain, 'Compiling an Atlas of Agriculture in England and Wales from the Tithe Surveys',
The Geographical Journal, 145 (1979), pp.225-235.
I gratefully acknowledge the financial support provided by the Social Science Research Council and the
work of my research assistant, Harriet Holt.
7.   Cox and Dittmer, 'Tithe Files....' pp.3-9.

8.   R.J.P. Kain, 'The Tithe Commutation Surveys', <u>Archaeologia Cantiana</u>, 89 (1974), pp.101-118.

9.   F.D. Hartley, <u>The Agricultural Geography of the Chilterns c.1840</u>, Unpublished University of London M.A. thesis (1953). p.12.

10.   Evans, <u>Tithe Commutation Act</u>, p.22.

11.   See, for example, the problems encountered by T.R.B. Dicks in <u>The South-Western Peninsula of England and Wales: Studies in Agricultural Geography 1550-1900</u>, unpublished University of Wales, Ph.D. thesis (1965).

12.   R.J.P. Kain, and H.M.E. Holt, 'Agriculture and Land Use in Cornwall <u>circa</u> 1840', <u>Southern History</u>,3(1981), pp.138-181.

13.   J.Chapman, <u>Agriculture and the 'Waste' in Monmouthshire from 1750 to the Present Day</u>, unpublished University of London Ph.D. thesis (1972), pp.21-26.

14.   Cox and Dittmer 'The Tithe Files....'; recent work is reviewed in H.C. Prince and R.J.P. Kain, <u>The Tithe Surveys of England and Wales</u>, (Cambridge University Press, forthcoming). See also, A.D.M. Phillips, 'A Study of Farming Practices and Soil Types in Staffordshire around 1840', <u>The North Staffordshire Journal of Field Studies</u>, 13 (1973), pp.27-52; A.D.M. Phillips, 'Agricultural Land Use, Soils and the Nottinghamshire Tithe Surveys <u>circa</u> 1840', <u>The East Midland Geographer</u>, 6 (1976), pp.284-301.

15.   For Staffordshire and Nottinghamshire see A.D.M. Phillips, 'A Study of Farming Practices ...' and 'Agricultural Land Use ...' respectively; for Essex, E.A. Cox, <u>An Agricultural Geography of Essex c.1840</u>, University of London M.A. thesis (1963); for Monmouth, J. Chapman, <u>Agriculture and the 'Waste'</u>...; for Kent, R.J.P. Kain, <u>The Land of Kent in the Middle of the Nineteenth Century</u>, University of London Ph.D. thesis (1973); for Surrey, A.G. Parton, <u>Town and Country in Surrey c.1800-1870: a Study in Historical Geography</u>, University of Hull Ph.D. thesis (1973); for Cornwall, R.J.P. Kain and H.M.E. Holt, 'Agriculture and Land Use ...' and similarly for Suffolk and Cheshire in the press. Other studies are listed in R.J.P. Kain, 'Compiling an Atlas ... from the Tithe Surveys', pp.233-234.

16.   R.J.P. Kain <u>et al</u>, <u>The Tithe Files of England and Wales: A Classified Index of PRO Class IR 18</u> (in preparation).

17.   I owe this quotation to Harriet Holt of the University of Exeter who is preparing a

Tithe Files

biographical essay on assistant tithe commissioner
Henry Pilkington.

Chapter Three

INDUSTRIAL LANDSCAPES OF THE EIGHTEENTH AND
NINETEENTH CENTURIES
M. Palmer

It is probably true to say that nothing has had a
greater effect on the British landscape than
industrial development. Yet it is an aspect of
landscape history that has, until recently, been
largely ignored, perhaps because of the often un-
pleasing nature of the landscape that industrial
development creates. For that reason also the
industrial landscape has tended to disappear without
any attempts being made to study, let alone preserve, it. Only during the last twenty years has
any serious attempt been made to record and interpret what is, after all, an essential element in
the making of the English landscape.
        The term 'industrial archaeology' is now a
familiar one. It was born in the Black Country in
the 1950s during efforts to record what still survived of the old chain-making industry which once
flourished there.(1) The industrial archaeologist
is essentially a field worker, attempting, like most
landscape historians, to record and interpret the
visual evidence of the past in the face of modern
development. The recreation of past landscapes,
even those of the recent past, cannot be attempted
entirely on field evidence, and the purpose of this
chapter is to describe what documentary materials
will be of most value to the industrial archaeologist. All too often, though, the documentary work
now being carried out by local groups or museum
staff to establish the county or regional distribution of past industries has to be broken off because of the urgent necessity of recording an eighteenth century brewery or nineteenth century blast
furnace which can no longer be retained in the landscape. The speed of modern development means that
the student of industrial landscapes has by necessity to be a field worker first and a user of doc-

uments second, even though this may not always be
the logical way to proceed.

Modern concentrations of industry give a misleading impression of the past industrial landscape
of Britain. Industry used to be far more widespread
than it is now. Obviously, extractive industries
have always been sited where the ore or clay or
stone lay beneath the surface, but studies of the
field evidence of mining in particular have shown
how even small deposits were once considered economic to work. These industries were therefore widely scattered, often in remote areas in the hills of
Wales, Scotland or the Pennines. Before the eighteenth century, too, most industries were dependent
on hand power and were often undertaken to supplement a livelihood earned in another way, most frequently in agriculture. Industrial tasks were undertaken where people lived rather than the people concentrating around industrial concerns as happened
later. The development of water power initiated a
change in this pattern although it did keep industry on a rural basis, high up on the slopes of the
Pennines, for example. Only the advent of steam
power in the late eighteenth century, combined with
improvements in transport facilities which enabled
coal to be taken to where it was needed, created the
industrial conurbations which were so familiar a
feature of the late nineteenth century landscape.

Another fact which contributed to the widespread nature of industrial activity was the unique
character of British landownership. Firstly, the
decline of peasant agriculture led to the domina-
tion of landownership by the aristocracy and gentry
which, whatever the social consequences, certainly
made the exploitation of raw materials considerably
easier. Secondly, the English landowners, unlike
many of their European counterparts, were prepared
to accept additions to their wealth from the profits
of industry and trade: they did not regard those
activities as solely the province of the bourgeoisie.
Thirdly, English landowners had from the late seventeenth century enjoyed the rights to mineral resources on their own lands. Only mines of gold and
silver belonged to the Crown, although earlier mon-
archs had laid claims to copper and lead mines if
they were thought to contain the slightest trace of
precious metals. The English landowner therefore
enjoyed a position very different to that of his
fellows in most of Europe, where the Crown often had
a monopoly of iron and copper as, for example, in
Sweden. Many estates all over the country were

exploited for minerals: landowners invested capital
in canals and railways and, by releasing land for
building purposes, played a central part in urban
development. Most areas of Britain have, then, experienced
some form of industrial activity in the past which
has left traces on the landscape. It is the task of
the industrial archaeologist to become as familiar
with those traces as the post-mediaeval archaeologist is with ridge and furrow. He must then, by
comparing field evidence and documentary evidence,
attempt both to delineate and to interpret the
industrial landscapes of the past, many of which
survive in altered form in the present day landscape. The two case-studies which follow suggest
how this might be done: one is an area of the East
Midlands and the other a remote mining site high in
the hills of central Wales.

TWO CASE-STUDIES

1. Moira: a nineteenth century coal and iron
community on the Leicestershire and South Derbyshire
Coalfield
An industrial archaeologist is usually attracted to
an area by some obvious industrial relic which he
tries to set in its historical environment. The
blast furnace shown in Fig. 15, now an isolated
building surrounded by woods and fields, is a good
example of such a relic which initiates the attempt
to recreate a past industrial landscape.
    The village of Moira lies in the area known as
Ashby Woulds, about three miles west of the better-
known town of Ashby-de-la-Zouch. The unusual name
derives from the Irish estates of the Rawdon family
who married into the Hastings family in the mid-
eighteenth century and who, in the person of Lord
Moira, first Marquis of Hastings, were responsible
for the industrial development of the area in the
early nineteenth century. Little new industrial
activity has been introduced since then and so there
is considerable visual evidence for the industrial
landscape of over 150 years ago. The two coal mines
close to the village were steam powered until fairly
recently and one still retains its engine. Moira
Pottery produces earthenware, a southern outpost of
the once extensive pottery and sanitary ware industry
centered on Swadlincote and Church Gresley. Several
rows of mid-nineteenth century miners' cottages,
still with cast-iron name and date plate, still

87

Fig. 15 Moira Furnace in 1979. The foundry was converted into cottages in the 19th century, hence the infilled windows. It is now a scheduled Ancient Monument in the care of the National Coal Board.

survive. By contrast, the iron furnace and foundry
are non-working relics of a no longer extant
industry. The furnace is about 11 metres high and
built of brick with quoins of local stone. The
most striking feature of the furnace, apart from its
excellent state of preservation, is the series of
arches, six on each side, which reveal the iron
bands around the inner part of the furnace. The
foundry building adjoins the furnace and the two
buildings are set on sloping ground, the base of the
furnace being about 4 metres below the base of the
foundry at the opposite end. Running alongside this
far end of the foundry is a wide cinder track and
below this, not far from the furnace, is a bank of
7 stone-faced kilns of brick construction, now
ruinous. These open out on to a field criss-crossed
with raised tracks, one of which passes by the very
tall brick building which can be seen in Fig. 16.
The thick walls, position of the infilled arches and
massive interior beams, one dated 1805, indicate
that this was an engine house for a steam engine,
probably of the Newcomen type, used for pumping or
winding up the shaft of a mine. Behind this building, now a cottage, is a wood full of humps and
hollows and the surrounding fields provide similar
evidence of past mining activity.

     What sources, then, can be used to reconstruct
the landscape of this area at the time industrial
activity began? The current metric Ordnance Survey
map does not identify any features in the area although 'Old Furnace' was marked on the previous
imperial 1" Ordnance Survey map. The reprint of the
first edition 1" Ordnance Survey map (Sheet 43) also
names the furnace and shows that in the mid-nineteenth century the Ashby Canal passed right by the
furnace - the line now marked by the çinder track.
The first edition 6" Ordnance Survey map furnishes
greater detail about the canal, which crossed the
village street at a point by the still extant
Navigation Inn, whose name is the only remaining
evidence of the presence of a canal.(2) On this map
the association of the furnace and the kilns with
the canal is very clear. When, however, one looks
at maps before the Ordnance Survey, such as John
Prior's map of the county in 1777, (Fig. 17) there
is no evidence of any industrial activity in the area
known as Ashby Woulds. The creation of the industrial landscape, then, dates from the last decades of
the eighteenth century and is presumably associated
with the building of the Ashby Canal of which, as we
have seen, no trace remains in the area today. One

Fig.16   Engine House Cottage, Moira, Leicestershire,
in 1980.   The shape of the building and position of
the infilled arch betrays its origins as a steam
engine house.

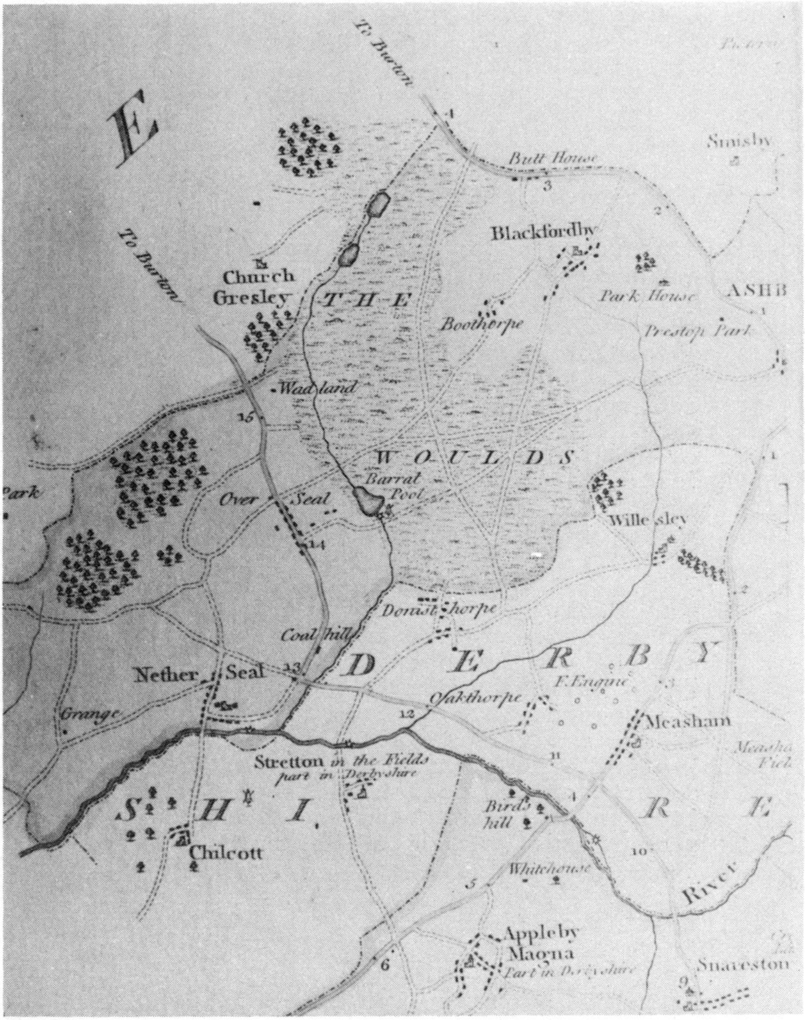

Fig.17 Part of John Prior's map of Leicestershire (1777). Coal is being mined between Measham and Oakthorpe but not yet on Ashby Woulds.

might, therefore, expect the Canal Company records
to be of some use in mapping the landscape, and
the Minute Books(3) do in fact deal at considerable
length with the industrial potential of the area as
the major reason for building a new canal. This was
opened in 1804, and the development of coal and iron
working seems to have followed rather than preceded
it.

The dating of this industrial landscape to the
first decade of the 19th century indicated another
possible useful source, the General Views commiss-
ioned by the newly established Board of Agriculture.
These obviously deal largely with the agrarian landscape but many do provide evidence for industry as
well, especially John Farey's account of Derbyshire.
Since Moira is on the border of the two counties,
it is mentioned in Farey's account as well as in the
Leicestershire General View by William Pitt. The
latter refers to the sinking of new coal pits on
Ashby Woulds, "lately established by the Earl of
Moira, at a great expense, the coal being raised
from a depth of near 200 yards, a three yard strata".
He adds:

> His Lordship has erected an iron foundry at a
> great expense, by the side of the Ashby Canal,
> where the ore has been smelted and cast into
> pigs as well as utensils for various purposes.
> The ironstone lays at from 5-8 yards from the
> surface, a 3 yard measure but mixed with two-
> thirds of a rubbishy blue bind, or clay marl.
> I understand the coal here is too valuable to
> make iron profitably and the foundry at present
> (October 1807) stands still, but it is meant
> to make further trials.(4)

Farey, listing collieries in the Leicestershire and
South Derbyshire Coalfield in 1811, refers to:

> Warren-Hill Furnace (or Ashby Woulds) 1m W.N.W.
> of Overseal in Leicestershire, an Iron Furnace
> and Mines: the deepest pits and the thickest
> coal in all this list, 202 yards deep and 21
> feet thick.(5)

He adds that the furnace had cost £30,000 to build
and that it was then resuming operations under the
direction of an engineer named Jonathan Woodhouse.
(6) Farey also shows that in Derbyshire iron ore
was roasted in kilns similar to lime kilns in order
to save both time and coal in the smelting process,

which suggests the original purpose of the battery
of kilns in Moira so close to the furnace.
   The Board of Agriculture writers, then, secure-
ly date the creation of Moira's industrial landscape
between the years 1804 and 1812. They also stress
the part played by Lord Moira in that creation and
it seemed logical to turn next to whatever family
papers still survived. Unfortunately most of the
estate maps are for periods either before or well
after the one under consideration, but Lord Moira's
personal correspondence goes some way to filling
that gap. He sent a box of iron ore specimens to
Robert Honeybourne of Fleet Street in 1793. He
reported favourably on its quality but tried to curb
Moira's enthusiastic belief in "inexhaustible
quantities of Iron ore on the Woulds" by emphasising
that only the discovery of a thick seam would make
it economic to mine.(7)   In 1802 a Mr. J. Case of
Dale Abbey Furnace in Derbyshire was appointed to
manage the furnace "that is to be built by his Lordship on his own account" and the Colliery Accounts
for 1806-7 show that half the coal mined in that
year (nearly 8000 tons) was used in the furnace or
for roasting ironstone.(8)   Moira's letters confirm
the statement made by Pitt that the furnace was
about to resume trials; in 1810 he wrote enthus-
iastically to his wife that the iron worker he had
hired, Mr. Shepherd,

         has on his first trial made exactly the same
         kind of iron which Woodhouse (his agent) had
         for some time past been purchasing at Shrop-
         shire for castings in my Foundry..... the
         people are quite wild with triumph.(9)

   But his later financial papers show that,
largely because of the state of the country at this
stage of the Napoleonic Wars and his own indebted-
ness which prevented the injection of further capital into his ironworks, the furnace was never the
financial success he had hoped it would be: in 1811
he had reckoned on an annual income of £7,400 from
the original furnace and a second one he had hoped
to build.(10)   The iron produced seems only to have
supplied the local market: for example, the Ashby
Canal Company placed orders for rails to repair
their horse tramways on five occasions between 1809
and 1818.(11)   An inventory of the furnace and
foundry in 1837 indicates that both were still in
occasional use, since "burnt ironstone at the limekiln and ironstone at the canal" are listed.(12)

Certainly the foundry was well equipped with
patterns for this kind of casting and the Newfield
Pit, opened in 1830, had received £1400 worth of
castings from the foundry. The tramway shown from
this pit to the furnace on the first edition 6"
Ordnance Survey map also indicates the continued
use of the furnace and foundry after 1830, coal
from this pit replacing that of now exhausted pits
nearer the furnace. This tramway can still be
clearly seen on the ground today. By 1841, however,
the Census Returns show that the engine house had
been converted into cottages, one occupied by a
limeburner whose sons were also employed at the
kilns, which were now obviously burning limestone
rather than ironstone. The intermittent use of the
furnace and its comparatively short active life help
to account for its excellent state of preservation.
    The family papers also describe the creation of
elements other than the furnace in the industrial
landscape of Moira. Various pits were sunk, the
earliest being Bye Pit and Engine Pit just south-
west of the furnace. Fig. 18 is based on a pencil
sketch found among the Hastings Papers and explains
the nature of the raised tracks, once railroads, in
the fields by the furnace, the converted engine
house - once Engine Pit - and the surface evidence
of mining activity in the wood behind. The Colliery
Accounts of 1811-12 refer to the sinking of another
pit, later Bath Pit, and the building of 'Moira
Town' at a cost of over £15,000 in that year. The
date plaque of Anno 1811, once on the now demolished
Stone Tows, confirmed that they were the core of the
'Town' built in that year. Lord Moira also sent
samples of clay found on the Woulds to Josiah Wedg-
wood, who was disparaging about its quality for use
by potters,(13) but suggested it would make good
firebricks, and these were soon being made in Moira.
The discovery of a brine spring in the coal seam
reached by shafts sunk in 1811-12 led Moira to hope
he could utilise this also, but the excise duty on
salt made it uneconomic to produce that and a letter
from the Treasury(14) informed him that he could not
use brine for any purpose other than extracting
salt. Moira appears to have suggested its use for
soap. Ever enterprising, he had a bath-house and
lodgings for visitors constructed in Moira to take
advantage of the fashion for sea-bathing at this
period: Moira was to become an inland resort! He
departed for India as Governor-General in 1813 but
his wife, returning for a period in 1816, was told
by their agent that "the Baths are going on extra-

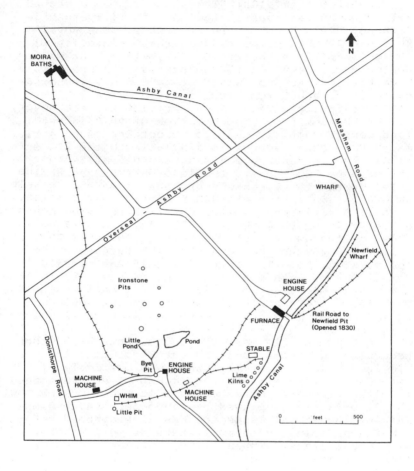

Fig.18 Moira in the early nineteenth century.
The shaded buildings still exist and the rail roads
survive as raised tracks in the fields. Scale 25"
to 1 mile. Based on O.S. 6" First Edition (1885)
Sheet XXII and a sketch in the Hastings Papers in
Dumfries House.

ordinary well, the Country people finding great benefit from them".(15) Thus encouraged, a second set of baths was constructed on a far larger scale at Ashby-de-la-Zouch, opened in 1822. The Royal Hotel in Ashby and the elegant railway station with its Doric pillars, built in 1849, still bear witness to its elevation to the status of a spa town - a reputation based on water brought daily in horse-drawn iron tanks from a colliery in Moira.

The family papers, then, provide a great deal of information about the creation of this industrial landscape to amplify that to be obtained from early maps. One other source is available to the student of nineteenth century landscapes and that is the photograph. So much of the landscape has been altered in the twentieth century that even photographs from early in that century can provide vital information. A series of photographs from the Edwardian era of Moira have come to light, several of them local postcards, one of which (Fig. 19) should be compared with the photograph of the furnace as it is today. (Fig. 15) The furnace itself was clearly in domestic use, with what look like pigsties built on to it. It was also somewhat higher than it is now. The old photograph also shows the engine house marked on earlier maps, then converted into housing and now demolished.

A considerable variety of documents have, then, been used to reconstruct and interpret this 150 year old industrial landscape. What was particularly interesting,however, was the amount of detail gained from the personal correspondence of the landowner. The important part played by landowners in developing the industrial landscape has already been referred to, and clearly their letters as well as the more usual leases, inventories, maps and accounts among family papers can be of considerable value.

2.   Esgair Hir: leadmining in Cardiganshire from the Seventeenth to the Twentieth century
Esgair Hir and Esgair Fraith (Fig. 20) are both parts of a mining sett situated at about 1500' O.D. in the remote area below Plynlimmon in central Wales. The site became familiar to the author while conducting a training week for industrial archaeologists during the summer of 1978. It was chosen for this purpose because of the numerous surface remains which needed recording urgently, partly because of the afforestation programme of the Forestry Commission(16) and partly because of the

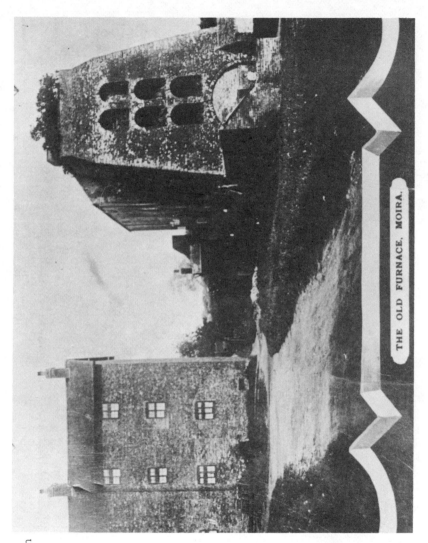

THE OLD FURNACE, MOIRA.

Fig.19 Moira
Furnace as shown
on an Edwardian
postcard

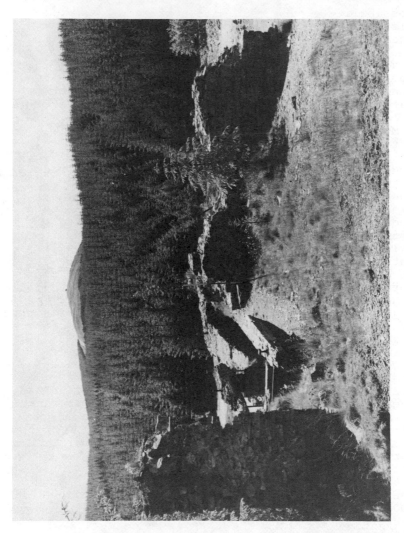

Fig.20 Remains of the ore crushing house and forty feet wheelpit at Esgair Fraith, Cardiganshire, 1979. Much of the site is clothed in conifers.

possibility of the reclamation of so-called dere-
lict areas such as this by the Welsh Development
Agency.
    The site is approached along a superbly graded
road from Tal-y-Bont on the coast road about 6 miles
north of Aberystwyth. Having travelled above the
steep valley of the Afon Ceulan and crossed the
watershed, the surfaced road continues southwards on
a leisure drive alongside the new reservoir of Nant-
y-Moch. The unsurfaced road which continues
straight ahead approaches a second pass, Banc Bwlch-
garreg, from the top of which there is a clear view
south-eastward   to Plynlimmon. The whole area is
littered with grass-grown tips and fenced-off shafts.
The ruins of an engine house stand midway between
two shafts which are completed with balance-bob pits
and the bases for horse-drawn capstans, implying
that they were used both for pumping and winding.
Half a mile further down the valley are three large
water-wheel pits, one raised above the ground with
an elevated tramway running to it, one with a plat-
form on which a winding drum had been fixed and the
other sunk into the ground with two balance-bob pits
adjoining it. Numerous dumps surrounding shafts can
be seen through the trees. The whole area was surveyed and the building remains recorded: excavation
was also carried out which revealed well-preserved
wooden ore-dressing apparatus.(17)   It was clear
that not all areas of the site had been in use at
the same time and so, following the fieldwork, came
the task of giving the site an historical dimension.
    The first document an industrial archaeologist
will turn to is the first edition of the 6" Ordnance
Survey map or, where available, the 25" Ordnance
Survey map. Although the Ordnance Survey agreed
after 1856 to cover the country on a 25" rather than
a 6" scale, the 25" survey was not carried out in
what were then uncultivated areas, usually above the
1000' contour line. Many mining areas were not,
therefore, published on a 25" scale and the 6" maps
are insufficiently detailed to be of much use. Of
course, mining engineers were usually surveyors
themselves and made their own maps, but one needs to
know something of the history and ownership of a
particular site in order to locate other maps. There
are two major printed sources which assist in this
search, firstly the nineteenth century Mining
Journal, a record of all public mining companies,
and secondly the Memoirs of the Geological Survey
for the same period.
    Esgair Hir was just above the limits for the

25" survey of Cardiganshire. The Memoirs, however,
provided two accounts of Cardiganshire mining before
1850(18) and these, together with various advertisements in the Mining Journal, indicated two further
lines of enquiry. Firstly, the site had been worked
by the Mines Adventurers in the late seventeenth
century and therefore the writings of Sir Humphrey
Mackworth and William Waller might prove useful.
Secondly, the site was on the estate of the Pryse
family of Gogerddan and their family papers might
provide additional maps and information.

The seventeenth century material, run to earth
in the National Library of Wales and the British
Library,(19) showed that mining in the area had
begun in 1690. After unsuccessful efforts due to
lack of capital, the mine had been worked by the
newly founded Company of Mines Adventurers with
William Waller as mine manager until his disgrace in
1709. During that period mining had taken place at
the summit of the pass, where a shaft called the
Great Work was sunk. Two adits or drainage levels
were driven towards this from each side of the pass
but had not connected with each other by the time
the Company abandoned the site. The West and East
Levels, marked A and L respectively on Waller's map
of 1704 reproduced as Fig.21, are still visible today and there are several run-in shafts at the head
of the pass where his mining efforts were centred.
This map also indicated Waller's intention to create
a new settlement at the site which he called New
Potosi, hoping to emulate the silver discoveries at
Potosi in Bolivia. The lead in the area is argent-
iferous, but Waller clearly never fulfilled his
ambitions. He may, however, have built the earliest
houses on the site where the ruined miners' barracks
still stand today.

Waller's writings revealed one of the problems
of mapping mining landscapes which is also true of
many of the nineteenth century documents concerning
this site, namely that of reporting discoveries in
an optimistic manner in order to attract further
shareholders to invest in the company. Waller
claimed while defending himself against charges of
inefficient management in 1710 that he "had Orders
to magnify everything with Shows and Outsides",(20)
hence perhaps his report on the discovery of a vein
of lead ore in 1700: "I have such a glorious sight
before me that I am resolved to work Night and Day
till I have cleared the Works of Water"(21). Such
reports were equally common in the nineteenth century although the mineral statistics do not support

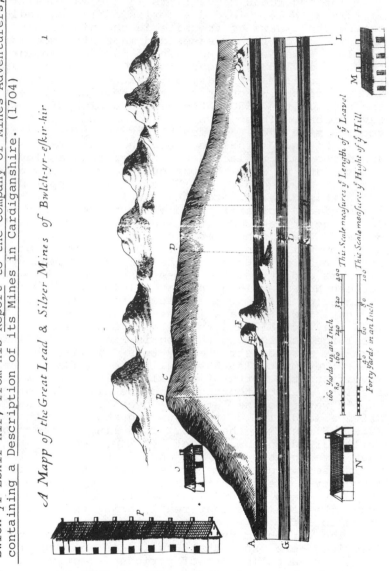

Fig.21 William Waller's Map of the Great Lead and Silver Mines of Bwlch-yr-Eskir-Hir, from his Report to the Company ot Mines Adventurers, containing a Description of its Mines in Cardiganshire. (1704)

A Mapp of the Great Lead & Silver Mines of Bwlch-yr-eſkir-hir such a view of the wealth of Esgair Hir.

The Gogerddan Manuscripts in the National
Library of Wales yielded a series of leases indicating the owners of the site in the nineteenth
century. Two of the leases had maps attached which
enabled comparison to be made of the development of
the site in 1853 and again in 1900. Further search
through their Map Library and that of the Mining
Record Office in London revealed two further maps of
the site in the 1850s, the period of its greatest
development. These have to be compared with the
reports made weekly or monthly by the mine captains
in the Mining Journal to check their accuracy -
again they may reflect hopes rather than achieve-
ments - and to date the various changes taking place.
Fig. 22, showing part of the site, was prepared
using this data. Where they survive, however, nothing gives a clearer picture of the development of
this kind of landscape than the day books or bargain
books of the mining companies, which detail the
tasks on which men were set. We know, for example,
from the Bargain Books of the Flintshire company of
Williams and Eyton, who leased the site in 1839, that
between November 1839 and March 1840 99 men were
employed on building the road up to Esgair Hir - not
a pleasant winter task in this bleak area.(22) The
lease map of 1853 and the Bargain Books show that
the large wheelpit at the Esgair Fraith end of the
site was also constructed by this Company, which
means they must also have built one of the two reservoirs to the north of the site, Llyn Dwfn, with
its long leat contouring round the hillside to
supply water to the large 42' overshot wheel used to
drive a long line of rods pumping shafts at the
Esgair Hir end of the site. This line of rods is
still marked on the present 2½" map, implying that
they were in use until the end of the life of the
mining sett, but their earliest existence is also
proved by a sketch on the back of a memorandum by
the mine agent in 1842.(23) It is such chance finds
among the documents that really bring the past landscape to life.

The various maps and documents, too many to be
described here, show that Esgair Hir and Esgair
Fraith are a palimpsest of periods of activity.
Mining began in the seventeenth century at the highest part of the site, but all that survives from
that date are run-in shafts, grass-grown tips and
the East and West Levels. The revival of lead mining by the Flintshire Company in 1839 created the
basic pattern of the western part of the site, two

Fig.22 Esgair Hir Sett in the period of maximum lead production c.1839-1857.

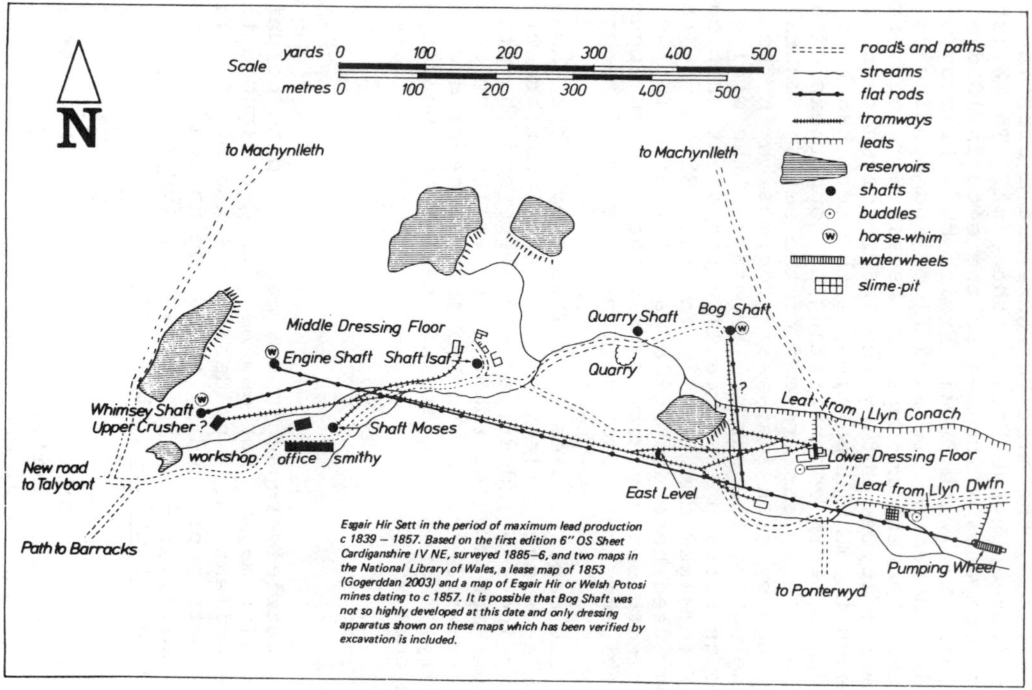
N
Scale
yards 0 100 200 300 400 500
metres 0 100 200 300 400 500
roads and paths
streams
flat rods
tramways
leats
reservoirs
shafts
buddles
horse-whim
waterwheels
slime-pit
to Machynlleth
to Machynlleth
Middle Dressing Floor
Engine Shaft
Shaft Isaf
Quarry Shaft
Bog Shaft
Quarry
?
Leat from Llyn Conach
Whimsey Shaft
Upper Crusher ?
Shaft Moses
workshop
office
smithy
New road to Talybont
Path to Barracks
Lower Dressing Floor
East Level
Leat from Llyn Dwfn
Pumping Wheel
to Ponterwyd
Esgair Hir Sett in the period of maximum lead production c 1839 – 1857. Based on the first edition 6" OS Sheet Cardiganshire IV NE, surveyed 1885–6, and two maps in the National Library of Wales, a lease map of 1853 (Gogerddan 2003) and a map of Esgair Hir or Welsh Potosi mines dating to c 1857. It is possible that Bog Shaft was not so highly developed at this date and only dressing apparatus shown on these maps which has been verified by excavation is included.

large shafts pumped by a wheel half-a-mile away, the
mine offices, the mine barracks and a dressing
floor just down the hill to the east. The Welsh
Potosi Company, which leased the site in 1853, linked Esgair Hir with Esgair Fraith by a tramway,
building a second dressing floor and opening up new
shafts. The engine house at Esgair Hir dates from
the early 1870s, but by the 1880s the western end
and even the middle portion of the sett had been
abandoned, work concentrating on copper exploitation
at the extreme eastern end of the sett. Generally,
then, there is an east-west progression in the
chronology of the surface remains on the mining sett
although certain features like the great pumping
wheel remained continually in use. Since the technology used here did not advance greatly in the
nineteenth century, it is only the map and documentary evidence that provide the basis for interpretation.
    The case studies described above were chosen to
illuminate the variety of documents that are of use
in mapping the industrial landscape and the problems
encountered in using them. The remainder of this
chapter will examine the various types of documents
and try to suggest what information may be derived
from them.

MAPS

No industrial archaeologist can afford to be unfam-
iliar with maps. Nor can he afford to ignore the
two excellent short guides to the use of historical
maps, both published by the Standing Conference for
Local History, J.B. Harley's Maps for the Local
Historian: A Guide to British Sources (1972) and
J.B. Harley and C.W. Phillips, The Historian's Guide
to Ordnance Survey Maps (1964). These not only indicate the range of maps available but also discuss
their uses and limitations: frequent references are
made to industrial and urban sites.

County Maps
Fortunately for the student of the industrial landscape, the main period of industrialisation was also
a time of great advance in county map-making. Between 1750 and 1800 most counties in Britain (excluding Wales and northern Scotland) were mapped on the
basis of scientific triangulation, generally at a
scale of 1" to the mile.(24) Conventions came to be

104

standardised, which enables comparisons to be made
between counties. For example, Nottinghamshire was
mapped by John Chapman in 1774 (published 1776) and
Leicestershire by John Prior in 1775 (published 1777).
The key to the conventions used on Prior's map
(Fig.23) indicates the kind of information about
industrial activity which can be elicited from
both maps, as does the extract from Prior's map in
Fig. 17, where even 'fire engines' or steam powered
mine pumping engines are marked. The conventions
do not, of course, enable the precise location to be
identified but at least their presence at that period is suggested. Additional information is also
given; Chapman identifies one of the mills on the
River Leen north of Nottingham as an iron forge, for
example. It must be remembered, however, that these
are private maps and the information given is selec-
tive. That a site does not appear on these maps
cannot be taken as evidence that it did not exist at
that time.
     County maps continued to be produced until
after the mid 19th century, despite the new Ordnance
Survey maps. The firm of C. and J. Greenwood systematically exploited Ordnance Survey data and re-
surveyed much of Britain in the 1820s and 1830s.
Neither their map for Leicestershire nor that for
Nottinghamshire, both 1826, provide so much detail
as the eighteenth century maps, but windmill and
watermill sites, for example, continue to be marked
and their distribution can be compared. Other
county maps were produced on a larger scale than the
1" Ordnance Survey and provide cartographic evidence
of industrial sites which had disappeared by the
time the first 6" Ordnance Survey maps were produced. For example, the survey made in 1830-34 and
published in 1835 by George Sanderson, a land surveyor of Mansfield in Nottinghamshire, of the area
20 miles around Mansfield, is on a scale of just
over 2" to the mile. Sanderson recorded field
boundaries and so enables a more accurate location
of sites he identifies, for example a large number
of brick kilns along the Derby Canal where all the
relevant buildings appear to be marked. His map is
also the only easily available cartographic source
for the important cotton mills belonging to the
Robinsons along the River Leen, in one of which the
first Boulton and Watt rotary steam engine was put
to work in 1786. The map names mill sites and marks
buildings, reservoirs and leats, most of which were
disused by the time of the Ordnance Survey first 6"
map of 1884. However, fieldwork and comparison with

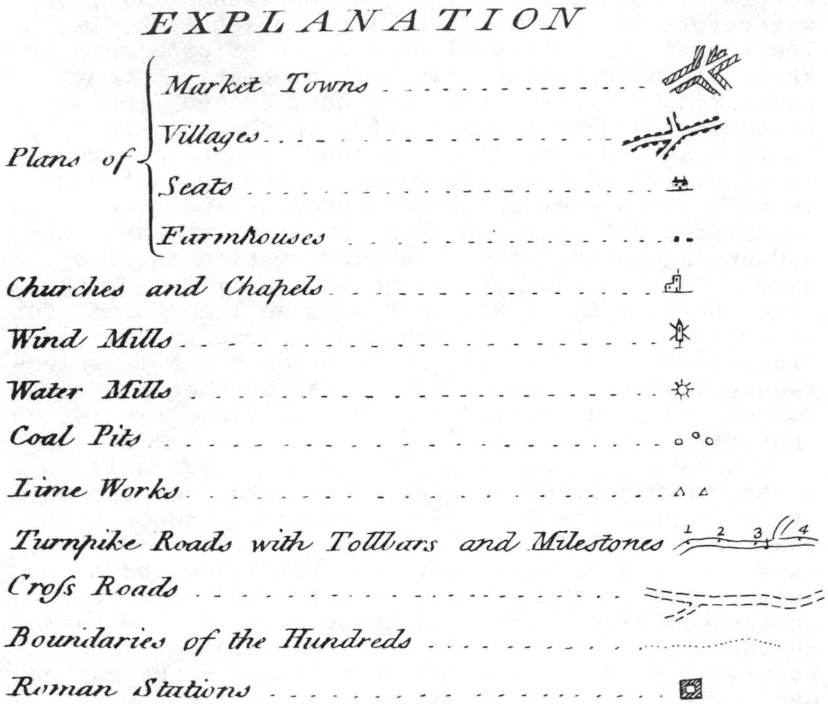

EXPLANATION

Plans of {
Market Towns . . . .
Villages . . . .
Seats . . . .
Farmhouses . . . .
}

Churches and Chapels . . . .

Wind Mills . . . .

Water Mills . . . .

Coal Pits . . . .

Lime Works . . . .

Turnpike Roads with Tollbars and Milestones

Cross Roads . . . .

Boundaries of the Hundreds . . . .

Roman Stations . . . .

Fig.23   Conventions used on John Prior's map of Leicestershire (1777).

estate maps has suggested that Sanderson's mapping
of the leat system may not have been entirely
accurate. It is possible that he was not familiar
with the intricacies of the complex system of leats
feeding the numerous waterwheels and so confused
their direction. Private cartographers had their
own specialisms and interests and, as with any other
historical document, the historian needs to find out
as much as possible about the author of his record
in order to identify any possible bias or inaccuracy.
It is so easy to regard maps as totally factual yet,
prior to the Ordnance Survey, they are likely to be
as subjective as any other product of an individual
hand.

Transport Maps
Maps of roads, railways and canals can be used for
two purposes, firstly as a record of the actual
undertaking and secondly for the ancillary information often included which, since so many transport
schemes were devised to serve industrial areas, is
often of great value in mapping the industrial landscape. These maps are, of course, linear and are
useful for specific areas rather than for mapping
county distributions of industry. Maps of canals
and railways in particular were the work of skilled
surveyors and can therefore be regarded as reliable,
although it must be remembered that only a small
proportion of the proposed schemes came to fruition.
These maps are also easily available as, after 1792,
promoters were required to submit exact plans accompanied by books of reference both to Parliament itself and to the local Clerk of the Peace. Those
submitted to Parliament are now to be found in the
House of Lords Record Office. Those submitted to
the Clerk of the Peace have usually found their way
into County Record Offices.
    John Ogilby's Britannia was published in 1675
and is our earliest specialised road map. The book
contains 100 plates each containing 6 or 7 strip
maps showing the road and marking features alongside.
Its use in mapping openfield and enclosed land has
long been known, but it is also of value to the industrial archaeologist because watermills, windmills
and, in some cases, types of bridges are indicated.
The road from London to Shrewsbury (24) portrays the
small size of Birmingham in 1675 and marks 'cole
pitts' to the north of Dudley. 'A Moore with a great
many Colepitts' is shown off the Oakham-Richmond
road to the north of Mansfield in Nottinghamshire

but in other areas where one might expect to find
these shown as, for example, near Newcastle, they do
not appear and it is probable that Ogilby was selec-
tive about what he recorded.

Eighteenth and nineteenth century road develop-
ments are well evidenced in records of enclosure and
of estate improvements, both of which were required
to deposit plans of alteration with Quarter Sessions.
Also available in County Record Offices in some
cases are the records of the Turnpike Trusts, which
usually contain a plan showing the location of toll-
houses and bars together with side roads which join
the turnpike and whose destination was frequently
recorded. In industrial areas this may well be coal
mines or lime quarries, whose traffic was a valuable
source of income to the Trusts.

Many late eighteenth century canals were specifically promoted to serve industrial areas and the
map which forms Fig.24 is a good example of the
information which can be derived from their plans.
(26) It is a plan of a branch of the intended
Navigation from Loughborough to Leicester which was
to serve the industrial area of west Leicestershire.
Limeworks, coal mines, pumping engines and even in
some cases the names of owners of industrial
concerns are recorded. Surveyors of river naviga-
tions were required to produce large scale plans of
proposed cuts to obviate obstructions in the river
such as mill dams. William Jessop produced in 1790
such a plan of 'the intended navigation in the
Rivers Wreake and Eye from the proposed Leicester
Navigation to Melton Mowbray'.(27) His papers also
include drawings for locks(28), all of which were to
be positioned at the upper end of the cuts. Fieldwork, however, indicated that the locks were eventually built at the lower end of the cuts, showing
how important it is to remember that canal plans are
indications of intention rather than records of fact.
The Syston to Peterborough Railway was built close
to the canal in 1846 and the survey maps for that
are in fact the best documentary source for the
river navigation as it was actually built, since the
survey maps for the latter were never updated with
changes of plan. The railway plans are on a scale
of 5 chains to 1 inch(29) and show the position of
locks at the lower ends of the cut where they were
in the end built, but what the plans do not actually
show is where the railway itself was built! The
intended route of the line is shown as a solid line
and the permissible margin of deviation by a dotted
line each side, but in some cases the railway was

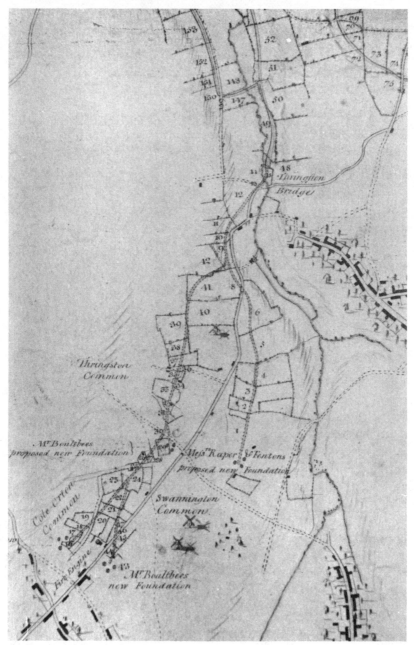

Fig.24 Christopher Staveley's map of 'An Intended Navigation from Loughborough to Leicester' 1790.

actually built outside the limits of deviation.
The importance of fieldwork to check map evidence
is as great as that of using maps to identify features in the field. (30)

Estate Maps and Mining Maps

The value of estate maps has been indicated in the
case studies. These, like county maps, became both
more professional and more numerous during the
eighteenth century. With increased industrial activity as well as agrarian improvement on the part
of landowners, areas not previously adequately surveyed were often covered for the first time. This
is particularly true of Wales, where mining development proceeded rapidly: the Gogerddan collection,
from which the maps of Esgair Hir were taken, contains 160 late eighteenth century and nineteenth
century maps of Cardiganshire. In the eighteenth
century, when industrial concerns were frequently
worked directly by the landowners, the estate maps
themselves provide evidence of the industrial landscape. The map in Fig.25 is taken from a volume of
maps of the estate of the Earl of Huntingdon in
Leicestershire and Derbyshire made in 1735. It
shows the charcoal iron furnace of Melbourne, Derbyshire, with its associated leats, ponds and so on.
(31) Corn mills are shown on other maps in the volume, while the names of closes indicate further industrial activity - Bleaching Close, Lime Kiln Close,
Coalpit Heath. Many areas of the country can furnish similar examples. (32)
    In the nineteenth century mineral rights were
frequently leased to companies prepared to raise the
necessary capital to exploit them. Lease maps, as
has already been shown in the case study of Esgair
Hir, are a useful source of information. Since,
however, they are intended to delineate boundaries
rather than indicate surface features, they may only
show the most obvious elements of the industrial
landscape. The mining companies themselves did not,
of course, produce their own detailed maps and plans.
Underground plans are frequently in the form of
sections and include surface features. Waller's map
of Esgair Hir (Fig.21) is an early example of such
a plan, while Fig.26 is based on a section of Esgair
Hir in 1857, made by the well known mining expert,
Robert Hunt. (33) The National Coal Board has located
plans of many disused collieries to prevent dis-
asters caused by flooding from old workings and information is available from the various Regional

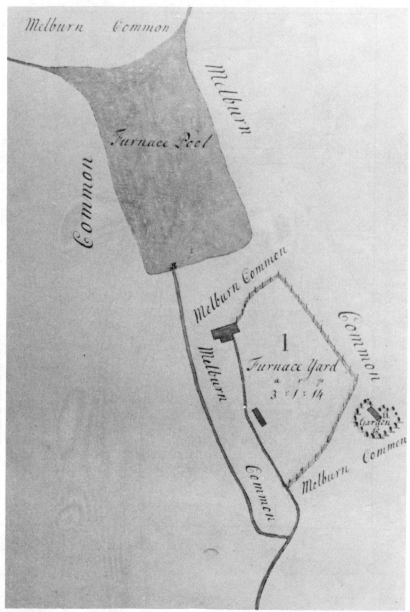

Fig.25 Melbourne Furnace, Derbyshire, from a book
of maps of the Huntingdon Estate of 1735 (Leicestershire County Record Office).

Fig.26 Part of a section of Esgair Hir drawn by Robert Hunt, dated 1857. (Mining Record Office, London.)

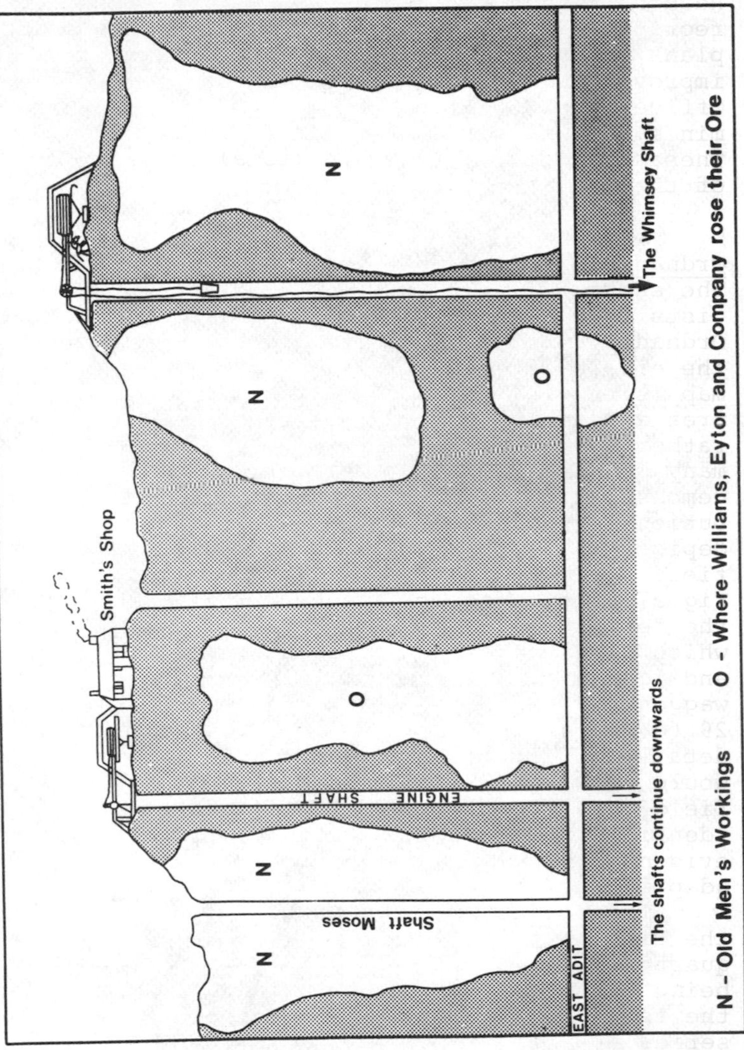

Industrial Landscapes

Headquarters. The Board naturally appreciates
recriprocal information from historians who locate
plans in other collections which can assist in
improving safety in coal mines today. The Home
Office has also produced lists of plans of abandoned
mines, including metal mines, from 1889 to 1920.
These can be seen in the Official Publications Room
of the British Library.

Ordnance Survey Maps
The starting point for most industrial archaeologists is the first edition of the 6" to the mile
Ordnance Survey map dating from the second half of
the nineteenth century. Where possible, the 25"
map is preferable which, since topographical features are shown to scale, is technically a plan
rather than a map. However, its non-existence for
many mountainous industrial areas has already been
demonstrated. The 6" map enables the county distribution of industries to be determined: the 25" map
depicts industrial concerns in such detail that
field survey work is often unnecessary. The map
Fig.27 is of Froghall Basin in Staffordshire,(34)
the terminus of the Caldon Canal and the point at
which limestone from nearby quarries was calcined
and loaded onto boats and later also onto railway
waggons. This should be compared with Figs. 28 and
29 to see how the area looks today; without the
detailed information provided by the 25" map it
would be very difficult to interpret the present
field remains. Industrial premises are usually also
identified on the 25" map, an invaluable source of
evidence when so many mills and factories have been
adapted for other uses in recent years.
     The oldest Ordnance Survey maps are, of course,
the First Edition 1" series which took nearly three-
quarters of a century to complete, the first map
being published for Essex in 1805 and the last for
the Isle of Man in 1873. The problems of using this
series are well outlined by J.B. Harley; the basic
one is to determine the date of the original survey,
revisions and printing of any particular sheet. The
publishers David and Charles have reprinted the
First Edition 1" for England and Wales using print-
ings of the 1860s, and so the material included
ranges over half a century. Dr. Harley's notes to
each sheet should be read carefully before any use
is made of these maps. They are particularly useful
for early railway development, showing the whole
range from plateways to locomotive railways. One

Fig.27 Map of Froghall Wharf, Staffordshire, based on O.S. 25" First Edition (1880) Sheet XIII.15.

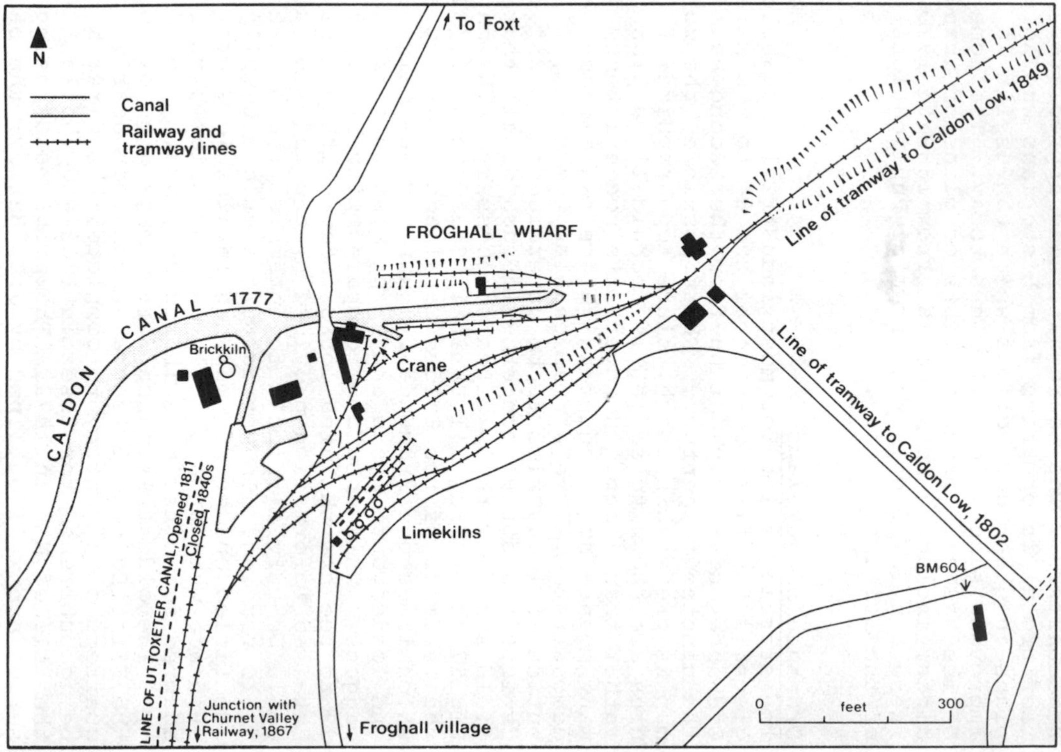

Fig.28 Froghall Wharf in 1904. The limestone was brought from Caldon Low, calcined here and sent away by either railway or canal.

Fig.29 Froghall Wharf in 1980 - an industrial area transformed into a picnic site and base for pleasure boats along the canal.

cannot, of course, be certain that all features
marked existed at the same time. The First Edition
1" Ordnance Survey does, however, provide evidence
of an earlier industrial landscape than the 6" or
25" series, but needs to be used, certainly in England, with the county maps already described.

Maps and Plans of Towns and Industrial Concerns

By the nineteenth century, with the introduction of
steam power and better means of communication, industry became wherever possible concentrated at the
source of labour, that is, in towns. Once again,
cartography kept pace with development. Before the
mid-nineteenth century maps of towns can be found in
directories, gazetteers and guidebooks, although
care needs to be taken as some of these are earlier
maps inserted without acknowledgement and remain
unchanged despite revised editions of the book itself. Some useful maps were produced as a result of
enquiries into health conditions in the 1840s;
William Lee's Enquiry into the Sanitary Conditions
of Loughborough (1849) extends well beyond the town
and marks railways, canals, wind and water mills
and brick kilns. Tithe maps may also indicate urban
areas, although in some cases the built-up areas
were left blank.

Plans are also available for many nineteenth
century towns and frequently identify industrial
premises. John Wood's plans of the 1820s and 1830s
are particularly valuable in this respect; a good
example is the plan of the Greenfield Valley below
Holywell, published in 1833, which identifies each
of the mills and other industrial buildings in this
busy valley.(35) From the mid 19th century onwards
the Ordnance Survey published a series of town plans
on scales of 1/1056, 1/528 and 1/500. The detail of
these enables, for example, the ground floor area of
industrial premises or the living space in terrace
houses to be calculated. Similarly large scale
plans, even earlier in date in some cases, exist for
public utility schemes. They are in themselves of
interest in detailing gas supply, sewerage, drainage,
water supply, lighting, dock and harbour improvements and so on, and they also locate and identify
other urban industries and should not be ignored in
an attempt to map the nineteenth century urban
landscape.

PRINTED SOURCES

Parliamentary and other Official Papers
This vast reservoir of information has been extensively used by social and economic historians but
less so by landscape historians. It does, however,
contain material of interest and merits attention,
despite the difficulties of finding one's way
through it. A fair knowledge of the chronology of
the area being studied is necessary before seeking
information from official papers. There is a published Guide to Parliamentary Papers by P. and G.
Ford, and the volumes of evidence from the nineteenth century Commissions of Inquiry published by
the Irish Universities Press are satisfactorily indexed and available in many reference libraries.
Until the First World War the oral evidence obtained
by the commissioners was printed in full and includes that submitted by, for example, engineers like
I.K. Brunel on the use of iron in railway bridges.
Factory owners were interviewed and frequently
describe their mills as well as the conditions of
labour in them. It must be remembered, of course,
that employers naturally tried to present their case
in the best possible light and that the Commissioners themselves had a specific task to perform and
directed their questions to this rather than conducting a general enquiry. However, the Commissioners personally visited many industrial concerns and
have left eye-witness accounts, including descriptions of mills, coal and metal mines and ironworks,
all arranged by region. For example, one of them
visited the leadmines of north-east England in 1842
and has described the ore-dressing and smelting
processes.(36) His account helps in the interpretation of an industrial feature such as that shown in
Fig.30:

> The most important circumstances connected with
> the smelting mill is the chimney by which the
> smoke and effluvia are carried off. About 20
> years ago they had begun to make what they
> called horizontal chimneys, about 100 yards in
> length, but they are much longer now. In going
> across from Stanhope to the Derwent Company's
> mines and smelting mills on the river Derwent,
> I saw at the top of a hill a tall, white cir-
> cular turret rising up out of the ground, and
> a cloud of white smoke issuing from the summit.
> The road came to within the distance of ¼ mile

Fig. 30 Flue alongside the lead smelt mill at
Grinton, Swaledale. These flues can be seen in
several places in the Yorkshire Dales.

from it and the smoke, as we passed through it,
was disagreeable. The ling, or common heather,
had its blossom and leaves entirely destroyed;
the bell heather (erica cinerea) was more hardy.
This chimney was a mile from the smelting mills,
and it was stated by the people that it proceeded under the ground all the way from the
mills up the side of the hill to the foot of
this turret, to carry off the destructive smoke.

The Geological Survey was founded in 1835 and
its series of Memoirs provides invaluable evidence
of mining activity throughout the nineteenth and
early twentieth centuries. Much of the information
is obviously mineralogical but a mining geologist
like Warington Smyth, who visited Cardiganshire in
1848, was also interested in the practical working
of the mines. He refers, for example, to the extensive use of water power and describes how

not only have streams been conducted for
several miles along the mountainside to assist
in expelling the waters from the depth of the
mine, but large reservoirs have been constructed in the main ridge, and natural lakes, such
as the Teifi Pools, have been made instrumental
to the same purpose.(37)

The Welsh landscape today is still being altered to
provide drinking water for town-dwellers, in much
the same way as in the past a surprising number of
its lakes and pools were constructed to provide
water for pumping and ore dressing at metal mines.

Newspapers, Journals and Magazines
The value of the Mining Journal has already been
referred to. Published weekly from 1835 to 1911, it
provides a comprehensive record of public companies
not only in mining but also in transport. As well
as weekly reports on productive mines, it contains
articles on mining areas, often with maps and engravings, reports of annual meetings of companies
and notices of sale, which often list the surface
and underground plant surviving. Similar journals
exist in other fields. For example the Hosiery
Trades Journal contains engravings of long vanished
or altered hosiery mills, and The Engineer, first
published in 1856, is particularly useful on transport: it contains some remarkably detailed engravings of construction work on bridges and tunnels.

The problem in using any of these is the lack of an
index, or in the case of later volumes of the
Mining Journal, an adequate index.
     The same is true of another well-thumbed
source, local newspapers. Most counties had their
own weekly newspaper at least from the mid-18th
century onwards, and they therefore provide invaluable reports about the building of canals and railways, the growth of towns and the development of
steam power, for example. Much useful detail is
contained in notices of sale and in advertisements,
which occasionally contain engravings of buildings.
They are best perhaps used, like official papers,
when a chronology has been established and the years
of greatest interest determined.(38)

Directories, Guidebooks and Gazetteers
County Directories were first published in the late
eighteenth century and proliferated in the nineteenth century. White's and Kelly's are probably
the most informative, particularly the earlier volume of White's where industries are classifed for
each town and village. Some directories only listed
firms on payment of a fee, and it cannot therefore
be assumed that because a particular firm or brick-
works, for example, has not an entry in a certain
edition that it did not exist at the date. Directories, in other words, need to be used for what they
contain but must not be regarded as comprehensive.
Their limitations are well described in Jane E.
Norton's Guide to the National and Provincial Directories of England and Wales Before 1850 (1950).
Once their use is understood, directories, together
with the first edition 6" Ordnance Survey maps, are
the starting points for determining the county
distribution of particular industries.
     County and town guidebooks are another useful
source which at the same time cannot be regarded as
comprehensive. Britton and Brayley's topographical
county guides of the early nineteenth century refer
to industrial concerns, but many must have passed
unnoticed. Later nineteenth century guides often
proudly describe a town's industries and are a
valuable source of engravings or early photographs
of sites and buildings.

Catalogues and Firms' Papers
These may have found their way into County Records
Offices, particularly if a firm became bankrupt,

because before the Bankruptcy Court was founded in
1824 the Clerk of the Peace was often the clerk to
local commissions of bankruptcy and the material
therefore was included in Quarter Sessions papers.
Some firms will make available archives they still
have, especially those in public ownership like the
National Coal Board, but access to the archives of
private firms is not always easy. Many catalogues,
of course, only deal with machinery but may still
enable the functions of different parts of an industrial plant to be identified. For some firms
whose products were widely distributed, like brick
and tile manufacturers and major iron founders, the
catalogues may help in dating particular buildings
where their products were used. The best example
is probably the firm of Boulton and Watt, who supplied so many steam engines to mining concerns and
textile mills in the late eighteenth and early nineteenth centuries. They insisted on having a drawing
of the part of the building where the engine was to
be situated, and the collection of these in Birmingham Reference Library has enabled the reconstruction
of many early industrial buildings and their immediate environment. The collection has been catalogued and selections from it are being published
by Dr. Jennifer Tann of the University of Aston in
Birmingham.
    Many firms have published histories for some
important anniversary and these may contain engravings and photographs of the various stages of the
development of sites or buildings belonging to them.
The map in Fig.31 is in the possession of Liberty's
of London and depicts a long vanished industrial
landscape of this country, the bleachfield, made
redundant by the development of chlorine bleaching
in the nineteenth century. The map should be compared with the lithograph that forms Fig.32 to
appreciate the true nature of the bleachfield, once
very common in textile districts. On the whole,
however, business archives are very difficult to
track down since so many lie uncatalogued, in
solicitors' offices for example, and even more have
been destroyed as so much waste paper.

MANUSCRIPT SOURCES

It is far more difficult to generalise about the use
of manuscript sources than of printed sources since
the availability of the former varies considerably
from area to area and industry to industry. A use-

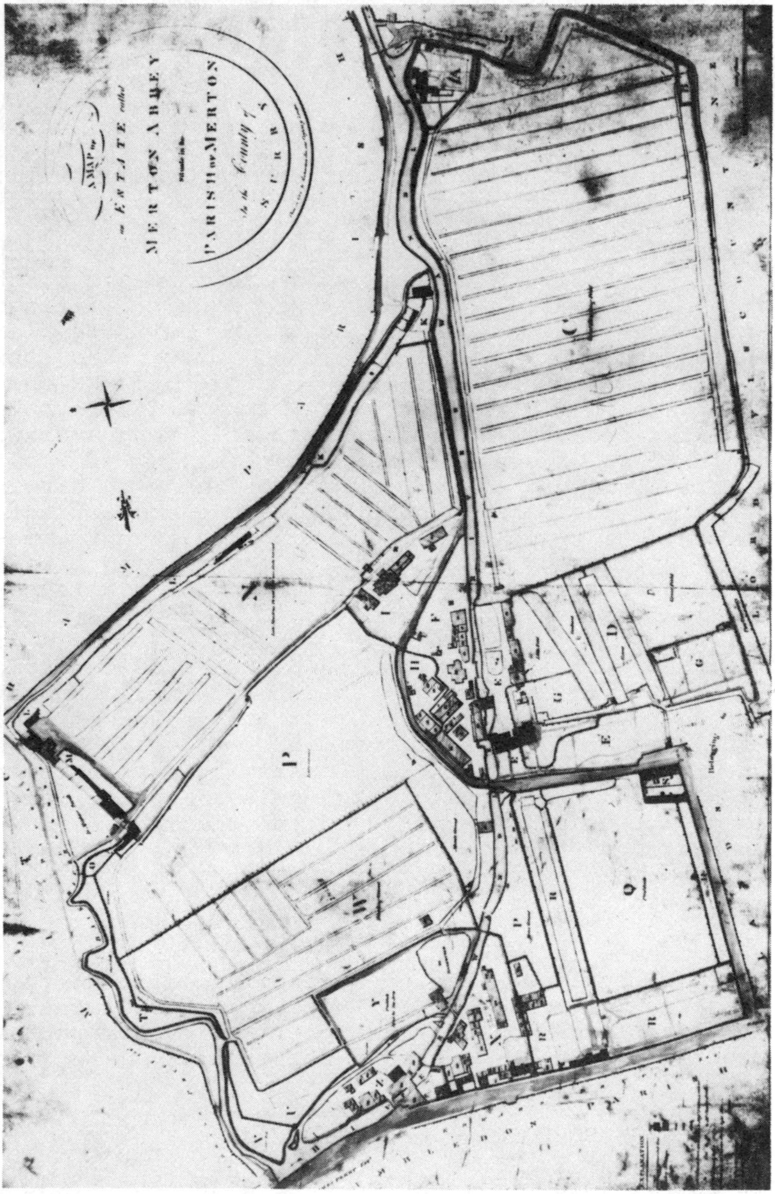

Fig.31 Map of Liberty's print works at Merton, Surrey, showing bleachfields. (1805)

Fig.32 A mid-19th century lithograph of Charley's bleachgreen near Dunmurry County Antrim.

Industrial Landscapes

ful method of determining what is available for a
particular county is to consult the footnotes of the
relevant chapters of the Victoria County History.
The first volumes of these were produced in the final
years of Victoria's reign and the series is still in
progress. Those published more recently generally
contain fuller accounts of industrial activities
than earlier volumes, reflecting the change in approach to history during this century. One must bear
in mind when using these volumes that they contain
summaries rather than detailed studies and that more
sources may be available than those consulted, but
nevertheless they are a valuable starting point for
the student of industrial landscapes.
    The use of family papers has already been re-
ferred to. Most County Records Offices publish
schedules of family collections in their possession
and some produce subject indexes which indicate
where material of interest may be found. If a
particular family proves to be of interest then it
may be possible to locate their archives through the
National Register of Archives, Quality Court,
Chancery Lane, London, which produces handlists of
family papers still in private possession. John
Bateman's Great Landowners of Great Britain and
Ireland, of which several editions were published in
the 1870s and 1880s, indicates which landowners had
major interests in industrial activities. Many
studies have been published based on family papers,
but they have usually been concerned with the
family's income and interests and only marginally
with changes in the landscape(40). Much more use
could be made by the landscape historian of this
source. Many estate papers, particularly leases,
are difficult documents to deal with, but help can
be obtained from the useful series of Helps for
Students of History, published by the Historical
Association, especially Alan Dibben's Title Deeds
(H.72, 1968).
    Minute books of companies, if they survive,
are another useful manuscript source which often
provide information ancillary to their main purpose.
For example,the minute books of railway and canal
companies often describe changes in the landscape
necessitated by their construction activities. The
following extract is taken from the Minute Books of
the Ashby Canal Company:

    to make the bridge over the canal in Measham on
    the east side of the turnpike of an Easy and
    moderate descent, it will be necessary to raise

>   the said Road higher or above the Chamber
>   floors in 6 houses on one side of the Road
>   belonging to Mr. Wilkes and in 3 other houses
>   on the same side of the Road. Resolved also
>   that Mr. Wilkes shall have liberty to make a
>   Bason above the said Bridge and an Additional
>   Arch under the road and under a Warehouse in-
>   tended to be built near thereto...(41)

The houses below the level of the road and the arch
under the now converted warehouses are still a
feature of the landscape today.

Diaries are a third manuscript source which may
be of interest although many of the major ones have
now been printed. A useful guide is British Diaries
1442-1942 (1950) by William Matthews, which ind-
idcates the profession of the diarist and whether
he included comments on other than his purely
personal concerns. Many diaries of nineteenth century engineers and other people with industrial
interests do survive and record details not obtainable from any other source.

PAINTINGS, ENGRAVINGS AND PHOTOGRAPHS

The industrial archaeologist is fortunate in having
a wider range of visual sources to assist him in his
re-creation of industrial landscapes of the eighteenth and nineteenth centuries than historians of
earlier landscapes. Nevertheless, paintings and engravings need to be subjected to the same scrutiny
which is applied to any other historical document:
they are one man's impression of a landscape and
highly subjective in their treatment. That impression,
however, may well indicate better than any other
source how the landscape appeared when industrial
activity was in full swing. The well-known painting, 'Coalbrookdale by Night', is a vivid evocation
of a landscape dominated by the iron industry. The
same is true of the impressive painting by William
Howell of the great open-cast copper workings on
Parys Mountain in Anglesey. Turner's paintings
include impressions of the Calstock Valley in Devon,
with its numerous water-wheels, while the series of
water-colours by H.E. Tidmarsh of Welsh lead mine
sites in the 1880s provides invaluable evidence.(42)
         Engravings vary from the highly accurate draw-
ings in the technical press to those produced by
artists as a means of disseminating their work.(43)
One important collection of engravings and other

illustrative material of eighteenth and nineteenth century engineering is that amassed by Sir Arthur Elton, now catalogued by his daughter Julia and available at Ironbridge, in Shropshire. Many libraries and record offices contain collections of local engravings and many others can be found in the guidebooks and local almanacs already referred to. They have been extensively used in books of illustrations but have rarely been systematically studied for the information they can provide concerning the historical landscape.

This is equally true of the books of photographs of past scenes which are now proliferating. Photography provides a valuable record of the late Victorian industrial landscape, so much of which has been destroyed in recent years. Early photographs are, of course, not so technically perfect as modern ones. For example, long exposures caused blurring of moving features such as water-wheels, and many old photographs have darkened with age. However, some industrial concerns began to use photography as a means of record in the late nineteenth century and some collections do survive. Thus the Stanton Ironworks Company (now part of the British Steel Corporation) possesses photographs of ironstone working at the end of the nineteenth century in Lincolnshire and east Leicestershire which, since the area has now been reclaimed, are our only indication of how features in the present landscape were formed.(44) Record offices also frequently possess photograph collections and some splendid examples have been published in recent years.

More local photographs record churches and public parks than industrial scenes, but it is surprising what was regarded as of interest. The photograph of Moira Furnace in Fig.19 is taken from a postcard of early this century. The two photographs in Figs. 28 and 29 are of Froghall Basin in Staffordshire, referred to earlier; Fig.28 is from a postcard of 1904, Fig.29 of the site today, transformed by Staffordshire County Council into a picnic area. The two should be compared with the map in Fig.27, based on the Ordnance Survey 25" first edition map, to understand the additional dimension that photographic evidence can give to the basic plan of an industrial landscape.

One other type of photograph which deserves mention is the aerial photograph, many of which date from before or just after the Second World War. These not only reveal industrial elements in the landscape which have since disappeared but, for the

industrial archaeologist as well as for the archaeologist, indicate the remains of earlier man-made
features such as bell-pits for iron and coal, leats
to water-powered sites and so on. The RAF vertical
survey, made in 1947, is often available locally
for a particular county. Large aerial photographic
collections have been built up by the professional
firm of Aerofilms and by Professor J.K.St. Joseph
of Cambridge University, and individual local collections also exist.

CONCLUSION

The student of the industrial landscape is, then,
faced with a bewildering variety of documents, each
of which presents its own special problems. In
general, however, difficulties can be overcome if
all kinds of documents, whether maps, plans, pictures or manuscripts, are subjected to the same
degree of scrutiny to assess authenticity, reliability and provenance. At least the study of eighteenth and nineteenth century industrial landscapes
rarely involves palaeographic problems!
    Finally, I would make a plea for the study of
the landscape in its totality. It is important to
remember that while a circular mound may be a Bronze
Age burial cairn, it might equally be a windmill
mound or even the spoil heap from a lead mine or the
construction waste from a canal or railway tunnel.
The landscape historian needs to be familiar with
the field evidence from all periods and should not
ignore that of the more recent past.

ACKNOWLEDGEMENTS

For assistance in using documents: Miss C. Armet,
archivist to the Marquis of Bute; the staff of
Leicestershire County Record Office, Surrey Record
Office, the Pilkington Library, Loughborough Univ-
ersity, and the National Library of Wales.
    For illustrations: Roy Day (Fig.22), Liberty
of London (Fig.31), Dr. W.A. McCutcheon, Ulster
Museum (Fig.32), British Library (Fig.21), Froghall
Wharf Passenger Services (Fig.28), Leicestershire
County Record Office (Figs.17,23,24 and 25), Mining
Record Office (Fig.26), my husband, D.S. Palmer,
for many photographs taken under difficult condi-
tions.

REFERENCES

Abbreviations
L.C.R.O. - Leicestershire County Record Office
N.L.W.   - National Library of Wales
P.R.O.   - Public Record Office
Hastings (Bute) Manuscripts in the possession of
the Marquis of Bute at Dumfries House, Ayrshire.
Hastings (L.C.R.O.) Manuscripts in the possession
of the Leicestershire County Record Office (Crane
and Walton Deposit)
B.L.   - British Library

1.   Michael Rix, 'Industrial Archaeology',
Amateur Historian, 2 (1955), pp.225-229.
2.   Inn names frequently provide a clue to
past industrial activity. In Leicestershire The
Limekiln at Barrow on Soar, The Engine at Donis-
thorpe, and the Railway at Shepshed are by sites
where the industry after which they were named has
entirely vanished.
3.   P.R.O. RAIL 803
4.   William Pitt, A General View of the Agriculture of the County of Leicester (1809), p.8.
5.   John Farey, A General View of the Agriculture and Minerals of Derbyshire Vol.1, (1811),
p.213.
6.   ibid. 401.
7.   Hastings (Bute), Box 35, Bundle 5.
8.   ibid.
9.   ibid. Letter to Lady Flora Hastings,2 June 1810
10.   ibid. Bundle 6: memorandum by Lord Moira.
11.   Ashby Canal Minute Books, 2 May 1809,
5 Nov. 1811, 3 May 1814, 6 Dec. 1814, 3 March 1818.
12.   Hastings (L.C.R.O.) DE/500/108
13.   Hastings (Bute), Box 35, Bundle 5
14.   ibid. Bundle 12
15.   ibid.
16.   It was reported in The Guardian, 21 August
1980, that the Forestry Commission had "plans to
create something like 5 million acres of new forest
over the next three decades". This is an area
roughly equivalent to the whole of Wales.
17.   A brief account of the survey and excavation of the site has appeared in Association for
Industrial Archaeology Bulletin, 7, No.1 (1979). A
fuller account is to be published by the Northern
Mines Research Group.
18.   Memoirs of the Geological Survey, 2, Part
2 (1848), 'Notices of the History of Lead Mines in

Cardiganshire' by the Keeper of Mining Records, Robert Hunt, and 'On the Mining District of Cardiganshire and Montgomeryshire' by Warington Smyth, Mining Geologist to the Survey.

19. William Waller, A Short Account of Sir Carbery Pryse's Lead Work (1693), B.L. 645 b 11(14). William Waller, An Essay on the Value of the Mines late of Sir Carbery Pryse (1698) N.L.W. Wing W5524. William Waller, Report to the Company of Mines Adventurers, containing a Description of its Mines in Cardiganshire (1704) B.L. 444 a 29. William Waller, Answer to Mr. Hawkins Report (1710), N.L.W. W6557. William Waller, The Mine Adventure Laid Open (1710) B.L. 444 a 50. W. Shiers, First, Second and Third Abstracts of the State of the Mines of Bwlch-yr-Eskir-Hir (1700) B.L. 959 a 8(1,2) and 522/M/12/6.

20. Waller, The Mine Adventure Laid Open, 46.
21. W. Shiers, The Second Abstract
22. Gogerddan Manuscripts 2030, N.L.W.
23. Druid Inn Manuscripts, Bundle 42, N.L.W.
24. See the excellent maps indicating the dates at which each county in Great Britain was surveyed in Harley, (1972)
25. Plate 50 in the facsimile published by Alexander Duckham in 1939.
26. L.C.R.O., QS/72/1
27. L.C.R.O., DE 336/11A
28. L.C.R.O., Leicester Navigation Papers, 3D42/M37/2/5/6.
29. L.C.R.O., Syston-Peterborough Railway Plans, QS 73/32.
30. I owe these references to Mrs. S.M. Fletcher, whose work on the Melton Mowbray Navigation (with M.G. Miller) is to be published by the Railway and Canal Historical Society.
31. Hastings (L.C.R.O.) DG 30/Ma
32. See the article and excellent footnotes by J.T. Ward, 'Landowners and Mining', in J.T. Ward and R.G. Wilson, (eds.), Land and Industry: the Landed Estate and the Industrial Revolution (1971) pp.65 et seq.
33. Plan Room, Health and Safety Executive, Baynards House, Chepstow Place, London.
34. O.S. 25" First Edition (1880) Sheet XIII. 15.
35. In K. Davies and C.J. Williams, The Greenfield Valley (1977) published by Clwyd Record Office.
36. Children's Employment Commission. Appendix to First Report of Commissioners. Mines. Part 2. Report of James Mitchell, Esq., LL.D., British Parliamentary Papers 1842 Vol.17, pp.735-736.

37.   W. Smyth (1848) op.cit., 669
38.   An adult education group in Leicester
under the direction of R.L. Greenall has recently
produced The Leicester Newspapers 1850-1874: A
Guide for Historians. Further indexes of this type
would be very welcome.
39.   J. Tann, Selected Papers of Boulton and
Watt. Vol.1, The Engine Partnership 1775-1825
(1981).
40.   e.g. T.J. Raybould, The Economic Emergence of the Black Country (1973), makes extensive
use of the Hatherton and Dudley Manuscripts but is
concerned with the activities of the Earls of Dudley rather than with the landscape of the Black
Country.
41.   P.R.O. RAIL 803/2, 37.
42.   National Library of Wales. Two are reproduced, along with other examples of the visual
sources discussed here, in C.J. Williams, Metal
Mines of North Wales (1980).
43.   see F. Klingender, Art and the Industrial
Revolution (1968) for ideas on assessing the reliability of engravings.
44.   Several of these were published by H.B.
Hewlett in The Quarries (1935), republished in 1979
by the Market Overton Industrial Railway Association.

Chapter Four

THE LANDSCAPE OF PARLIAMENTARY ENCLOSURE

M. Turner

"God made the country, and man made the town".
This line from William Cowper's longest poem seems
to embody the very antithesis of the impact of enclosure on the landscape; it was not a God-made
country but one increasingly fossilised under generations of human interference; it was in short a
manscape.(1) Cowper's observation is all the more
disappointing because his residence at the time was
in north Buckinghamshire amidst a revolution in the
countryside. Not only did this occur in his native
Olney but also throughout the Midlands, essentially
the clay lands from the south east in Oxfordshire
and Buckinghamshire northwards into Northamptonshire, Leicestershire, and Warwickshire, and in the
wold and clay country of Lincolnshire and Yorkshire
East Riding.
     This is an appropriate perambulation across the
landscape because it naturally and necessarily introduces a discussion of extent and chronology of
parliamentary enclosure; extent because the hand of
eighteenth and nineteenth century enclosing man did
not reach every corner of England, and chronology
because this despoliation of God's country was relatively recent in the history of the landscape. As
Christopher Taylor reminds us, the landscape effect
of parliamentary enclosure "for all its apparent
antiquity" "... is relatively modern in the long
development of English fields", and this landscape
effect is perfectly captured by H.C. Darby in his
criticisms of Cowper's observations because quite
clearly "the English countryside in general is as
artificial as any urban scene".(2) Perhaps it is
this sense of 'unnaturalness' which partly intrigues
us in this collection of essays since it is man's
impact on the landscape which is our focus of attention; it is our efforts to repossess the landscape

of whichever centuries concern us which is one of
our motives today; and in this sense my brief simply
is to repossess, as far as documentation allows, the
eighteenth and nineteenth century enclosure landscapes. In truth much of it is still on the ground
but it is so familiar to us that we often fail to
recognise it. But whether Parliamentary enclosure
produced a new farming landscape which is easy to
identify, as F.V. Emery suggests, is debatable;
whether "we find a high degree of similarity in the
field patterns created by the enclosure commissioners, on the same kind of ground, whether it was in
Oxfordshire or Durham or Dorset, the economic circumstances of improvement gave rise to a predictable,
almost blueprinted layout of the new fields and much
else that appeared with them" will only be confirmed
by considerable and detailed research, quite outside
our brief here.(3)   This then is a warning. We are
not in search of blueprints, even if they exist. We
are not in search of rules and laws governing the
landscape, because there are many variations within
many typologies.

The documents exist (mostly). The landscape
fossilised or subsequently altered also exists, but
the actors have long gone. What therefore was the
impact of these actors?   In rounded terms there were
about 5,300 acts of enclosure in England in the
eighteenth and nineteenth centuries, though with
antecedents in the early seventeenth century. These
acts include all those passed as private and public
local acts and those under the general acts of 1836,
1840, 1845 et seq.(4) They account for close on
seven million acres, or about 21 per cent of the
area of England. But Parliamentary enclosures did
not have the same impact everywhere. In some places
they dominated the transformation from open fields
to enclosed ones, as in Oxfordshire and Northamptonshire, where over 50 per cent of the county area in
each case was enclosed by act; but in some counties
Parliamentary enclosure was either a trivial finale
to what had been a long-term process of agricultural
reorganisation or else was almost unknown in places
where open fields had never existed to any great
extent. Thus in Kent, Cornwall, Devon, Sussex and
Essex less than five per cent of the county area in
each case was enclosed by act. Figure 33 is a composite picture of the impact of Parliamentary enclosure in England showing on a county basis the density of enclosure. This is measured as the percentage of each county enclosed by act.(5) The dominance of Parliamentary enclosure in the Midland and

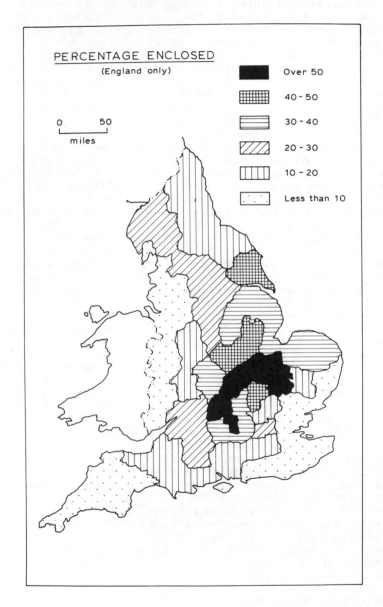

Fig.33   The density of Parliamentary enclosure in England.

East of England counties is clear.
The densities in Figure 33 hide important distributional disparities within counties. The subdivision into East and West Suffolk brings this out
rather forcefully for this county, but for most
counties these regional disparities are obscured.(6)
For example, Figure 34, a map of density of enclosure for Buckinghamshire based on individual parishes, shows clearly that nearly all of the parishes
in the north of the county were affected to some
degree by parliamentary enclosure, and in this sense
it serves a distributional purpose. Conversely
large areas in the south of the county were not
touched at all by Parliamentary enclosure. But the
map is distributional in another way because quite
clearly most parishes in the north were greatly
affected by Parliamentary enclosure with densities
of at least 30 per cent and in many cases over 50
per cent, but those in the south had densities of
enclosure mainly less than 30 per cent. The composite density of enclosure for the county is 35 per
cent but in the light of Fig.34 this is misleading
because of the variation from 44 per cent for the
five northern hundreds (highest at 58 per cent is
Cottesloe along the eastern border with Bedfordshire) to less than 20 per cent for the three southern hundreds (lowest at 7 per cent is Burnham in
the central Chilterns).

The distinction between the south and the north
of the county is sharper than even this map indicates and can be associated directly with the scarp
of the Chiltern Hills. This runs roughly north-east
to south-west through the middle of the county. To
the north and west lies a succession of clay vales,
the home of several classical examples of Midland
open field villages, including Padbury and Maids
Moreton. Southeast of the scarp lie the Chiltern
Hills, dominated by woodlands and old enclosures.(7)
This is more clearly indicated in Fig.35, a transect
across the Chiltern escarpment and based on the enclosure awards and plans of the Buckinghamshire
parishes which lie along that transect. It is ther-
fore a composite landscape map for the period from
1795, the date of the Wendover award, to 1865, the
date of the Edlesborough award.

We have in these simple maps indicated variations in distribution and density of Parliamentary
enclosure, and we have indicated the spatial variations in this transforming hand of man. Of course
the mirror or negative image of these maps is an
attempt to recreate the degree of openness of the

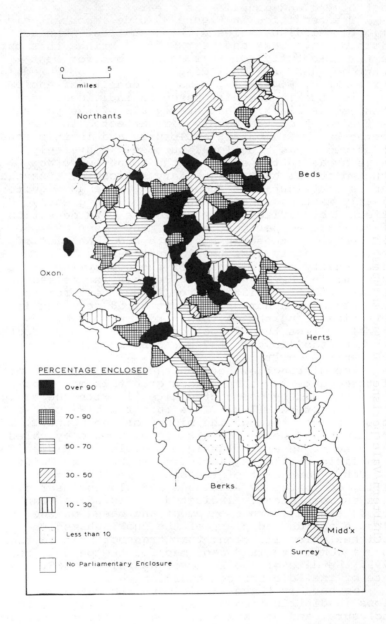

Fig.34   The density of Parliamentary enclosure in Buckinghamshire.

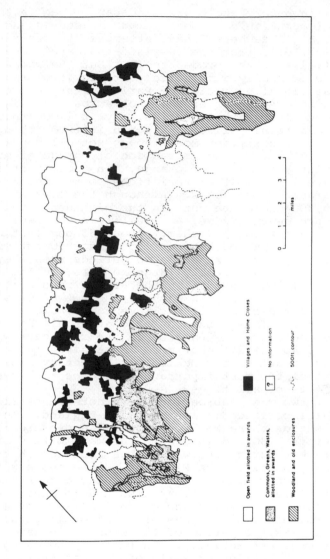

Fig.35 The impact of Parliamentary enclosure in the Chiltern/Vale parishes of Buckinghamshire.

pre-Parliamentary enclosure landscape, open in the
sense of open fields, open commons, pastures and
wastes.(8) Elsewhere I have attempted to separate
the open fields from the rest and indicated some of
the pitfalls in the procedure.(9) But the whole
exercise is really a relatively static, two-stage,
cross-sectional depiction of Parliamentary enclosure; a before and after snapshot across the eighteenth and nineteenth centuries, say in 1700 (though
more realistically 1750) and again in 1900 (though
more realistically for most though not all counties
in 1830). There is no impression of change or more
particularly the rate of change. In fact, just as
there are large spatial variations so are there
also large temporal ones. Although there were
about 5,300 enclosure acts in the eighteenth and
nineteenth centuries we can identify a narrower
chronology for most of them. About 85 per cent of
all acts were passed between 1750 and 1830 but within this 80 years there were two periods when they
were passed in noticeably large numbers: in the
1760s and 1770s; and during the French revolutionary
and Napoleonic wars. In each of these two periods
about 40 per cent of all Parliamentary enclosure
was enacted. Thus about 80 per cent of all Parliamentary enclosure was enacted in the very narrow
window of 40 years. What more impressive credentials are required for making Parliamentary enclosure one of the most important landscape architectural feats of all times?

The two main sub-periods were not necessarily
of equal importance in all parts of England. In
some counties there was a pronounced enclosure movement before 1780 and in others the main period of
activity was during the war. Thus counties on the
heavy clay soils of the Midlands like Leicestershire,
Northamptonshire and Warwickshire had a markedly
early enclosure movement, as also did Yorkshire East
Riding and Lincolnshire though to a lesser degree.
In others, especially areas of light or marginal
soils, it was the period of the Napoleonic Wars that
saw the greatest activity. In this second category
we think of the lighter soils of Eastern England as
found in Norfolk, or the marginal soil areas found
in the heaths of Surrey, the mosses and carrs of
Lancashire, the lakeland fells of Cumberland and so
on. Yet other counties exhibit a balance between
the two peak periods, counties like Derbyshire,
Rutland, and Yorkshire North and West Riding. No
hard and fast rules are intended here because there
were variations also within counties. However, it

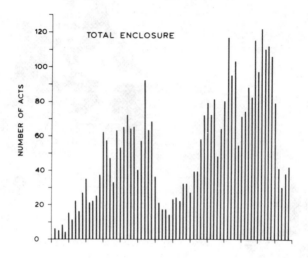

Fig.36 The chronology of English Parliamentary
enclosure 1750-1820.

is true to say that this process of Parliamentary
enclosure had almost run its course in Warwickshire,
Leicestershire, and Northamptonshire by 1793, but
in Norfolk and Cambridgeshire it had hardly begun.
W.G. Hoskins' observations that "the student of the
Leicestershire landscape must be prepared to find a
sixteenth- or a seventeenth-century field-and-hedge
pattern more often than he will find that of Georg-
ian days" is not disputed, but an appreciation of
the rate of landscape change is of the first importance.(10)
     Figure 37 is a demonstration for Oxfordshire
of the temporal sequence of enclosure for that
county, conveying an impression of movement both
across space and through time. A slightly more
complex version of this map could also indicate the
parish density of enclosure.
     How do we know so much about density and chron-
ology of Parliamentary enclosure in England and in
the parishes and townships within the separate

Parliamentary Enclosures

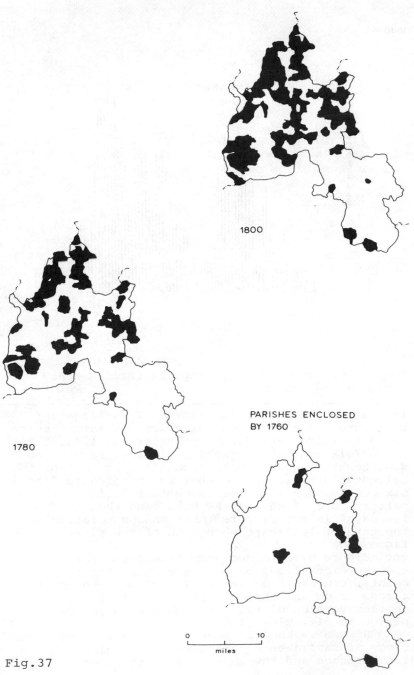

1800

1780

PARISHES ENCLOSED
BY 1760

0   10
miles

Fig.37

140

1840

1820

0   10

miles

Fig.37 contd.   The chronology of Parliamentary
enclosure in Oxfordshire.

counties? A lengthy discussion of the sources need
detain us little on this occasion because such a
discussion is well known in the literature. Need-
less to say there are many problems associated with
the use of the records, problems of record survival
as well as interpretation. The reader is directed
towards the most recent publications with a particular eye on these problems.(11) For the 5,300
parliamentary enclosures the basic document, the
enclosure commissioners' award, has usually survived, either as an enrolment in the county clerks'
records (now usually with the respective county
record office), or in the national archives (enrol-
ments in the public records in the Public Record
Office), or as an original award initially deposited
locally, either with the parish records or elsewhere
in the parish but now usually with the county records office, or lastly as copies made for a variety
of reasons and available in a variety of miscellaneous locations. Perhaps for only about 250 of the
5,300 enclosures is there no surviving 'copy' of an
award, and of these perhaps 120 were Parliamentary
enclosures by dint of an act confirming an existing
enclosure agreement or for some other reason not
necessarily requiring a subsequent award. The
agreements if they survive might also be the award.

The awards are invaluable documents for a
study of the economic and social history and the
historical geography, not only of individual enclosures but also of those for a region or a district.
For the purposes of the present study it should be
emphasised that it is a document which locates in a
time and space cross-section a wide range of different kinds of boundaries, not only of parcels of
land but also of roads and other public and private
rights of way, and boundaries of parishes or townships. With a large enough base map (aerial photographs or the 6" or 25" Ordnance Survey maps which
already have field and other boundaries), it should
be possible to reconstruct the landscape, or at
least certain features of it, by a careful reading
of the award. Changes in the field and fencing
patterns will have occurred since enclosure and
these will cause some headaches; nevertheless, not
only is the exercise possible but in a number of
cases it has been accomplished. The "conjectural
map" which is obtained may be indistinguishable from
an original survey made at the time of enclosure.
The collection of Worcestershire enclosure awards
has been used in this way to construct "conjectural
maps" where enclosure maps have not survived.(12)

But such effort is not normally required since most
enclosure acts required a map of some description
to be made and these maps have usually survived.
Even if the originals or enrolled copies have not
survived there is very often some copy or draft map
made at or near the time of enclosure. These may be
supplemented by a contemporary estate or parish map
or a pre-enclosure survey from which a conjectural
map may easily be made. Table 2 indicates the survival rate of these maps, and they are predominantly
originals or enrolled copies. In fact of all enclosures made after 1830 upwards of 96 per cent of
awards have surviving maps. There was as a result
of all this enclosure activity, a considerable spin-
off into the land surveying profession. In Bedfordshire for example, for the period 1760-1779 only 24

Table 1: The Survival Rate of Enclosure Maps for
England

Period	Number of enclosures	Number of maps	Survival rate of maps
1730-69	588	191	32.5%
1770-89	877	475	54.2%
1790-1809	1,459	1,167	80.0%
1810-39	1,120	1,020	91.1%
Total			
1730-1839	4,044	2,853	70.5%

Source: W.E. Tate, A Domesday of English Enclosure
Acts and Awards (1978)

per cent of the surviving maps in the county record
office are enclosure maps but for the period 1790-
1815 60 per cent of all surviving maps are enclosure maps.(13) This partly reflects the dominance
of the war years in Bedfordshire enclosure history,
although we do find that the survival of enclosure
maps also improves. Before 1790 something over 70
per cent of Bedfordshire enclosure awards have maps.
After 1790 a little under 95 per cent have maps.
    Tate's Domesday was an attempt to bring to-
gether for all English enclosures the basic information concerning acts, awards and maps, including
dates of acts and awards, acreages enclosed as stated in the documents, and survival and location in
record repositories of awards and maps. For some
counties more detailed information can be found;
for example the catalogue of West Riding enclosures
by Barbara English and the similar one for the East

143

Riding by Vanessa Neave, and the remarkably detailed
catalogue of Somerset maps in Tate's handlist of
enclosures for that county.(14)   The acts, awards
and maps therefore are the main body of evidence but
there are other sources. Sometimes some or most of
the administrative material associated with enclosures has survived, essentially what we might gene-
rically term the enclosure commissioners' working
papers.(15)   In some very few cases these papers
exist where the awards and maps have not survived.
(16)
        In 1946 M.W. Beresford published the results
of a pioneer survey into the survival and location
of enclosure and commissioners' papers, mainly minute books but including other items as well such as
accounts, claims and letters.(17) Not only are
these papers useful for reconstructing aspects of
the pre-enclosure period but they may also include a
map, not the enclosure award map itself but perhaps
a copy or draft of it, or an early version of the
award map on which may be depicted the approximate
or even precise boundaries of the parish and also
the pre-enclosure field and strip boundaries. From
this the precise relationship between the pre- and
the post-enclosure landscape may be identified.
There have been many minute books and other enclosure papers uncovered since 1946 from the dust of
solicitors', surveyors', estate agents', and auc-
tioneers' attics and now deposited in record offices.
Beresford listed eight sets of minutes for Buckinghamshire enclosures in the County Record Office.
Today there are well over twenty. From a cursory
inspection of the National Register of Archives'
Annual Reports we can say that for most counties
Beresford's list can be added to. For example
there are at least 11 more minute books for Bedfordshire, as well as over a dozen more for Cambridgeshire to add to what was already the largest single
collection. A similar story applies to most counties. The dates of acquisition vary from the mid-
1950s (entirely for the subsequent Bedfordshire
minute books) to the early 1960s and early 1970s
for Cambridgeshire, to the middle 1950s for Leicestershire items and the early 1960s and early 1970s
for Lincolnshire items. Recent survey evidence from
the county record offices tells a similar tale of
the impressive survival and continuing discovery of
enclosure commissioners' papers.(18)
        This then is our basic information; awards,
maps, enclosure papers; to which can be added contemporary maps and papers, institutional maps like

the Ordnance Survey and aerial photographs, Government Papers, and lastly of course, 'the ground itself'. J.R. Green's aphorism that "the ground itself, where we can read the information it affords
us, is .... the fullest and the most certain of documents", is certainly open to debate but nevertheless the near indelible print of man on the ground
is an indispensable tool.(19)   It was a sentiment
paraphrased 85 years later by the doyen of English landscape historians, W.G. Hoskins: "The English landscape itself, to those who know how to read it
aright, is the richest historical record we possess".
(20)
     At the macro level we can produce reconstruc-
tions of the landscape (as in Figure 34) showing by
one particular measure the overall impact of parliamentary enclosure. From that national level
there are successively lower levels, such as the
impact at county level portrayed in Fig.35 for Buckinghamshire and Fig.37 for Oxfordshire, showing in
the first case the parish density of enclosure and
in the second the parish chronology of enclosure.
Ultimately we come to micro levels, regions within
counties or parishes within regions or fields within
parishes. At this micro level we might investigate
two types of landscape to encapsulate the work of
Parliamentary enclosure as an agent of landscape
change under two broad headings: the passive and the
active; Parliamentary enclosure as a fossilising
agent and Parliamentary enclosure as a moulding or
creating agent.
     Let us first consider Parliamentary enclosure
as a fossilising agent, this is an agent which fixes
and emphasises either an existing landscape phenomenon or else an ancient one, as an indelible mark on
the ground. Here we have in mind the old strip,
furlong and field boundaries. Fig.38, by picking
out the landowning interest of one owner in the surviving open fields of Clifton Reynes in 1792 from a
pre-enclosure survey, also picks out the strip and
furlong pattern that then prevailed. Also fossilised were the ancient paths and routeways across the
ground, and ridge and furrow features as well. The
twentieth century survival of ridge and furrow is
important in field system research, not least for
dating the feature as pre-enclosure in origin. This
is shown in the way that hedgerows very often cut
across the direction of the ridge and furrow, suggesting that the ridge and furrow ante-dated enclosure, although, as Christopher Taylor reminds us,
some of this ridge and furrow, especially the

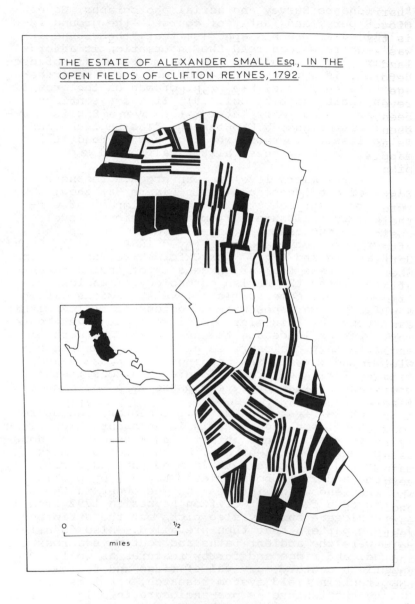

THE ESTATE OF ALEXANDER SMALL Esq., IN THE
OPEN FIELDS OF CLIFTON REYNES, 1792.

0   ½
miles

Fig.38   The estate of Alexander Small Esq. in the
open fields of Clifton Reynes, 1792.

"narrow rig", may date from the Napoleonic war ploughing up of marginal land. (21) Of great help is the fact that so much of the ridge and furrow was and is located in the heavy clay lands of Midland England, an area much enclosed in the period before 1790 and with extensive conversion from tillage to pasture. (22) Much of this pasture has never reverted to tillage and so the ridge and furrow has been preserved and has not, as it has in some areas, been subject to cross-ploughing in order to level it. We now have a number of studies available on the mapping of ridge and furrow features building on the pioneering work of W.R. Mead in Buckinghamshire. (23)
     The modern rural road plan is in many areas a fossilisation of its eighteenth century pre-enclosure counterpart. The enclosure commissioners in their awards sometimes committed to paper what custom had already created, something which had often been created centuries beforehand. Alan Harris suggests that this was more likely to occur where pre-Parliamentary enclosure was a protracted affair. In other words piecemeal enclosure was likely to create a relatively disordered rather than a planned road pattern. (24) The widths of roads can also help in the dating of the transport network. As F.V. Emery observed for Oxfordshire "the enclosure roads give themselves away by their surplus grass verges", that is 40 to 60 feet between hedges, a width sufficient to allow alternative courses for road users in wet weather. By the early nineteenth century however, with civil engineering improvements in road construction, there was no longer the need for such wide roads, and consequently roads became narrower in overall width. (25) This usually meant that the road part of the surface remained the same size but that the amount of grass verge on each side became smaller. Another reason why road widths tend to get smaller for the later enclosures is that the expansive verges of the early Parliamentary enclosures became convenient resting places for 'gypsies, vagabonds, and wastrels', as eighteenth century parlance would have it, and of course if allowed to settle and erect hovels these people might eventually become a charge on the parish rates.
     At the Bierton enclosure of 1779-80 in Buckinghamshire it is clear from the wording in the enclosure award that the old routeways were merely ratified at enclosure. They have right angled bends in them and a disposition in general which fossilises many of the old furlong and field boundaries

as well as the ancient routeways across the former
open fields. The first road described was ordered
to be 55 feet wide and to proceed to Aylesbury "in
the same direction the said road went before the
passing of the said Act". Other roads were also
laid out "in the same direction etc." The same is
true for many other contemporary enclosures.(26)
This fossilising agency attributable to enclosures
cannot be taken too far however, because, as Alan
Harris and Keith Allison both show for Yorkshire East
Riding, many new roads were established at enclosure, or diversions and realignments of existing
tracks were undertaken.(27) To establish the certainty or otherwise of the antiquity of landscape
features requires a knowledge of the enclosure award
and map, although only the survival of a pre-enclosure survey can yield positive proof of their pre-
enclosure origins. Lastly one would require the
evidence from the present day landscape. As near as
makes little difference for the last item of course,
the Ordnance Survey maps and the evidence from
aerial photographs is sufficient.

For example, in the region north and west of
Aylesbury in Buckinghamshire we see that the road
from Aston Abbots (enclosed 1795-6) to Cublington
(enclosed 1769-70) has pronounced double right
angled bends, which from the 6" map reveal a coinci-
dence with the parish boundary. The road from Whitchurch (enclosed 1771-2) to Cublington, which takes
in a corner of Aston Abbots as well, has three
successive right angled bends at the boundaries of
the parishes.

In a small area of Leicestershire, just south
of Leicester, a number of these landscape features
have been observed on the ground.(28) In the parishes of Wistow, Fleckney, Kilby, Saddington,
Shearsby, Kibworth Harcourt and Kibworth Beauchamp
the ground is littered with roads which have right-
angled bends, many of them at parish boundaries.
Ridge and furrow is fossilised in pastures and its
dispositional relationship with routeways is evident. Hence ridge and furrow, routeways and hedge-
rows act in concert as fossilising agents for
ancient strip and furlong boundaries.(29) Near the
boundary between Wistow and Newton Harcourt not only
is the ridge and furrow in different fields juxtaposed at right angles suggesting the boundary between old furlongs, but also at one stage the road
is adjacent to pronounced reversed 'S' shaped ridge
and furrow with one end of the 'S' remarkably coin-
cident with the direction of the road. This strongly

suggests that the road marks the headland of a former open field furlong. The ridge and furrow on the
opposite side of the road is parallel to the road,
that is at right angles to the ridge and furrow just
described, again suggesting a furlong boundary. In
neighbouring Fleckney, using the evidence of the
roads, or rather the bends in them, the ridge and
furrow markings, the 6" map and aerial photographs,
and finally lubricated with some imagination, it
might be possible to re-create the furlong patterns
around the village. The land adjacent to the road
leading westwards out of Fleckney seems to show that
the boundaries of the fields use the old furlong
boundaries. The assumption is made here of course
that strong, though not necessarily watertight,
relationships existed between ridge and furrow,
strip boundaries, and furlong boundaries. Thus
while it is easy to show the antiquity of ridge and
furrow because it appears to travel underneath hedges it is equally easy to show hedges coinciding
with changes in direction of the ridge and furrow,
although this may prove to be a feature of pre-Parliamentary enclosure. Christopher Taylor for the
Northamptonshire village of Raunds, part of which
was enclosed in 1664, noticed that "the fields have
long curving sides that follow exactly the ridge and
furrow of the earlier open furlongs, which is still
visible inside them".(30) In Cambridgeshire he
tells us that seventeenth century piecemeal enclosure created fields which were "relatively large,
between two and four hectares, generally rectangular
but with slightly sinuous sides".(31) Note also
Taylor's general remarks on the relationship between
enclosure boundaries of the period 1650-1750 and
ridge and furrow features.(32)
     To return to Leicestershire. Westwards out of
Fleckney into neighbouring Kilby similar features
are apparent even from a cursory inspection from
the roadside, even from a slow moving car. These
Leicestershire examples have all been observations
taken from parishes enclosed in the 1760s and 1770s,
the period of most Leicestershire Parliamentary enclosure. Proceeding in a north north-west to south
south-east direction out of Kilby brings us into
the parish of Arnesby and hence to Shearsby, three
parishes enclosed in 1771, 1794 and 1773 respectively. It is quite clear that on leaving Kilby the
carriageway and grass verge of about 60 feet in
width narrows to about 40 feet and continues so
throughout Arnesby to become about 60 feet again on
entering Shearsby, confirming the suggestion made

earlier that varying road widths are related to the
chronology of enclosure.
    This has been an exercise in conjectural hist-
ory. It has to be tested against the evidence in
enclosure awards and maps and where possible with
pre-enclosure surveys, but the ground itself has
provided the initial documentation, of which Ordnance Survey maps and aerial photographs form part.
Some of these conjectures can be refuted, and so no
hard and fast rules are offered, nor intended, but
first lines of investigation are suggested.
    Similar puzzles can be found when taking an-
other region, for example the East Yorkshire coastal
lowland district of Holderness between Hull and
Hornsea. Here there is a group of parishes of essentially, although not exclusively, old enclosure.
(33) The similarity between the landscape of Holderness and that of south Leicestershire is striking.
The road pattern on the 2½ inch map is distinctively
one punctuated with numerous right angled bends,
for example the road from Great Hatfield to Little
Hatfield to Sigglesthorne, and also the road from
Sigglesthorne to Rise to Skirlaugh. It is a landscape of old enclosure or at the least pre-1780 enclosure and stands in sharp contrast to the landscape, or at least the road pattern of the landscape, of the chalk based Wolds of central East
Riding.(34) Here the landscape varies from places
enclosed after 1816 (Lund, Dalton, Lockington, Etton
and Cherry Burton), to those enclosed during the
Napoleonic wars (Walkington and Rowley) to those
enclosed between 1760 and 1789 (Bishop Burton, Newbald and South Cave). Here, regardless of the age
of enclosure, the roads are straighter, more direct
between settlements and less 'dense' on the ground
than those in the old enclosed areas of Holderness.
    Perhaps the two landscapes in the East Riding
suggest that the Wolds were always more 'open'
before enclosure than the adjacent lowlands, in the
sense of being uncluttered with regimented furlongs,
strips and routeways. Of course one of the traditional uses of the Wolds was as extensive sheep
pastures, and this is a feature of much of Woldland
Yorkshire and Lincolnshire, and Downland Dorset,
Wiltshire, Sussex and Hampshire,(35) and it is in
such extremely 'open' environments that the eighteenth and nineteenth century surveyor could ply
his trade and produce his pattern of straighter
roads. In the open field arable lands of the Midlands however the more complex field systems may
have rendered the possibility of such large-scale

replanning more remote, and perhaps therefore the
fossilisation of the routeway pattern in the old
enclosed townships of Holderness is akin to the
early Parliamentary enclosure in the Midlands, such
as in Leicestershire, already referred to.

Nevertheless, the Wold road pattern is not
entirely one of straight roads between settlements.
Right angled bends still occur, but significantly
at parish boundaries, for example between Walkington and Bishop Burton, Walkington and Newbald, and
Cherry Burton and Etton(36) In addition, the parish boundaries are often co-extensive with stretches
of road eventually producing double right angled
bends or two sharp bends in succession. We have
discovered this also near Aylesbury in Buckinghamshire and we might also note some Cambridgeshire
examples.(37) This may suggest that historically
the boundaries between parishes or townships were
easily adopted as roads or other routeways, perhaps
one consequence of the practice of perambulating
them, something that goes back to before the Norman
Conquest. It may also suggest that the furlongs on
either side of a parish or other boundary did not
always 'mesh' very well, producing that 'step' pattern of boundaries which may well be due to the
drawing, in pre-Conquest times, of the boundaries
of those estates which eventually became parishes
around the headlands of existing furlongs (see
further Chapter 8 below). Thus if furlong boundaries became the chosen routeway across the open
fields we might see this translated by the twentieth century into double right angled bends on roads
at parish boundaries. Pre-enclosure strip maps
showing furlong patterns and old routeways do not
survive in large numbers, but clearly some testing
of what must be treated as conjecture is possible.

Another possible reason for the road pattern
differences detected between the Yorkshire Wold
parishes and the coastal lowland parishes is that
at enclosure a rationalisation of an existing
routeway pattern took place. For example, in a
region of mixed chronology of enclosure, like the
central north Wolds, where enclosure extended from
pre-1760 to post 1816 (the Heslerton, Ganton and
Sledmore region in general) there is once again a
familiar Wold pattern of straighter, more direct
routes, and fewer roads or a less 'dense' pattern
of roads than in the old enclosed parishes of Holderness. But in contrast, if rationalisation took
place on the Wolds it was related more to the characteristics of the Wolds than to the chronology of

enclosure, because in the parishes of Holderness,
which were enclosed in the eighteenth century, no
such <u>obvious</u> rationalisation took place. Instead
there is the same, or nearly the same, road pattern
as in the neighbouring parishes of old enclosure,
(38) i.e. an ample distribution of roads with right-
angled bends. Perhaps what we have discovered is a
topographical relationship allied to pre-eighteenth
century field systems, land uses, etc.; or at least
a topographical relationship with sufficient antiquity which conspired to create open field relationships which were eventually fossilised on the
ground and in the route-ways to a greater degree in
Holderness than in the Wolds; finally to be picked
out or created afresh by the enclosure commissioners in different ways in countryside only a few
miles apart. Also, as Alan Harris has indicated,
enclosure in the eighteenth and nineteenth centuries on the Yorkshire Wolds is chronologically more
concentrated than the much more protracted process
in Holderness, where it was spread over many centuries and thus resulted in a greater variety of
field patterns.(39) We have here therefore the
difference between one artist's canvas already
cluttered with detail (Holderness) compared with
another artist's fresh canvas (Wolds). W.G. Hoskins
has noted similar findings in Norfolk where in the
east and centre of the county the landscape grew up
piecemeal over the centuries whereas in the west it
was almost entirely planned, or replanned, by Parliamentary enclosure on a large scale.(40)
     Two working hypotheses have emerged therefore:
one based on topographical relationships and a
second on chronological ones. Perhaps the two are
inseparable. Nevertheless conjecture rather than
hard and fast rules should govern our approach to
the problem.
     These last few paragraphs have been an exercise
in combining the detail contained in maps with that
which survives on the ground, and the 2½" map seems
to be the correct scale to accommodate enough parishes or townships without losing detail. Rex
Russell advocates the 6" and this will give greater
detail but accommodate fewer parishes and townships.
(41) However, when it comes to detecting differences in field shapes between parishes and different
chronologies of enclosure, for the example area of
Yorkshire East Riding at least, neither map is
wholly acceptable. It seems to this eye at least
that nearly all of the fields are straight sided,
the product of near precise surveying, an attribute

we claim for eighteenth century surveyors perhaps.
Larger scale maps may help to overcome the problem
but better still is the representation obtained from
aerial photographs. If we look at the Wolds and
Holderness of the East Riding again, the classic,
regular, straight sided, roughly rectangular, field
pattern so often attributed to the enclosure commissioners and their surveyors, shows up well for
the parishes of the Wolds,(42) and is in direct contrast to the old enclosed parishes and townships of
Holderness where there is a much more irregular
field pattern.(43) The exception in this small
sample area of Holderness seems to be the parish of
Coniston, enclosed 1789-90, where the great regularity of size and shape of field, perhaps the hallmark
of the enclosure commissioners, is evident. The
aerial photographs have the advantage in that, as
well as picking out differences in field shapes and
sizes they also, in a photographic metaphor, expose
the old enclosed fields which have blurred boundaries in contrast to the sharper boundaries of the
eighteenth and nineteenth century enclosures. Alan
Harris has indicated this for the three Holderness
parishes or townships of Burstwick, Preston and
Lelley, where the ancient enclosures of the first
are sandwiched between the straight sided fields of
the other two, enclosed in 1777 and 1770 respectively. Thus "what appears at first view to be a
countryside of rather uniform character proves on
closer inspection to be one of considerable variety".
(44) F.V. Emery for Oxfordshire has illustrated
the same characteristics. In an aerial photograph
the rectilinear pattern of fields in Salford, enclosed in 1770, is juxtaposed with the old enclosed
larger pastures of the deserted settlement of Little
Rollright.(45)

In some areas not only is the shape and size of
old enclosed fields different from those of later
enclosures, but also their location in the parishes
may betray their great antiquity. Figure 34, showing the density of Parliamentary enclosure in Buckinghamshire parishes, displays the great variety
from parish to parish. Five examples from that map
are brought together in Figure 39. They vary from
Astwood, a late enclosure where only 26 per cent of
the open and common fields remained intact, to the
wartime enclosure of Weedon where a massive 95 per
cent was enclosed, to the earlier enclosure of Great
Brickhill where 61 per cent was enclosed. There was
a tendency for old enclosures to be formed either at
or close to the village, or else at the remoter

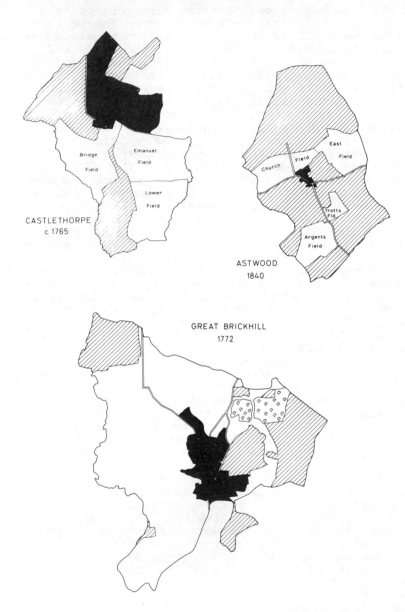

CASTLETHORPE
c.1765

Bridge
Field

Emanuel
Field

Lower
Field

ASTWOOD
1840

Church   Field

East
Field

Trotts
Fld.

Argents
Field

GREAT BRICKHILL
1772

Fig.39 Variations in the open fields of five
Buckinghamshire parishes enclosed in the eighteenth
and nineteenth centuries.

Parliamentary Enclosures

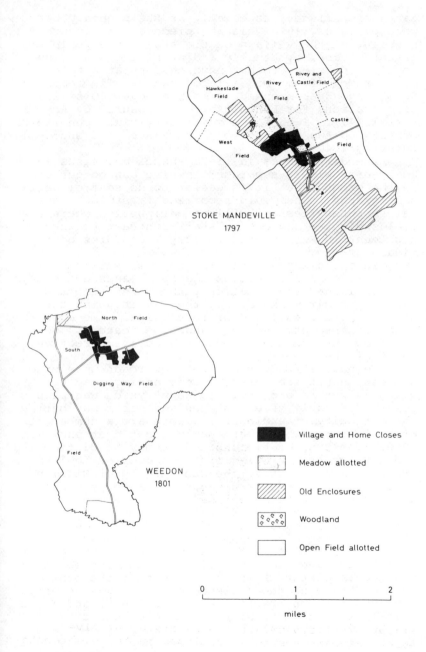

STOKE MANDEVILLE
1797

Rivey and
Castle Field

Rivey
Field

Hawkeslade
Field

Castle
Field

West
Field

WEEDON
1801

North   Field

South

Digging Way Field

Field

Village and Home Closes

Meadow allotted

Old Enclosures

Woodland

Open Field allotted

0   1   2

miles

Fig.39 contd.

parts of parishes, especially at the boundary between parishes.(46) This was piecemeal enclosure
nibbling at the village centre and at the periphery
of the parish, eventually isolating the surviving
open fields close to but nevertheless at a home
close remove from the village centre. The reader
is strongly recommended to look at over 40 similar
illustrations for Lincolnshire enclosures by Rex
Russell(47). Two of the small surviving open fields
of Astwood had been surrounded by such old enclosures by 1840.

The differences in field shapes and sizes in
enclosures widely separated in time can be detected
on the ground, but it is easier to do so from aerial
photographs. One would recommend first looking at
parish boundaries and village peripheries where the
fields might stand out in stark contrast to the
eighteenth and nineteenth century enclosures of the
middle ground.

In our discussion of the work of Parliamentary
enclosure commissioners as agents of landscape change
we have looked so far at only the first, the passive,
facet of their work, namely the way in which their
actions have fossilised or regularised some existing, perhaps very ancient, landscape feature. We
must now turn to the second, the active, creative,
facet of their work.

We have already seen that new roads were often
created, and in some areas a contrasting road pattern
with respect to old enclosed countryside was produced. Similarly, field shapes and sizes may betray
the antiquity of enclosure. There are a number of
other features which were newly created at enclosure. The type of field boundary may be distinctive
and here we are thinking of the hedges of Lowland
Britain in contrast to the stone walls of Highland
Britain. Such differences are not a feature peculiar to Parliamentary enclosure but instead reflect
the availability of different kinds of fencing
materials throughout enclosing history. These in
their turn are often based upon differences in underlying geological structures. Nevertheless hedges are
distinctive and characteristic of the eighteenth and
nineteenth centuries in the sense that the heart-
land of Britain, the Midland counties, was so very
much dominated by Parliamentary enclosure and is so
thickly wooded today with those hedgerows created
two hundred or so years ago. This is in contrast
to the Pennine and Lake counties where a great deal
of enclosure, mainly of common and waste, took place
during the Napoleonic wars and in the middle de-

cades of the nineteenth century. Here, however,
boundaries were marked by miles of drystone walling.
Then again, both of these landscapes, the hedges
and the stone walls, stand in complete contrast to
those enclosures associated with drainage schemes,
as in large tracts of Somerset, Lincolnshire and
Cambridgeshire, where often all that acts as a
boundary is a drainage channel. In Yorkshire East
Riding, along the Humber estuary and the river Hull,
similar ditches or channels abound, but here they
may again act as a fossilising agent, fixing on the
ground existing boundaries and existing attempts at
drainage. Witness to this are some of the similar-
ities in the road pattern created at enclosure in
Holderness with right-angled bends in roads and
drainage ditches alike.(48)

There are a number of features associated with
parliamentary enclosures which were created in the
landscape after and sometimes as a direct result of
Parliamentary enclosure. In particular we have in
mind new farmsteads and other buildings, as well as
the numerous small pieces of woodland set aside by
landowners in corners of the newly created fields
to act as fox coverts for future generations of
squires and gentleman farmers. These coverts are
rarely very large,from 2 to 20 acres in East Leicestershire.(49) They were not by any means created
in all parts of England, but in parts of the Midland
counties they can be picked out on the ground, on
maps and on aerial photographs, dotted over the
landscape like an outbreak of measles. Raymond Carr,
the modern historian of English fox hunting, points
to three factors which combined "to create the
primacy of the Midland hunts as centres for the
fashionable world: better roads, grass and enclosures".(50) The roads gave convenience and access-
ibility. Conversion to grass meant fewer objections
on the grounds of damage to crops. Enclosures created the hedges, with their obvious relationship to
steeplechasing. However, as John Patten observes,
the first effect of enclosures in creating hedges
and fields was to destroy the openness of the countryside in which the existing nature of hunting had
grown up, hence the subsequent need to create the
gathering places for the quarry, the coverts.(51)
The first two of Carr's factors, roads and grass,
are clearly tied up with the third, especially in
the 'Shires' (Leicestershire, Northamptonshire,
and Rutland) where up to the 1790s there was clearly
an extension of greensward. Elsewhere, outside the
Midlands, enclosures, as Carr explains, were not

always a blessing to fox hunting because, instead
of maintaining or extending the pastures, they may
have increased the area of land under grain. The
wrath of the peasant proprietor was therefore easier
to incur.(52)

Another creation of the enclosure commissioners
was the gravel pit, but unlike fox coverts it was an
institutional creation rather than one merely following in the wake of enclosure as if by accident.
Pits were set aside specifically to provide places
where stones, gravel, and other material could be
collected to help in the making and repair of the
roads set out at enclosure. These pits may now
serve as ad hoc nature reserves because they harbour
wild plants and animals. They may be water-filled
and in some cases they have been reclaimed, legally
or otherwise by encroachments, and put over to
agricultural purposes. These pits rarely extended
over many acres, and very often more than one pit
was created. At Iver in Buckinghamshire, for example, six pits were allotted. In the same county in
the enclosures before 1830 the largest gravel or
stone pit allotment was $14\frac{3}{4}$ acres, at Wavendon in
1788-91 in two separate allotments, and the range
of the remainder was between one and $5\frac{3}{4}$ acres. Before 1780 only 25 per cent of all Buckinghamshire
enclosures made provision for gravel pits, but from
1780 to 1830 the proportion rose to 70 per cent.
Perhaps there is a relationship here with the general civil engineering improvements of the late eighteenth and early nineteenth centuries, together with
an awareness of the likely difficulties of obtaining
sand and gravel locally for enclosure. In the Wolds
and Holderness regions of Yorkshire East Riding the
largest gravel, sand or stone pit allotment was 9
acres, at South Cave in 1785-7, and made up of three
separate allotments. The range of the remainder was
from $\frac{1}{4}$ acre to 8 acres. The rate at which pits were
allotted in Holderness was in 30 per cent of enclosures before 1780 and nearly 40 per cent after 1780
but in the Wolds nearly 80 per cent before 1780 and
nearly 85 per cent thereafter. Isaac Leatham gives
a clue as to why so few Holderness enclosures included gravel pits, "in the east division [of the East
Riding] it is very common to fetch gravel from the
sea shore",(53) therefore special pits, perhaps,
were rendered unnecessary.

The text book approach to Parliamentary enclosure suggests that one major effect was to bring
about a migration of activity away from the village
nucleus into the newly created fields. The

creation of landholdings in severalty encouraging
the re-siting of farms and farmbuildings away from
the village out among the fields. That this
occurred is without doubt, but as W.G. Hoskins and
others have pointed out, it may have been delayed
for many years after the respective enclosure.(54)
Not only had much capital been sunk into the process of enclosing, perhaps to starve the individual
farms of capital for future expenditure, but of
course it was not the practice under open field
cultivation to have scattered settlements. One
would expect therefore a considerable inertia to
prevail. One major study of post-enclosure settlement adjustments is that by M.B. Gleave for the
Yorkshire Wolds in the period 1770-1850.(55) He
found that before enclosure "Outlying farmsteads
were the exception rather than the rule" and that in
any case they were associated with pre-Parliamentary
enclosure. But the implication is that dispersal,
regardless of the date of enclosure, was associated
with enclosure. As a result of enclosures between
1770-1850 on the Wolds "A rash of new outlying farmsteads" was created, but the spatial and economic
centres of the villages or townships remained intact
and did not decline because of farmstead dispersion.
This secondary effect was precisely what occurred in
parts of Denmark and Ireland.(56) Further, the
commissioners could give positive encouragement to
the continued location of farmsteads in a village by
scattering an individual's allotment of enclosed
land over the parish. This would serve to reinforce
the existing settlement pattern.(57) On the other
hand, some landowners, and not just the small ones
or cottagers, must have been awarded land close to
the village nucleus and therefore had no reason to
move their farms out into the hedged fields. Nevertheless, throughout the length and breadth of England there are examples of farms in villages, their
presence being quite unrelated to the fragmentation
of holdings upon enclosure. On the Dorset chalk-
lands new isolated farmsteads are a rarity because
"on the whole the newly enclosed land continued to
be worked from the old village centres".(58) Gleave
indicates that the combination of factors such as
large farms, few owners and rapid expansion of rural
population may have resulted in a post-enclosure
development of a settlement pattern of nucleus
expansion rather than movement away from the nucleus,
the typology of which was peculiar, or nearly peculiar, to the Yorkshire Wolds.(59)
    These then are some of the features of the

landscape of Parliamentary enclosure. Much has
been left out, not least a detailed study of the
element in the landscape most profoundly affected
by the changes, namely the fields themselves. In
addition the regional nuances have barely been
touched on at a national level, instead one or two
specific localities have been concentrated on. This
is indeed error, but the error would be greater
still if these closing paragraphs were not in their
own way a dedication to the 'agents' of Parliamentary enclosure landscape change, the actors in the
story. Who could claim better credentials as the
architects of the English countryside than the eighteenth and nineteenth century enclosure commissioners and their entourage of collaborators, the surveyors and road and fence contractors? For the area
of land they worked over, the relatively few decades
during which most of their work was accomplished, in
some parts of England these men were truly some of
the most thorough going 'despoilers' of the land,
and in some areas perhaps the most efficient agents
of landscape change ever. As Marc Bloch put it,
"Behind the features of the landscape... there are
men, and it is men that history seeks to grasp."(60)
      Take Buckinghamshire, for example, where the
most active commissioner was John Fellows of Foscott
near Buckingham.(61) He served as a commissioner
29 times between 1788 and 1825, as a surveyor 8
times and as an umpire 3 times. In one way or another he was partly responsible for fashioning and
refashioning the road and field patterns, and subsequent farm patterns, of over 63,000 acres, or
about 13 per cent of the county. But more significant, remembering the distribution of enclosure
(Fig.34), this accounted for about 38 per cent of
all the land enclosed by act in the county. In
large measure they were rightly his fields, his
hedges, his roads and his bridlepaths, and in the
majority of cases they still survive. But he was
also active elsewhere: a surveyor 4 times and commissioner 15 times in Bedfordshire; once a surveyor
and once a commissioner in Oxfordshire; seven times
a commissioner in Northamptonshire; and a commissioner once in each of Hertfordshire and Somerset.
The reason for this last appearance so far from his
home territory appears to be through the landed
interests of the Marquis and Duke of Buckingham of
Stowe, for whom both Fellows and his father were
tenants at various times.
      Much more impressive than Fellows' record is
that of John Davis of Bloxham, near Banbury in

Oxfordshire, at least for the number of commissions
he was engaged on, although his actual record of
attendance at meetings of commissioners is less
than impressive. He worked in many counties in
southern England from the 1790s to the 1820s: in
Buckinghamshire on 13 commissions; in Berkshire on
35; in Oxfordshire on 34; in Gloucestershire on 6;
in Leicestershire on 5; and in Hampshire on 2; a
total of 113 commissions. He was always a commissioner except on the seven occasions when he acted
as an umpire. He was therefore responsible in part
at least for the manscape of something over 180,000
acres and was thus of monumental importance as an
agent of landscape change. Figure 40 locates his
appearance.(62) He was the busiest commissioner
yet unearthed from the archives, eclipsing the
impressive record of John Burcham of Coningsby in
Lincolnshire who served on at least 70 enclosures.
From a variety of sources it can be established that
Davis never served on enclosures in Middlesex, East
and West Yorkshire, Sussex, Cumberland, Nottinghamshire, Staffordshire and Cambridgeshire, but from
Figure 40 it is quite clear that his spatial compass
from his native Bloxham was considerable. Like his
fellow commissioners the length and breadth of the
country, this relatively unsung hero (or villain) of
the landscape is what this study has been about, if
not in biography then in inheritance.

REFERENCES

1. From W. Cowper, The Task, Book 1, line 749.
2. C. Taylor, Fields in the English Landscape
(1975), p.140, my emphasis; H.C. Darby, 'On the
Relation of Geography and History', Transactions of
the Institute of British Geographers, 19 (1953), p.6.
3. F.V. Emery, The Oxfordshire Landscape
(1974), p.138.
4. For more detail see W.E. Tate, A Domesday
of English Enclosure Acts and Awards (1978), Introduction.
5. Taking Yorkshire as three counties (the
Ridings), Lincolnshire as three (the Divisions) and
Sussex and Suffolk as two each (East and West in
both cases).
6. See M.E. Turner, English Parliamentary
Enclosure (1980), chapter 2 for a detailed discussion of this point; see also J. Chapman, 'The Parliamentary Enclosures of West Sussex', Southern
History, 2 (1980), pp.73-91.
7. There is a fuller discussion in Turner,

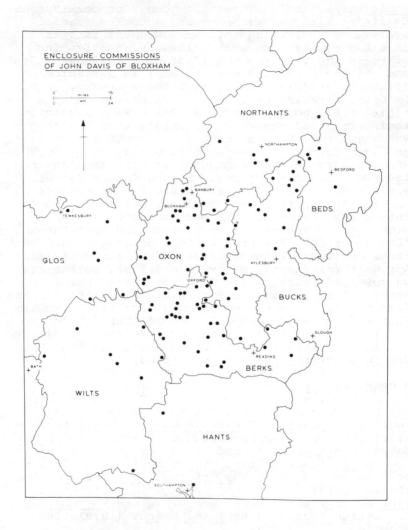

Fig.40   Enclosure commissions of John Davis of
Bloxham, Oxfordshire.

Enclosures, pp.39-42; see also J.T. Coppock, The
Chilterns (1968), pp.14-15 and D. Roden, 'Field
Systems of the Chiltern Hills and their Environs',
in A.R.H. Baker and R.A. Butlin, (eds.), Studies
of Field Systems in the British Isles (1973), p.366,
and it is a pattern which is carried over into
neighbouring Oxfordshire, for which see Emery,
Oxfordshire, p.111.
    8. Without some measure of non-parliamentary
enclosure we shall never be able to accomplish this
exactly.
    9. Turner, Enclosure, pp.20-31.
    10. W.H. Hoskins, Leicestershire: an Illustra-
ted Essay on the History of the Landscape (1957),
p.87.
    11. For procedural history see Tate, Domesday,
Introduction, Turner Enclosure, chapter 1. For
problems of use and interpretation see also Chapman,
'Enclosures of West Sussex', and J. Chapman, 'Some
Problems in the Interpretation of Enclosure Awards',
Agricultural History Review, 26 (1978), pp.108-14.
On general issues about documentation see R.C.
Russell, 'Parliamentary Enclosure and the Documents
for its study', pp.27-40 of A. Rogers and T. Rowley,
(eds.), Landscapes and Documents (1974).
    12. See Tate, Domesday, pp.279-83.
    13. F.M.L. Thompson, Chartered Surveyors: the
Growth of a Profession (1968), p.33.
    14. B.A. English, Handlist of West Riding En-
closure Awards (1965); V. Neave, Handlist of East
Riding Enclosure Awards (1971); W.E. Tate, 'Somerset Enclosure Acts and Awards', Somerset Archaeological and Natural History Society (1948); for
Wales the reader is referred to I. Bowen, The Great
Enclosures of Common Lands in Wales (1914).
    15. See particularly the pamphlets prepared by
or under the supervision of R.C. Russell and listed
in J.G. Brewer, Enclosure and the Open Fields: a
Bibliography (1972), pp.10-11.
    16. For example Moulsoe in Buckinghamshire,
enclosed in 1802, where a map and the minute book
have survived but the enclosure award has not,
Buckinghamshire County Record Office, Carrington
Mss, Box 8a, Bundle no II.
    17. M.W. Beresford, 'Bibliographical Aids to
Research no.XI: Minutes of Enclosure Commissioners',
Bulletin of the Institute of Historical Research,
21 (1946), pp.59-69.
    18. Based on a survey in progress by the
author and Mr. Trevor Wray with a view to producing
a catalogue of enclosure commissioners' papers for

England.
    19. J.R. Green, The Making of England (1885),
p.vii; Russell, 'Parliamentary Enclosure and the
Documents', lists as the three "absolutely essential
sources": the enclosure award with surveyor's map;
the modern 6" Ordnance Survey maps; and the landscape, in which "the landscape must be used, not
merely seen", p.27, my emphasis.
    20. Editor's Introduction to C. Taylor, Dorset
(1970), p.18.
    21. Taylor, Fields, p.143.
    22. See Turner, Enclosure, chapter 6.
    23. W.R. Mead, 'Ridge-and-Furrow in Buckingham-
shire', Geographical Journal, 120 (1954), pp.34-42;
M.J. Harrison, W.R. Mead and D.J. Pannett, 'A Midland Ridge-and-Furrow Map', Geographical Journal,
131 (1965), pp.365-9; W.R. Mead and R.J.P. Kain,
'Ridge-and-Furrow in Kent', Archaeologia Cantiana,
92 (1976), pp.165-71.
    24. A. Harris, The Rural Landscape of the East
Riding of Yorkshire 1700-1850 (1961), p.59.
    25. Emery, Oxfordshire, p.142; see also
Hoskins, Leicestershire, p.98.
    26. Bierton Enclosure Award, Bucks. C.R.O.,
Inrolment vol.2
    27. Harris, The East Riding of Yorkshire, pp.
79-81; K.J. Allison, The East Riding of Yorkshire
Landscape (1976), p.156.
    28. From observations made on 15 September 1980.
    29. See also Hoskins, Leicestershire, especia-
lly p.96, "in the open field landscape the "road"
from one village to the next was often only a green
path along the common balks, sometimes a fairly
direct route but more often making numerous right-
angled bends around blocks of strips "furlongs"
which lay across the direct line".
    30. Taylor, Fields, p.120. In general for the
relationship between the surviving seventeenth and
eighteenth century open field features in the present day landscape and the role of piecemeal enclosure see his chapters 7 and 8, pp.118-52.
    31. Taylor, Fields, p.124.
    32. In C. Taylor, The Cambridgeshire Landscape
(1973), pp.178-80.
    33. The parishes of Brandesburton, Seaton,
Catwick, Sigglesthorne, Riston, Rise, etc. on O.S.
2½" sheets TA13 and TA14. Much of this old enclosure east of the River Hull is by no means ancient,
rather, much of it dates from the seventeenth century. See Harris, The East Riding of Yorkshire,
p.10.

34. On O.S. 2½" sheets SE94 and SE84.
35. On the differences generally between the landscapes of the Wolds and Holderness at the time of enclosure see Allison, The East Riding Landscape, pp.150-52. For some Dorset Downland examples see Taylor, Dorset, pp.133-4.
36. On roads changing direction and discontinuity of field patterns at parish boundaries see Russell, 'Parliamentary Enclosure and the Documents', pp.31-2.
37. Taylor, Cambridgeshire, p.183.
38. On O.S. 2½" sheets SE87 and SE97.
39. Harris, The East Riding of Yorkshire, p.39.
40. W.G. Hoskins, The Making of the English Landscape (1955), p.142.
41. Russell, 'Parliamentary Enclosure and the Documents', p.27.
42. Hull University Geography Library, Aerial Photograph Collection. Runs of 28 October 1971 ref. 401(a) numbers 0408-0416, and 402(b) numbers 0487-0497, for the parishes of Cherry Burton, Bishop Burton and Walkington, enclosed by acts of 1823, 1767 and 1794 respectively. See also Allison, The East Riding Landscape, p.152 for an aerial photograph of part of Walkington parish. The same pattern can be seen in Downland Cambridgeshire as in Taylor, Cambridgeshire, pp.182-5.
43. Hull Univ. Aerial Photograph Coll. Runs of 2 May 1971 ref. 409 numbers 0276-0281, and 410 numbers 0252-0257, for the parishes of Benningholme, South Skirlaugh, Swine, Ellerby, Ganstead and Coniston, of which only Coniston was enclosed by act of parliament, in 1789.
44. Harris, The East Riding of Yorkshire, pp. 39-40.
45. Emery, Oxfordshire, p.121.
46. As explained in Turner, Enclosure, pp.137-45.
47. R.C. Russell, The Logic of Open Field Systems (1974).
48. These last few observations are speculation rather than proven facts.
49. Hoskins, Leicestershire, p.100 based on C. Ellis, Leicestershire and the Quorn Hunt (1951).
50. R. Carr, English Fox Hunting: a History (1976), p.68.
51. J. Patten, 'Fox Coverts for the Squirearchy', Country Life (September 23 1971), pp.736-8.
52. Carr, Fox Hunting, p.70.
53. I. Leatham, General View of the Agriculture of the East Riding of Yorkshire (1794), p.16. This

quote from Leatham and the raw data on which the
Holderness and Wolds gravel pit calculations are
based was generously supplied by Mrs. Jan Crowther
of Cottingham, to whom I am very grateful.
54. Hoskins, Leicestershire, p.99; Hoskins,
English Landscape, pp.157-9; See also Harris, The
East Riding of Yorkshire, pp.15-16, and 71-2,
Allison, The East Riding Landscape, pp.160-1 and
Taylor, Cambridgeshire, pp.184-5.
55. M.B. Gleave, 'Dispersed and Nucleated
Settlements in the Yorkshire Wolds, 1770-1850',
Transactions of the Institute of British Geographers
30 (1962), pp.105-18.
56. Gleave, 'Dispersed and Nucleated Settlements', pp.105-7.
57. Gleave, 'Dispersed and Nucleated Settlements', p.112.
58. Taylor, Dorset, p.153.
59. Gleave, 'Dispersed and Nucleated Settlements', p.118.
60. Marc Bloch, The Historian's Craft (English
Edition, 1954), p.26.
61. For an extended discussion see M.E. Turner,
'Enclosure Commissioners and Buckingham Parliamentary Enclosure', Agricultural History Review, 25
(1977), pp.120-29. The remainder of this chapter
is based on this article.
62. His five Leicestershire appearances have
not been included because these are unspecified in
the source, namely, H.G. Hunt, The Parliamentary
Enclosure Movement in Leicestershire 1730-1850 (Unpublished PhD thesis, University of London, 1956).

Chapter Five

PROBATE INVENTORIES AND THE RECONSTRUCTION OF
AGRICULTURAL LANDSCAPES
M. Overton

INTRODUCTION

Reconstructing a landscape of early modern England
presents something of a dilemma. Given the historical sources available we can either build up a
detailed picture of a small area, using several
kinds of documents in combination and for which the
pattern of survival is sporadic; or we can generalise for a larger area using a single source, though
such generalisations answer a more restricted range
of questions about the past. Piecing together
fragments of information about a single parish can
be extremely rewarding, but the extant sources
determine which parishes can be studied, and generalising from such studies is difficult if not impossible.(1) This chapter is concerned with the problems and possibilities of reconstructing some aspects of the farming economies of pre-industrial
England on a larger scale - with those macro studies
that are essential in setting the scene for micro
scale investigations. The only source with which
this can be done is farmers' probate inventories;
lists of crops, livestock and farm equipment, which
survive for most parts of England and Wales(2) for
a period of over two hundred years.
    Inventories cannot, however, answer direct
questions about agrarian landscapes as such, if
these are simply taken to consist of relic features
in the present landscape, or the morphology of past
landscapes. Nevertheless inventories do provide
essential material for making sense of such features
within the context of rural society in general and
farming practice in particular. Because they exist
in large numbers and are relatively consistent in
content and coverage for two centuries we can use
inventories to reconstruct patterns of agricultural

activity and to explore the dynamics of agricultural
change on a broad scale. But they offer more than
simply the raw materials for building aggregate
estimates. By their nature inventories remind us
that the past is about people: the idiosyncrasies
of the people who wrote them mean they are rarely
dull, but more importantly by referring to individuals they give a uniquely personal glimpse of the
past. Thus they help us to avoid focussing, 'upon
landscapes transformed by man, rather than upon man
as an agent of landscape change'.(3)

The first part of this chapter discusses the
nature of inventories as an historical source, for
clearly we cannot 'approach historical source material de novo and immediately extract data to be
mapped and analysed'.(4) Thus we need to examine
the ways in which inventories were produced, the
content and form of the documents, their coverage
in time and space and their representativeness of
social groups. It is then possible to evaluate
the contribution of inventories to the measurement
of agricultural change, and to discuss the work of
some historians and geographers who have used inventories to this end.

THE DOCUMENTS

Although inventories of goods and chattels were
produced in England for a variety of reasons and
date from at least the fourth century, those made
for probate purposes dating from the mid sixteenth
century are by far the most numerous. An act of
1529 re-established the practice that executors or
administrators of an estate were responsible for
exhibiting an inventory at the time of probate to
safeguard themselves against excessive claims on the
estate, to assist in a just distribution of the
deceased's assets and thus help prevent fraud, and
to determine the fees that the probate court was to
receive. Except for occasional examples inventories
are not available for the period 1640-1660 and they
gradually cease to be made in the period after 1750.
(5)

Inventories were drawn up (or 'appraised') by
two or more people, in most cases shortly after the
death of the deceased. The appraisers usually started with the money and clothes on the body. They
then proceeded round the house, room by room, recording the values of goods and chattels before them.
When they were valuing the goods of a farmer they

would then move to the yards, barns and stables,
and finally into the fields. At the head of the
document they wrote the deceased's name and sometimes his status or occupation, the date, and the
name of the parish in which he lived. One copy of
the indented inventory was presented to the appropriate ecclesiastical probate court and retained in
the archives of that court. During the 1960s some
tens of thousands of inventories were transferred
to county record offices, where they may now be consulted.(6)

Contents
The Statute of 1529 called for a 'true and perfect
inventory of all the goods, chattels, wares, merch-
andises..., of the person deceased'. Goods included
'all the testator's cattle, as bulls, cows, oxen,
sheep, horses, swine,and all poultry, household
stuff, money, plate, jewels, corn, hay, wood severed
from the ground and such like moveables'.(7) Comprehensive as this list might seem it contains some
important omissions. Most crucial is the absence of
real estate (but not documents referring to real
estate like bonds or leases which are chattels real)
for without this we cannot calculate total farm
acreages and do not have a complete picture of all
the buildings on a farm.(8) Since the names of
farms are not usually recorded, and the appraisers
rarely named the fields in which crops were growing,
it is not normally possible to locate the farm in
the present landscape using inventories alone.
Nevertheless we should expect an inventory to list
and value growing and stored crops, livestock and
farm equipment.
     There are, however, several categories of info-
rmation that inventories do not include. Some of
these can be determined from contemporary legal
texts which were quite explicit as to what should,
and what should not, be recorded in an inventory.
Some of these are not very important: 'fishes in
the pond, conies in a warren, deer in a park, pig-
eons in a dove house... are not chattels at all...
and are not to be put in the inventory', the rule
being that only tame animals were included.(9) More
relevant, and not usually mentioned by historians
using inventories in the study of agricultural
change is the statement that, 'Corn growing upon the
ground ought to be put into the inventory; seeing as
it belongeth to the executor; but not the grass or
trees so growing; which belongeth to the heir and

not the executor'. Further, 'If a man ... sows the
ground with corn but dies before it is ripe; his
executors shall have it, and not the wife or heir:
But grass ready to be cut for hay, apples, pears
and other fruits shall not go to the executors'.
The principle here was that grass and trees came
'merely from the soil', whereas corn was grown with
the 'industry and manurance of man'.(10) Towards
the end of the seventeenth century, new fodder crops
like clover and turnips were introduced into farming
practice and would be included in an inventory since
they were grown with such 'industry and manurance'.
Thus a direct comparison of either total acreage,
or fodder acreages, between the early sixteenth
century and the late seventeenth century, is misleading if new crops were replacing former areas of
pasture or meadow. Trees and woodland are also excluded, and as timber made an important contribution
to the income of many large farmers in the sixteenth
and seventeenth centuries,(11) inventories cannot be
used to estimate total incomes from the land. It is
difficult to determine whether inventory appraisers
followed these rules and regulations laid down in
legal text books. Less than a dozen of the four
thousand or so farmers' inventories presented to the
Consistory Court at Norwich, for example, mention
growing grass or standing timber, but they do record grass cut for hay, new fodder crops and felled
timber.(12)
    There are two further questions we must ask
about the contents of inventories. With the exceptions of those items that could legally be excluded,
are inventories a complete record of moveable goods
and chattels on a farm and are the quantities and
values they contain accurate? Unfortunately a satisfactory answer to the first question is impossible,
if only because inventories are such a unique
source. It is sometimes possible to match inventories with tithe or farm accounts(13) but the opportunities for such comparisons are too few to
allow any generalisations. Checks with the wills
that often accompany inventories can be made more
often although few such comparisons have so far been
published.(14) Occasional items may be missing for
a wide variety of reasons. Longman, working with
Hertfordshire inventories, found instances where
the number of cattle and horses is understated
because the lord of the manor exercised his right
to heriot; yet a 'heriot cowe' appears in a Cumberland inventory.(15)
    Aside from these specific examples it is worth

emphasising that inventories refer to individuals whereas our concern should logically be with the farming unit. In some parts of England this could have been the whole village, or a group of farmers working together. In Norfolk for example, some smaller farmers had no sheep, yet sheep were grazed over their land by another farmer (often the manorial lord) who had the right to run his sheep over a foldcourse.(16) Some farmers may have 'retired', passing goods to their heirs before they died, so that the goods in a farmer's inventory would refer to only some of the goods on the farm where he lived. Marshall considers this practice to have been 'rare' in Cumberland yet it seems to have been more common in Somerset.(17) In any collection of inventories some are bound to arouse suspicion and are therefore best ignored. An inventory referring to a large farm for example, made during the summer, with a list of the implements of arable husbandry, yet with no growing crops, would obviously have to be used with care.

In the absence of other sources in sufficient quantity it is impossible to check the accuracy of quantities recorded in inventories directly. Valuations, on the other hand, can sometimes be compared with independent price series. In one case where this has been carried out systematically a close correlation was established between a series of inventory valuations of the main grain crops and a series of market prices, although there is an absolute difference between the two series.(18) More impressionistic analyses have produced equivocal conclusions; comments range from, 'few items are appraised at values which are totally at variance with the general levels', to 'some... valuations are ridiculously low'.(19) The problem is that we rarely have enough specific information about an item - its age or condition for example - to compare it with some other price evidence. In any case sale or auction prices for the same commodity can vary considerably. However, there does seem to be some consensus among historians that inventory valuations are underestimates, but that the trend of valuations, based on large numbers of inventories, can be used as a guide to relative price movements.

This discussion of the accuracy of information in inventories cannot be very conclusive, simply because much of that information is unique to inventories. Perhaps the most important point is that while an individual inventory is liable to error for a depressing variety of reasons, general conclusions

drawn from a collection of inventories are less
likely to be misleading. Errors there must be, but
unless they are biased in a particular direction (as
might be the case with valuations) it is reasonable
to expect the errors to approximate to a normal distribution if the number of inventories is sufficiently large (say above 30). At the same time the
information in inventories can only be used in a
positive way. Because something is not mentioned
as being on a farm it does not mean that it was not
there. Even so, as Holderness puts it, 'the quality
of inventories as source material must largely be
taken on trust', and we must hope that Moore is
correct when he says, 'most appraisers would have
serious qualms about falsifying a document made
under solemn oath'.(20)

The form of information
The form in which appraisers recorded information
is one of the great attractions of inventories as
historical documents, not least because of the ways
in which their comments can stimulate our historical
imagination, but at the same time it makes their
analysis more complicated, and sometimes more frust-
rating, than is the case with more orthodox agricultural statistics. While inventories are broadly
consistent in the kinds of information they contain,
the manner in which that information is presented
is not consistent, and so varies from inventory to
inventory. Two such inconsistencies have been discussed in a paper by the author.(21) One is the
way in which variations in the basic formula 'quantity item value' can conceal information, and the
other is in the level of detail at which information
is expressed. As the appraisers had no pre-defined
categories to follow they concocted their own, giving
rise to a sometimes bewildering variety. Thus categories of information must be imposed in an analysis
of inventories. If the appraisers' categories are
used with no modification a most confusing picture
results.(22)
    Variations in the form of information mean that
inventories vary in the amount of useful information
they contain. For example, one item may be mentioned alone (say '6 acres of wheat 12^{li}') and then
mentioned again in combination with another item
('2 acres of wheat and rye 5^{li}'). Further, it may
also be concealed in a more general category ('corn
10^{li}'). Clearly, if these three entries existed in
the same inventory a figure for the acreage of wheat

could not be derived, even though we knew that the
farmer was growing wheat. One strategy for dealing
with these problems has been outlined which manages
to make use of all available information in an inventory.(23) While the specific computer techniques
it mentions are rapidly becoming outdated(24) the
general principles put forward are applicable to
any analysis of the agricultural content of inventories whether by hand or by computer.

A third inconsistency has to do with the season of the year when the inventory was made. The
acreage of winter cereals for example, can only be
extracted from inventories made between November
and August and for spring crops between April and
August (the exact dates will vary from place to
place and from year to year). Until the mid seventeenth century all the crops grown during the year
on a particular farm should be mentioned in the
farmer's inventory if it were made between April and
August, but once turnips were grown as a catch crop
after the harvest there would be no single point in
the year when all the crops for a harvest year would
be in the ground at the same time. The general
effect of these inconsistencies is to reduce considerably the number of inventories from which a
particular measure can be derived.(25) At the same
time most inventories can provide summary statistics
of agricultural practice. Since values are rarely
omitted and livestock and crop values seldom combined in the same entry, almost all farm inventories
can yield a figure of the ratio of the value of
crops to the value of livestock.

Representativeness

These comments about the contents of inventories
apply whether the documents are used for describing
a single farm or for generalising about farming
practice over a wide area. In the latter case,
however, it is also important to be aware of the
extent to which farms with an extant inventory represent all the farms within a particular area.
The ratio of the number of deaths in a year to the
number of extant inventories seems to vary considerably between different areas and for different periods. The proportion of entries in burial registers
referring to males over 21 to which an inventory can
be linked ranges from 8% in the Vale of Evesham for
1705-09, 20% for a Nottinghamshire village between
1660 and 1725, 32% for the Vale of Berkeley in the
late seventeenth century, and 40% for Hawkshead in

Cumbria over the period 1661-1750.(26)   As far as
farmers are concerned it has been calculated that
roughly 15% of farmers who died in Norfolk and
Suffolk aged 20 or over in the decade 1600-10, have
an inventory referring to their farm and for the
1670s some 6%.(27)
     More important is the social bias in a collec-
tion of inventories. 'Wills or testaments made by
any woman covert, [i.e. married] shall not be taken
to be good or effectual in law'(28) so that the
proportion of extant inventories referring to women
(widows and spinsters) is usually of the order of
five percent. The law also stipulated that those
with goods worth less than five pounds did not have
to make a will, so we would expect inventories to
have an upward social bias. In any case common
sense tells us that there would be little point in
making an inventory for a person who left virtually
nothing. While this point has generally been ack-
nowledged for some time, its most conclusive dem-
onstration is in a recent paper by Lindert,(29)
again relating inventories to burial entries. Another example can be given for Norfolk and Suffolk,
where, in the 1760s, some 2% of farmers leaving a
Consistory Court inventory were esquires, 15% gentlemen, 41% yeomen and 6% husbandmen. For the same
period using a variety of other sources it has been
estimated that roughly 4% of all farmers were esquires or gentlemen, 28% yeomen and 68% husbandmen.
(30)
     That farms described by inventories are larger
than average is suggested by the social status of
their occupants; in fact the average acreage under
crops (which must be less than average farm size)
in Norfolk and Suffolk for the early seventeenth
century is about 20, compared with an average farm
size of 15 acres calculated from a sample of manorial surveys.(31)   The extent to which this distorts
our impressions of the general farming pattern for
a particular area depends on the behaviour of farmers of differing social status working farms of
different sizes. While it is possible to speculate
about this (for example, that larger farmers were
more innovative, or had more specialised farms), in
the absence of other sources it is difficult to verify such speculations at a general level.
     The social groups to which a collection of in-
ventories from a particular ecclesiastical court
refers depends in part on the status of the court.
For any area probate could be proved at one of
three types of court. At the lowest level were the
174

Archdeaconry Courts, next came the Consistory Courts, and finally the Prerogative Courts of Canterbury and York. A few parishes were 'Peculiars' under the jurisdication of different bodies such as the lord of a manor or the dean and chapter of a cathedral. The probate of people who left goods valued at more than five pounds (sometimes a higher level was agreed) in more than one diocese was dealt with by the Prerogative Court of Canterbury if the dioceses were in the Southern Province, or by the Court in York if they were in the Northern Province. If the deceased had goods in more than one Archdeaconry his will was proved in the Consistory Court. The arrangements for the division of the remaining probate work between courts varied from diocese to diocese, but, generally speaking, the smallest estates were handled by the Archdeaconry Courts and the larger ones by the Consistory Courts. In the Norwich diocese for example, the Bishop's Court proved the wills and granted the administrations of knights, esquires, gentlemen and clergymen as well as those with goods in more than one Archdeaconry, while the four Archdeaconry Courts dealt with those of lower status. Thus the mean value of inventories is usually higher in the Consistory Courts than in the Archdeaconry Courts. In Suffolk in 1674, for example, the mean value of yeoman inventories is £193 in the Archdeaconry Court of Sudbury but £303 for the inventories from the same area presented to the Consistory Court. For the late sixteenth century in Oxfordshire the mean value of the Consistory Court inventories transcribed by Havinden is £45 compared with £24 for those for the Archdeaconry Courts.(32)

Because each level in the hierarchy of courts dealt with people of different status it is unwise to make comparisons between collections of inventories drawn from different courts. The spatial units within which inventories survive are determined by areas covered by the courts, so that using them within other regional units may cause problems. Thus if all available inventories are used for say a county it is likely that there will be periods when some courts have no surviving records so that inventories will exhibit spatial as well as social bias. In Norfolk for example, Consistory Court inventories survive for the period 1584-1740 and Prerogative court inventories for 1660-1782; none survive for the Norwich Archdeaconry before 1674 and those for the Norfolk Archdeaconry are extant only between 1728 and 1740. To cover say, the

period 1660-1740 an analysis of these inventories
should confine itself to those from the Consistory
and Prerogative courts; if the whole spectrum of
farms represented by inventories from all courts
for the whole county are to be considered then only
the period 1728-40 could be studied.(33)
It should be apparent that inventories are not
the straightforward source that they might appear
at first sight. While we can be fairly specific
about some of their limitations others must remain
more speculative. We do know that inventories only
represent certain sections of the farming community,
that some items did not have to be included, and
that in general we can only use inventories in a
positive way. Since a single inventory could be
subject to so many sources of error, it is unwise
to place too much emphasis on the evidence that any
one document provides. However, individual errors
have less influence when statistics are derived from
a large number of inventories, indeed they may can-
cel out. In calculating a mean for example, random
errors for particular quantities or values will have
no effect provided they are normally distributed
around the mean.

INVENTORIES AND THE MEASUREMENT OF AGRICULTURAL
CHANGE

Given the rather forbidding catalogue of limitations
which inventories seem to have it is apparent that
the extraction of data on agricultural change is not
particularly straightforward, and that in the light
of these limitations some historians appear to have
been rather cavalier in their use of them. In this
section we discuss some measures of agricultural
practice that inventories provide, and how these
may be presented.
The extent to which inventories cover only limited elements of the farm enterprise is emphasised
by Table 3 which shows some measures we should like
to be able to make for a seventeenth century farm.
The table is merely a checklist of some of the attributes of a farm that we might wish to measure.
What we actually wish to measure depends of course
on the specific questions in hand and on the particular theoretical framework in which they are answered. It could be made more complicated by introducing the links and interrelationships between the
attributes for example,(34) and is included here
simply for the suggestions it might offer for a

particular resarch project.

The main contribution of inventories is in the analysis of crops and stock in the enterprise. They reveal nothing about tenure (although wills can be of some help) or about labour supplies; because they omit real estate they are an unreliable guide to fixed capital, though they do list working capital and give some information on debt and credit.(35) Even within the production pattern inventories cannot show land use in the way that the tithe surveys can for example.(36) Since inventories only tell us about growing crops it is impossible to extract the total acreage of any land use category mentioned in the table. By their nature inventories give us a picture of a farm that is static. It is difficult to discover the rhythms of the farming year, of the patterns of inputs and outputs to the farm system. We can only guess at what animals ate for example.

Table 2   Some Measures of a Seventeenth Century Farm

A. FIXED FORMS

1. Morphology: Location, area, field shape, field boundaries, buildings.

2. Physical environment: Climate, relief, soils.

3. Relative location: to markets for inputs, outputs and innovation centres.

B. ORGANISATION

1. Tenure: Type (e.g. freehold or leasehold), security, communal obligations, degree of control (e.g. by lease or manorial court).

2. Capital: Quantity of fixed and working capital, location of supply, seasonal requirements, patterns of debt and credit, cost, productivity (return per unit invested).

3. Labour: Quantity, skill, location, seasonal requirements, cost, productivity (output per man).

C. PRODUCTION PATTERN

1. Type of production: For subsistence or the market, for human food, animal food or industry, degree of specialisation, labour intensive, capital intensive, land intensive, level of optimality.

2. <u>Land use</u>: Arable, pasture, meadow, orchards, market gardening, woodland, waste.

3. <u>Enterprises</u>: Quantity, value, crop and stock combinations, seasonal and spatial rotation patterns. <u>Crops</u> (exhaustive, restorative, cleansing, seasonal patterns of inputs and outputs, productivity per acre and per seed). <u>Livestock</u> (feed requirements, output of manure, seasonal patterns of inputs and outputs, productivity.

4. <u>Equipment</u>: Tools, implements, vehicles.

Fortunately there is much that inventories do measure. They give us three methods of measuring the attributes of the farm enterprise; by the frequency with which items appear,(37) by their quantity, and by their value. The first method is of little use when considering common items (like wheat or cattle) although all inventories may be used. Frequency counts of the presence or absence of a particular commodity indicate how common it was but not necessarily how important to the farming economy. Quantities of particular items are also fairly straightforward (unless customary measures introduce complications(38)) so that given enough inventories with useable information it is relatively easy to calculate average acreages of particular crops, or average herd sizes.(39) Before comparisons can be made between such figures, either over space or over time, we have of course to ensure that the collections of inventories from which they are drawn are comparable in terms of the range of farms to which they refer. Several statistical methods are available for determining which combinations of crops are significant in some sense, (40) but it is important to stress that these cannot reveal crop rotations directly. Since we cannot locate crops to specific pieces of ground, and it is almost unknown for inventories of the same farm to survive for successive years, actual rotational patterns can only be inferred.(41)

Values have the advantage in that most inventories usually include them. However, it is necessary to be absolutely clear what these values mean when we use them to measure a farm enterprise. Some of the ways in which appraisers might have arrived at crop valuations have been discussed in a previous paper.(42) Of the three possible ways in which appraisers might have valued crops, by some fixed or notional value, by the costs incurred in their

production, or by the price which the crop would
fetch at market, it seems that the third was employed except when crops were newly sown. It is
also likely that variations of animals are estimates
of market price, and that the wide diversity in valuations of stock is a reflection of differences in
the quality and age of the animals. Indeed by comparing a particular valuation to the average for a
group of farms it is possible to produce a rough
categorisation of animal quality.

The values of crops and stock are best considered as indicators of the amount of working capital
tied up in the two branches of the farm enterprise.
It is important to stress that they are not measures
of output, and that we cannot use inventories to
measure the relative importance of crop and livestock output.(43) While the value of growing crops
just before the harvest is probably an estimate of
the sum they would fetch when sold and so represents
the value of crop output for one year, stored crops
on the farm after the harvest may or may not represent the output from the previous harvest year, for
we have no way of knowing whether grain had been
sold off the farm or bought in. The real problems
though, are with valuations of animals. The output
from animals could consist of meat, leather, wool,
tallow, cheese, butter and milk. While inventories
mention these products we do not know to what period of output they refer. It might be possible to
estimate the value of output from livestock very
roughly, but to do so we would need to know for
what purposes the animals were kept, the length of
time they were on the farm, and the yields of their
products. Further, in comparing the values of
livestock with those of crops, although both are
expressed in a common unit, the comparison is not
necessarily of like with like. The value of crops
on the farm just before the harvest represents their
value for a single year, while the value of animals
at one point in the year depends on the length of
time they were kept on the farm.

An alternative method of relating crops and
livestock is to deal with quantities rather than
with values. The difficulty here is that the units
involved (numbers of different animal types and
volumes or areas of grain) are not directly comparable. Varying types of livestock may be equated using livestock units (whereby sheep equals 0.1 of a
cow for example).(44) Modern stock units are usually based on labour or feed requirements,(45) but
it is virtually impossible to derive these for

early modern England, given the diversity of farming practice and the absence of sufficient sources.
In any case we do not know how such units may have
changed over space and time, so that maps of livestock based on them are more likely to reflect our
assumptions and expectations than something approaching the reality of farming conditions. Even
today, 'each British university agricultural department recommends local variations for use in its own
region'.(46)

The way round this problem is simply not to
equate different animal types, but to express the
crop/stock balance in terms of one specific type,
say the number of cropped acres per milk cow or per
ewe. Relating the two branches of farming by values remains the best way of summarising farm types
in a single measure provided that we realise what
we are measuring. It is a relatively simple index
to produce, uses all the farming information that
inventories provide, and can be derived from nearly
all inventories referring to a farm. For these
reasons it has been adopted in most quantitative
studies of probate inventories.

Because inventories are so tantalising in that
they remain silent about so much that we would like
to know, most historians working with them have been
tempted to interpolate the gaps, to estimate data
(with varying degrees of statistical sophistication)
rather than simply record what is given. Farm size
(in acres) has been derived in various ways by a
number of authors. In his pioneering study of Leicestershire inventories Hoskins assumed one third of
the arable to be fallow (and so not recorded) and
estimated total arable accordingly, although he
states elsewhere in the article that, 'it is wholly
false to imagine a stereotyped and fixed pattern of
arable farming'.(47) Kenyon performed a similar
exercise,(48) while Skipp goes further in estimating
farm size. He assumed one third of arable to be
fallow and calculates the acreage of grass from the
number of livestock on the farm.(49) While such
techniques may provide some rough guidelines for
particular areas where farming practice is known
to be consistent, they are not to be recommended,
particularly since inventories themselves can demonstrate quite wide differences between farms within
a small area, reflecting different farming practice
in farms of different sizes and local adjustments to
soil and topography. Even if animals were fed entirely on grass it is impossible to calculate yields.
In any case many farmers must have fed grain to

their animals. Once again maps of the distribution
of farm sizes based on such calculations will probably reveal the assumptions behind them and very
little else. Fortunately it is not really necessary to bother with farm sizes in acres at all. There
is no particular virtue in this measure for it begs
the question 'acres of what?' The value of crops
and stock is generally a much more helpful measure
of the size of a farm than its area.

On a different tack estimates have been produced of crop yields in probate inventories, data
which cannot be calculated directly (except in a
very few instances) because an inventory provides
either the area of crops for the current harvest
year or the volume of stored crops from the previous
harvest year, and not both area and volume for the
same year. For the same harvest year we could relate the average area from one set of farms to the
average volume from another set, provided both
groups came from the same statistical population,
but we cannot be sure that the stocks of grain on a
farm represent the sole output from the previous
harvest, or that estimates of area and volume are
accurate. It is, however, possible to estimate
yields in bushels per acre by the mathematical man-
ipulation of an assumption about the unit valuations
of growing and stored grain linked to a statistical
analysis based on sampling theory(50) If this
technique is accepted then the way is open to chart
the progress of productivity changes, and, by relating yields to crop acreages, to produce estimates
of changing output.(51)

Mapping agricultural change

Given the essentially quantitative character of inventories it is not surprising that analyses of
them have usually presented their results in a quantitative form of some kind, though it must be admitted that few studies have employed the powerful
tools of statistical inference to help make sense of
the numbers that are presented.(52) Other historians have been content to cite individual examples
to verify their generalisations.(53) It is, of
course, a matter of personal preference as to which
approach provides the most convincing arguments: it
is the present author's view that if the citation
of occasional instances is regarded as proof then
it is possible to prove almost anything.(54) Historians working with inventories have also been concerned to emphasise regional variations in farming

practice but have rarely resorted to cartography to demonstrate this. (55) It is not the intention of this section to provide a general guide to drawing maps, but to illustrate some particular problems in showing spatial variations in farming practice and in so doing provide some examples of the use of inventories in measuring specific aspects of agricultural change from Norfolk and Suffolk.

Table 4 shows the three ways in which inventories measure the introduction of two new crops into East Anglian farming, root crops (mostly turnips) and grass substitutes (mostly clover). All extant farm inventories can contribute to the frequency count (expressed as a percentage) but the number

Table 3   Fodder Crops in Norfolk and Suffolk Inventories 1587-1729

	Root crops						Grass substitutes					
	(1)	N	(2)	N	(3)	N	(1)	N	(2)	N	(3)	N
1587-96	0.8	674	*	211	*	521	0.0	674		156		280
1629-38	0.9	713	*	180	0.06	584	0.0	713		146		304
1660-69	1.6	416	*	119	0.19	318	0.7	416	*	98	*	173
1670-79	9.3	362	0.63	100	0.45	236	3.7	362	*	86	*	133
1680-89	19.1	240	0.74	63	0.46	154	4.3	240	*	55	*	105
1690-99	29.4	153	2.23	37	1.29	92	6.3	153	*	39	0.24	75
1700-09	40.2	272	1.27	71	1.25	173	11.7	272	0.10	78	0.32	140
1710-19	47.4	334	2.15	99	1.52	217	17.4	334	1.01	95	0.32	125
1720-29	52.7	380	2.21	120	1.81	242	23.6	380	1.49	97	1.04	171

Notes: (1) Percentage of inventories mentioning the crop
(2) Mean acreage
(3) Mean value
N   Number of inventories used
*   Insufficient data

reduces considerably for the other measures. It is worth pointing out that inventories do not date the actual introduction of new crops, only the date by which they had been introduced (when the farmer died). Further, some inventory entries are ambiguous, so that the entry 'fodder' could conceal the presence of a new crop. Even so these figures give us a good idea of the chronology of innovation. Figure 41 shows how we may map one measure, the frequency count of grass substitutes. For each ten kilometre grid square the number of inventories mentioning the crops is expressed as a percentage of all the inventories in that square. A square has

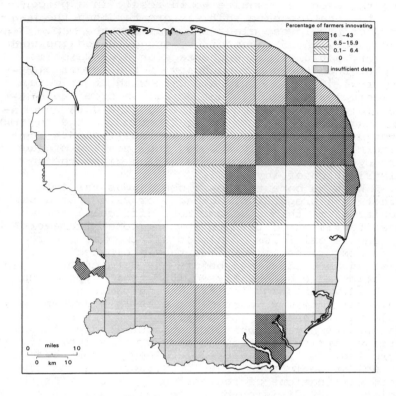

Fig.41   Density of inventories mentioning grass
substitutes in East Anglia, 1660-1730.

'insufficient data' when a single inventory mentioning the crop in a square would result in a percentage for that square that was greater than the boundary of the lowest class interval for the map. Thus
a square with 15 inventories, one of which included
clover, would give a percentage of 6.67 which is
higher than the upper boundary of the lowest class
interval (6.64) so only a square with 16 or more
inventories has sufficient data. In order to have
sufficient information for the map the data have
been aggregated into a 70 year period, but even with
over 2,000 inventories there are still gaps. The
alternative of simply showing the location of adopt-
ers by a point symbol is misleading given the uneven
distribution of inventories.

When we come to show a continuous variable
(that is a proportion, acreage, or value for a particular farm) things become more difficult, for we
need to fit our data into some regional framework.
A general criticism of almost all the farming regions historians use is that they are based on soil
type and predetermined before any data on farming
practice have been analysed.(56) Soil type is undoubtedly important in influencing patterns of agricultural activity, particularly in an era when agricultural technology (especially for draining land)
was relatively unsophisticated, but it did not determine farming practice as many writers imply.(57)
More important, using predetermined regions based
on soil type introduces an inevitable circularity
into explanations of regional differences. As Long
pointed out, division based on soil, 'assumes a
result that might be expected'.(58) If we derive
regional boundaries from the data itself - the attributes of a farm enterprise - we face the impossible task of trying to describe farming changes
over time for a series of regions whose boundaries
are also changing. The obvious solution is to adopt
an arbitrary framework (the grid in Figure 41 for
example) whose size depends on the scale of regionalisation and the quantity of data. This is preferable to the method of Yelling who based his division
of east Worcestershire on a 'preliminary inspection
of the inventories parish by parish', which again
could lead to circularity in subsequent arguments.
(59)
Where the adoption of an arbitrary grid results
in too coarse a framework for a given time period,
or too long a period for a given grid size, an alternative is to dispense with discrete regions altogether and to work with the concept of surfaces.

This is all the more justified when we realise that different patterns can result when the same data is mapped on to grids of different sizes.(60) In producing a contoured surface each farm is regarded as a point in three dimensional space, its location defining its position in two dimensions and its value on some attribute on the third. The resulting surface is then contoured. An example of such an exercise using inventories has already been published,(61) and gives a very generalised representation of the balance between crops and livestock using the value method for Norfolk and Suffolk between 1587 and 1797. The problem with this approach is again the density of information. When the distance between points (farms) is large the interpolation process (filling in the gaps between data points) produces misleading patterns since one farm influences the mapped values for a large area surrounding it. Thus the maps all too easily have a spurious air of accuracy. A second problem is that it is only possible to contour one aspect of the farm enterprise at a time.

While it may seem rather unoriginal, and may produce maps that seem harder to interpret, it is sometimes safest to map agricultural data from inventories using point symbols, particularly when the density of inventories is quite low. An example of this technique is given in Figures 42 and 43 which show the distribution of farming types in Norfolk and Suffolk in the late sixteenth century. The farm types were defined using the technique of cluster analysis,(62) which gathers farms into 'natural groups', such that the differences within each group are minimised and that between groups maximised. The variables used in the analysis were the percentage contribution of cattle, horses, sheep, winter corn, spring corn and fodder to the total value of crops and stock on the farm.

Figure 42 shows the characteristics of 13 types of farm revealed by the analysis in comparison with the average for all farms. Groups indicated by a square have an emphasis on crops, those with a diamond on cattle, and those with a circle on sheep. Of the remaining groups E represents an 'average' farm, G has an emphasis on horses and J on fodder crops. The map (Figure 43) indicates the boundaries between 'sheep corn' and 'wood pasture' farming regions defined by Thirsk(63) and indicates that those generalised regions need some modification. While there is a predominance of cattle farms in the 'wood pasture' area of High Suffolk, and crop farms

185

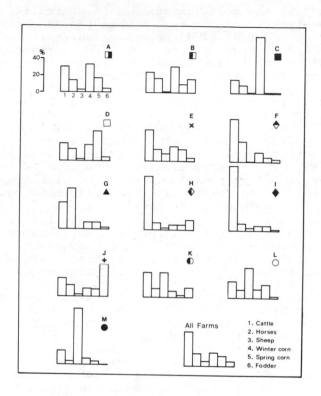

Fig.42 Percentages of cattle, horses, sheep, winter corn, spring corn and fodder by value for farm types, 1586-1597.

are more common on the 'sheep corn' area of Norfolk and the Suffolk coast, an alternative set of boundaries could make the differences more pronounced. Further, while 'sheep corn' farms are revealed by the analysis (type L) they are not very common, and we may have been misled by contemporaries into thinking this farming type was more common than it actually was.

These examples are offered simply as suggestions as to how we can use inventories to describe and analyse farming practice on a general scale. Aside from the articles already mentioned, inventories have been employed in several studies of particular aspects of farming including, dairying and cheese-

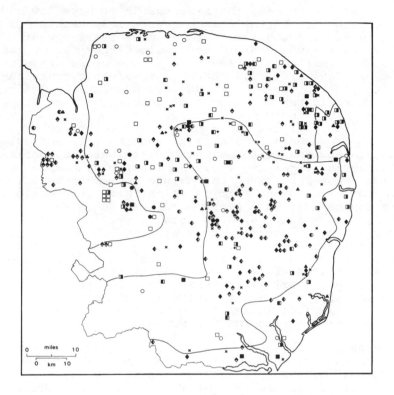

Fig.43 Distribution of farming types in East
Anglia, 1586-1597. Key as for Fig.42.

making,(64) farm equipment, (65) buildings,(66) and
the relation of farming and industrial activity.(67)
Many other studies of the early modern period using
inventories are also relevant to agriculture,(68) as
are some of the methods employed with inventories in
other countries.(69)

CONCLUSION

Inventories are a deservedly popular source for analysing agricultural patterns and processes in early
modern England. Before we can use them, however, it
is essential to understand the purposes for which

they were produced, their status in probate law and the machinery of the church courts responsible for administering the law. Provided we realise what inventories did and did not include they can be taken as a fairly reliable guide to the crops and stock on particular farms. Their most valuable contribution lies in large scale studies of farming practice, where estimates based on many documents iron out many of the individual errors.

Such analyses can employ many of the techniques which are commonplace amongst contemporary agricultural geographers for mapping distributions, defining agricultural regions, and describing change over time. However, given the nature and content of inventories, and the form in which their information is expressed, these techniques must be chosen carefully. Comparing studies using inventories with work on more modern sources also emphasises that inventories can only measure some of the attributes of a farm, and depending on the problem in hand these are not necessarily the most important or significant. Above all we must be clear about what we want to measure, what we are actually able to measure, and the implications of the ways in which we choose to portray the information we do measure.

REFERENCES

1. W.B. Stephens, 'Sources for the History of Agriculture in the English Village and their Treatment', Agricultural History, 43 (1969), pp.225-238 and J. Thirsk, 'The Content and Sources of English Agrarian History after 1500', Agricultural History Review, 3 (1955), pp.66-79, introduce other agrarian sources. A good example of a small scale study is M. Spufford, Contrasting Communities: English Villagers in the Sixteenth and Seventeenth Centuries (1974), pp.58-104.

2. And indeed for the known world, see the theme issue of A.A.G. Bijdragen 23 (Wageningen, 1980). The first published inventories date from the early nineteenth century, but G.E. Fussell and V.G.B. Atwater, 'Farmers' Goods and Chattels: 1500 to 1800', History, 20 (1935), pp.211-20 first brought inventories to the attention of agricultural historians; the first systematic analysis of them was in W.G. Hoskins, 'The Leicestershire Farmer in the Sixteenth Century', Transactions of the Leicestershire Archaeological Society, 22 (1945), pp. 33-95.

3. A.R.H. Baker, 'On the Historical Geography

of France', Journal of Historical Geography, 6 (1980)
p.75.
    4. A.R.H. Baker, J.D. Hamshere and J. Langton,
(eds.), Geographical Interpretations of Historical
Sources (1970), p.17.
    5. Early inventories are discussed in M.M.
Sheehan, The Will in Medieval England (1963), pp.
211-14, 321-2. The legal context on inventories is
set out in H. Swinbourne, A Treatise of Testaments
and Last Wills (first edition, 1590) and R.S. Burn,
Ecclesiastical Law (third edition, 1775) and partly
reviewed in R.A. Marchant, The Church under the Law
(1969) and R. Houlbrooke, Church Courts and the
People during the English Reformation 1520-1570
(1979). Works that introduce inventories include
O. Ashmore, 'Inventories as a Source of Local History II Farmers', Amateur Historian, 4 (1959), pp.
186-95, J. West, Village Records (1962), pp.92-131;
and the introductions to F.W. Steer, 'Farm and Cottage Inventories of Mid Essex, 1635-1749', Essex
Record Office Publication 8 (1950) (revised edition
Chichester, 1965), J.S. Moore, The Goods and Chattels of our Forefathers: Frampton Cotterell and
District Probate Inventories, 1539-1804 (1977)
B. Trinder, and J. Cox, Yeomen and Colliers in Telford: Probate Inventories for Dudley, Lilleshall,
Wellington and Wrockwardine, 1660-1750 (1980), M.A.
Havinden, (ed.), Household and Farm Inventories in
Oxfordshire, 1550-90' Oxfordshire Record Society, 44
and Historical Manuscripts Commission Joint Publication, 10 (1965). Printed examples of farmers'
inventories include, G. Clinch, 'The Inventory of a
Surrey Farmer', Surrey Archaeological Collections,
23 (1910), pp.77-82, P.N. Dawe, 'A Dorset Farm Inventory of 1704', Somerset and Dorset Notes and
Queries, 27 (1958), pp.160-73 and F.W. Steer, 'The
Inventory of Arthur Coke of Bramfield, 1629', Proceedings of the Suffolk Institute of Archaeology,
25 (1952), pp.264-87. A more complete bibliography
will be found in M. Overton, 'Probate inventories:
a guide and bibliography', Historical Geography
Research Series (forthcoming, 1982).
    6. John Moore of the University of Bristol
is currently investigating the locations and numbers
of extant inventories (SSRC grant no. HR7487), A.J.
Camp, Wills and their Whereabouts (fourth edition,
1974) gives the dates for which inventories survive
but not their numbers. Prerogative Court of Canterbury inventories are discussed in J.S.W. Gibson,
'Inventories in the records of the Prerogative
Court of Canterbury', Local Historian, 14 (1980),

pp.222-5.
    7.   21 Henry VIII c. 5.
    8.   Burn, Ecclesiastical Law, vol.4 p.238,
Houlbrooke, Church Courts, p.113.
    9.   Burn, Ecclesiastical Law, vol.4 p.238.
    10. Burn, Ecclesiastical Law, vol.4 p.240.
    11. P.J. Bowden, 'Agricultural Prices, Farm
Profits, and Rents', in J. Thirsk (ed.), The Agra-
rian History of England and Wales Volume IV (1967),
p.677.
    12. M. Overton, Agricultural Change in Norfolk
and Suffolk, 1580-1740, (Unpublished University of
Cambridge Ph.D. Thesis, 1981), p.31.
    13. N. Evans, 'Tithe Books as a Source for the
Local Historian', Local Historian, 14 (1980) 24-7,
G. Longman, A Corner of England's Garden: An Agrarian
History of South-west Hertfordshire, 1600-1850 (2
volumes, 1977), vol.1 pp.28-9, Overton, Agricultural
Change, p.32.
    14. R.P. Garrard, 'English Probate Inventories
and their use in studying the Domestic Interior,
1570-1700', A.A.G. Bijdragen, 23 (1980), p.69.
    15. Longman, A Corner of England's Garden, vol.
1 p.12, C. Moor, 'The old statesman families of
Irton, Cumberland', Transactions of the Cumberland
and Westmorland Antiquarian and Archaeological
Society, New Series, 10 (1910), p.154.
    16. K.J. Allison, 'The Sheep Corn Husbandry of
Norfolk in the Sixteenth and Seventeenth Centuries',
Agricultural History Review, 5 (1957), pp.12-30.
    17. J.D. Marshall, 'Social Structure and Wealth
in pre-industrial England', Economic History Review,
Second Series, 33 (1980), p.517, R. Machin, Probate
Inventories and Manorial Excerpts of Chetnole, Leigh
and Yetminster (1976), pp.26-8.
    18. M. Overton, 'Estimating Crop Yields from
Probate Inventories: an example from East Anglia,
1585-1735', Journal of Economic History, 39 (1979),
pp.363-78.
    19. Trinder and Cox, Yeoman and colliers, p.6,
Steer, 'Farm and Cottage Inventories', p.5.
    20. B.A. Holderness, 'Credit and a Rural Comm-
unity, 1660-1800, Some Neglected Aspects of Probate
Inventories', Midland History, 3 (1975), p.95, J.S.
Moore, The Goods and Chattels of our Forefathers,
p.4.
    21. M. Overton, 'Computer Analysis of an Incon-
sistent Data Source: the Case of Probate Inventories',
Journal of Historical Geography, 3 (1977), pp.317-26.
    22. For example, F.W. Steer, 'Farm and Cottage
Inventories', pp.52-3.

23. Overton, 'Computer Analysis'; the method of J.H. Bettey and D.S. Wilde, 'Using a Computer for a Local History Project' Local Historian, 11 (1974) pp.129-33 discards information.

24. R.P. Garrard, 'English Probate Inventories', briefly discusses a more flexible method applicable to non-farming items. Overton, 'Probate Inventories: A Guide', discusses this issue further.

25. M. Overton, 'English Probate Inventories and the Measurement of Agricultural Change', A.A.G. Bijdragen, 23 (1980), p.211.

26. J.A. Johnston, 'The Vale of Evesham, 1702-8: The Evidence from Probate Inventories and Wills', Vale of Evesham Historical Society, Research Papers, 4 (1973), p.87, M.W. Barley, 'Farmhouses and Cottages, 1550-1725, Economic History Review, Second Series, 7 (1955), p.292, J.P.P. Horn, 'The Distribution of Wealth in the Vale of Berkeley Gloucestershire, 1660-1700', Southern History, 3 (1981), pp. 85-6, J.D. Marshall, 'Social Structure and Wealth', p.507.

27. Overton, Agricultural change, pp.26-8.

28. 34 and 35 Henry VIII c.5.

29. P.H. Lindert, 'An Algorithm for Probate Sampling', Journal of Interdisciplinary History, 11 (1981), pp.649-68.

30. Overton, 'English Probate Inventories', p.209, D.A. Cressy, Education and Literacy in London and East Anglia, 1580-1700, (unpublished University of Cambridge Ph.D. Thesis, 1972), p.15.

31. Overton, Agricultural change, p.26.

32. J. Cox, The Records of the Prerogative Court of Canterbury and the Death Duty Registers (Public Record Office Guide, 1980), p.1, Marchant, The Church under the Law, p.24, Houlbrooke, Church Courts and the People, p.91. Figures calculated from Suffolk inventories analysed by the author for the Consistory Court and by R. Garrard for the Archdeaconry of Sudbury; the Oxfordshire data is derived from Havinden, Household and Farm Inventories, pp. 41-316.

33. Rough maps showing the boundaries of the Ecclesiastical courts are in J.S.W. Gibson, A Simplified Guide to Probate Jurisdictions (1980).

34. W.B. Morgan and R.J.C. Munton, Agricultural Geography (1971), p.22.

35. B.A. Holderness, 'Credit in English Rural Society before the Nineteenth Century, with special reference to the period 1650-1720', Agricultural History Review 24 (1976), pp.97-109, Holderness, 'Credit in a rural community'.

36. See the Chapters above by R. Kain and J.T. Coppock.
37. Longman, A Corner of England's Garden, vol. 1 pp.9-10 describes this method as 'content analysis'.
38. A useful guide here is, 'A return for each county in England and Wales, of the different measures... under which wheat, barley, oats and flour are sold' British Parliamentary Papers, 65 (1854).
39. For example, J.A. Johnston, 'The probate inventories and wills of a Worcestershire parish, 1676-1775', Midland History, 1 (1971), 26-7, J. Thirsk, Fenland Farming in the Sixteenth Century (1965), pp.29-41, Havinden, (ed.) Household and Farm Inventories', p.39.
40. J.C. Weaver, 'Crop Combination Regions in the Middle West', Geographical Review, 44 (1954), 175-200, Morgan and Munton, Agricultural Geography, pp.120-2.
41. W.G. Hoskins, 'The Leicestershire Farmer in the Sixteenth Century' (revised version), in W.G. Hoskins, (ed.), Essays in Leicestershire History (1950), pp.123-83 emphasises this point, J. Cornwall, 'Farming in Sussex, 1560-1640', Sussex Archaeological Collections, 92 (1954), pp.70-2 finds it impossible to discover rotations, but G.H. Kenyon, 'Kirdford inventories, 1611-1776, with particular reference to the Weald clay farming', Sussex Archaeological Collections, 93 (1955), pp.96-100 makes the attempt.
42. Overton, 'Estimating crop yields', pp.370-73.
43. J.A. Yelling, 'Probate Inventories and the Geography of Livestock Farming: a study of east Worcestershire, 1540-1750', Transactions of the Institute of British Geographers, 51 (1970), p.114 claims he can.
44. Yelling, 'Probate Inventories and the Geography of Livestock Farming', J.A. Yelling, Common Field and Enclosure in England, 1450-1850 (1977).
45. See for example, B.M. Church et. al., 'A type of farming map based on agricultural census data', Outlook on Agriculture, 5 (1968), pp.191-6 and J.T. Coppock, 'Crop, Livestock and Enterprise Combinations in England and Wales', Economic Geography, 40 (1964), 65-81.
46. Morgan and Munton, Agricultural Geography, p.107.
47. Hoskins, 'The Leicestershire Farmer in the Sixteenth Century (revised version)', pp.137, 164.
48. Kenyon, 'Kirdford inventories', pp.101-3.

49. V.H.T. Skipp, 'Economic and Social Change in the Forest of Arden, 1530-1649', Agricultural History Review, Supplement, 18 (1970), pp.89-90.
50. Overton, 'Estimating Crop Yields'.
51. Overton, 'English Probate Inventories', p.214.
52. J. Thirsk, English Peasant Farming: the Agrarian History of Lincolnshire from Tudor to Recent Times (1957) and J. Whetter, Cornwall in the Seventeenth Century (1974) show their results in the form of frequency tables for example.
53. E. Kerridge, The Agricultural Revolution (1967) is one of the best examples of this type of approach.
54. W.O. Aydelotte, 'Quantification in History', American Historical Review, 71 (1966), pp.803-25.
55. Not unexpectedly geographers have drawn maps, for example, F. Emery, 'The Mechanics of Innovation: Clover Cultivation in Wales before 1750', Journal of Historical Geography, 2 (1976), pp.35-48, J.A. Yelling, 'The Combination and Rotation of Crops in East Worcestershire, 1540-1640', Agricultural History Review, 17 (1969), 24-43, Yelling, 'Probate Inventories and the Geography of Livestock Farming', J.A. Yelling, 'Changes in Crop Production in East Worcestershire, 1540-1867', Agricultural History Review, 21 (1973), 18-34.
56. W.H. Long, 'Regional Farming in Seventeenth Century Yorkshire', Agricultural History Review, 8 (1960), pp.103-4, Cornwall, 'Farming in Sussex', p. 48, Bettey and Wilde, 'Using a Computer', p.131, C.W. Chalklin, Seventeenth Century Kent (1965), p. 77, Thirsk, English Peasant Farming.
57. J.T. Coppock, 'Land Use and Classification', in Classification of Agricultural Land in Britain, Agricultural Land Service Technical Report, 8 (1962), pp.65-80.
58. Long, 'Regional Farming', p.215.
59. Yelling, 'The Combination and Rotation of Crops', p.26.
60. J.R. Tarrant, Agricultural Geography (1974) p.147, P. Haggett, A.D. Cliff and E. Frey, Locational Analysis in Human Geography (1977), pp.349-51.
61. Overton, 'Computer Analysis', p.324.
62. Two Introductions are, B. Everitt, Cluster Analysis (1974) and R.J. Johnston, Classification in Geography, Concepts and Techniques in Modern Geography, 8 (1976).
63. J. Thirsk, 'The Farming Regions of England', in J. Thirsk (ed.), The Agrarian History of England and Wales Volume IV (1967), p.4.

64. For example, A. Clark, 'An Essex Dairy Farm in 1629', Essex Review, 21 (1920), pp.156-9, P.R. Edwards, 'The Development of Dairy Farming on the North Staffordshire Plain in the Seventeenth Century', Midland History, 4 (1977), pp.175-90, A. Henstock, 'Cheese Manufacture and Marketing in Derbyshire and North Staffordshire, 1670-1870, Derbyshire Archaeological Journal, 89 (1970).

65. Long, 'Regional Farming', is one of the few people who discuss this rather neglected topic.

66. N.W. Alcock, 'Devonshire Farmhouses Part II, some Dartmoore Houses', Transactions of the Devonshire Association, 101 (1969), pp.83-106, M.W. Barley, 'Farmhouses and Cottages, 1550-1725', Economic History Review, Second Series, 7 (1955), pp.291-306, M.W. Barley, The English Farmhouse and Cottage (1961), W.G. Hoskins, 'The Rebuilding of Rural England, 1570-1640', Past and Present, 4 (1953), pp. 44-59, R. Machin, 'The Great Rebuilding: A Reassessment', Past and Present, 77 (1977), pp.33-56.

67. D. Hey, 'A Dual Economy in South Yorkshire', Agricultural History Review, 17 (1969), pp.108-19, P. Frost, 'Yeomen and Metalsmiths: Livestock in the Dual Economy in South Staffordshire 1560-1720', Agricultural History Review, 29 (1981), pp.29-41.

68. For example, P. Clark, 'The Ownership of Books in England 1560-1640: the example of some Kentish townsfolk', in L. Stone (ed.), Schooling and Society (1976), pp.95-111, D.G. Hey, 'The Use of Probate Inventories for Industrial Archaeology, Industrial Archaeology, 10 (1973), pp.201-13, B.A. Holderness, 'Rural Tradesmen, 1660-1850: a regional study in Lindsey', Lincolnshire History and Archaeology, 7 (1972), pp.77-83, D.G. Vaisey, 'A Charlbury Mercer's Shop, 1623', Oxoniensia, 31 (1966), pp.106-16.

69. For example, D.E. Ball and G.M. Walton, 'Agricultural Productivity Change in Eighteenth Century Pennsylvania', Journal of Economic History, 36 (1976), pp.102-17.

Chapter Six

TOPOGRAPHY OF THE EARLY MODERN TOWN, c.1500-c.1750

C.F. Slade

INTRODUCTION

At the beginning of the period of our concern the
Tudor Henry VII had been for fifteen years on the
English throne and by its end the King was the Han-
overian George II; and the intervening two and a
half centuries had been a period of major development in almost all aspects of national life. Towns,
however, certainly as far as their topography (1)
is concerned, show far less disturbance and change
than do most other things. By 1500 the great formative age was long since over, and by 1750 the re-
voluntionary changes that were to bring about the
present-day urban pattern had not begun. Most certainly, the dramatic changes that profoundly affected the townsfolk were not reflected in their physical urban environment, where emphasis falls on
the evolutionary aspects of unity and continuity.
But this is not to characterise these two and a half
centuries as a time of no, or even slight, change.
Normal processes of rebuilding were continuous due
both to natural decay and to desire for improvement;
and each rebuilding, of both public and private
buildings, was liable to reflect changes in style,
frequently with some alteration of ground plan.
There was also some expansion in the built-up areas
of towns, but this tended to be limited to better-
class dwellings, the increase in urban population
being accommodated by infilling. There were, of
course, certain periods when private rebuilding was
more sustained. Somewhere in Tudor times most towns
saw a period of concentrated activity, although it
may be that more work than was once realised had
started before the beginning of our period.(2) Another period was the earlier eighteenth century,
where those who could afford it could best take ad-

vantage of new standards of comfort by rebuilding.
But in addition to these routine processes there
were periods that resulted in widespread destruction
on a national scale, a destruction that might subsequently involve making good by rebuilding or building anew. The first such period was that of the
religious changes of the sixteenth century, which
saw the destruction or adaptation of many buildings
of religious use. However, this must not be exaggerated, for the spiritual upheaval was by no means
reflected in topography, which shows nothing of the
major changes that occurred to church interiors.
And the physical appearance of many religious buildings remained superficially the same: for example,
that the nave of the church of the grey friars in
Reading became the town's new guildhall would not
affect the street-scape. Domestic buildings of religious establishments, coming into private or public
possession, frequently continued with minor or no
modifications. Many major monastic churches such
as those of the great abbeys of St. Alban or St.
Edmund continued; and even where destruction occurred, as in the cases of the imposing churches of
Abingdon or Reading, it was a slow process. Some
parish churches went out of religious use, but this
was by no means a new phenomenon, and on this occasion there was little immediate destruction of buildings. The second period, that of the Civil Wars
of the seventeenth century, saw some indiscriminate
destruction of lay and ecclesiastical buildings a-
like in the many towns that were attached or besieg-
ed. Some, like Bedford, escaped with alarms and ex-
cursions; others, like Bristol and Colchester, suffered considerable damage to buildings. In most
cases damage rather than destruction of buildings
was the outcome for weapons were limited in destructive power and looting only incidentally involved
destruction of buildings. Destruction, however, did
occur for military reasons: town walls and castles
were slighted to deny their use to the enemy, and
the list of castles totally or partially destroyed
is long. The construction of defences could also
involve the destruction of buildings: it was the
need to create a clear field of fire that caused
major destruction to what survived of the church
and claustral buildings of Reading Abbey. Other
occasions of destruction more concentrated than
usual varied from town to town and were usually the
result of fire, for the combination of flammable
materials and primitive fire-fighting appliances
- little more than firehooks and buckets for much

of the period - and techniques involved nearly certain destruction of any building or group of buildings that caught alight. Towns do not seem to have
suffered as much from fire in this period as in earlier centuries, although destruction could be considerable.(3) London, of course, was unique in its
Great Fire of 1666, both in extent of destruction
and in its subsequent rebuilding pattern. Where
lesser destruction occurred there was normally
little or no modification to the street plan, and
rebuilding potentialities were very much at the
mercy of property boundaries; in fact, the rebuilding of a recent house in the same style on the
same foundations leaves things for the topographer
essentially as they were, although in the guise of
local historian he or she can be very conscious of
the danger, misery and crisis that conflagration
brings to the lives of individuals. Other destructive forces - wind, lightning, floods, frost and
snow - have been seven-day wonders in most towns,(4)
but by this period they have little effect on the
topography of towns: any town liable to be washed
away in floods would have gone long since.

So the townscape saw continuous change, but it
is very limited in comparison with that of later
periods. In fact, the visual impact was considerably reduced, for lower-class housing changed comparatively little: simple rebuilding of a simple
structure gives no significant change, and in any
case repair was easier than rebuilding. Fashionable
rebuilding by the more affluent often involved a
move to the outskirts with the previous dwelling
declining into use as tenements for the poor; and
such would leave its appearance much as ever. Obviously the emphasis that falls on continuity and
limited change is very important for the urban topographer.

THE TOPOGRAPHER'S INFORMATION

So the topographer is concerned with the various
elements that make up the physical appearance of
the town. Strictly speaking he or she is not concerned with the life of the town, but it is undesi-
rable if not impossible to avoid drifting in and
out of local history; the activities of families;
the enforcement of by-laws; prosperity and decay;
government attitudes; changing fashion; and a host
of other aspects engage attention. In practice, of
course, local topographer is also local historian,

and at times historical information will allow selection among various topographical possibilities.
It should never be forgotten that the history is
there, but our present concern is only with the
topography. Although knowledge is said to be indi-
visible it is simplest to differentiate the four
forms under which information comes to the topographer and to consider them individually. They are
objects, illustrations, descriptions, plans.

OBJECTS

Objects are the actual houses, features, roads,
monuments and so forth that are currently present.
How many survive from our period varies greatly
from one town to another: there can be no general
rules, and it is a matter of local investigation on
the ground. Quite frequently an older building will
survive behind a false front or incorporated into a
later. Precise dating from the building itself is
normally impossible, but general knowledge will usually give an acceptable date-bracket. Information
from buildings is reasonably accurate but tedious
to acquire, becoming progressively more so with
pursuit of ever more precision about date and dimensions. The desirable outcome is when a standing
building or part can be identified on an earlier
plan, and this can greatly reduce the topographer's
work. Unfortunately it too often happens that older work incorporated can only be seen when a building is being demolished.
      Foundations of buildings can be brought to
light during the course of demolition or by archaeological excavation, and frequently the two go together, but foundations, obviously, give little
information about the elevation of a building. In
general archaeology is of little assistance over
the buildings of our period, no matter how useful
it may be for earlier epochs of a town's history.
Even were it not prohibitively expensive to open up
large urban areas, it is doubtful whether enough
has survived Victorian cellar-building to be of
more than occasional assistance. In addition, there
is the major problem of dating where nondescript
footings are involved: the coin set in the original
mortar is almost without exception an archaeological day dream. Where archaeology may give assistance under favourable conditions is in establishing
the alignments and limits of roads, paths, water-
courses and such linear features. Any aid here is

useful because so much tidying-up and rationalisation has taken place since the late eighteenth century that present lines are not those of former
times and, indeed, can give a very false impression.
The recovery of other linear features of an earlier
day - town walls, banks and ditches - that may have
survived into our period but have since been destroyed unplanned may have to rely entirely on archaeology.

ILLUSTRATIONS

Drawings and paintings are done for a variety of
purposes, and their scope extends from part of a
building or feature to whole streets and even districts. One variety is the architecturally accurate
drawing, strictly to scale, and examples of good
modern work on domestic architecture can be seen in
the R.C.H.M. volume for Stamford.(5) The best-
known early work is that of Stukeley, and there has
been a steady succession since his day.(6) All
towns possess these architectural drawings, some
published in local histories and periodicals, the
bulk still in manuscript. At the other extreme
from these architectural drawings are impressionistic works designed to catch what the artist perceived as the spirit of the building or the scene,
but the topographer can get little detailed aid
from such works, especially when buildings on either
side are faded out or symbolically indicated. But
most oils, sketches and water-colours are straightforward. Although they are primarily works of art
many are topographically accurate; others, however,
can be sadly deceiving in purporting an accuracy
that is spurious. But what art does not demand is
comprehensive cover - as of back and sides and out-
buildings and such - so that all except one face
may remain a mystery. Frequently a pictured building stands in no shown relationship with any adjoining, and exact relationships of buildings to streets
are rarely indicated. Artistic portrayal of groups
or streets of buildings involves perspective, which
can give an excellent topographical impression but
which usually defies construction of precise elevations. It is obvious that we are not limited to
illustrations done in the period of our concern.
If a building can be dated to pre-1750 then illustrations done in the nineteenth and twentieth centuries can be quite acceptable, although allowance
must be made for any post-1750 modifications. An

inevitable weakness of later illustration - certainly if much later than 1800 - is that it cannot give
the former relationship of buildings to streets and
footways, for footways came within the view of the
Improvement Acts of the late eighteenth century onwards; and the nineteenth century saw the creation
of new road-lines and even new roads in old town
areas. The question might be asked as to how far
illustrations can be trusted. There can be no sure
answer, but if two independent illustrations of the
same thing are similar there can be little quibbling;
and, generally, the work of someone drawing for the
purse or the praise of his contemporaries has to
be presumed accurate unless there is evidence to the
contrary. A painter producing historical works of
streets or buildings of a time long before his own
is topographer rather than artist, and it is from
the former point of view that his work must be regarded. All towns possess much of this illustrative
material, from large canvases to small sketches. It
is to be found mainly in local art galleries as well
as in museums, reference libraries and record offices, with an unknown quantity, albeit reducing, in
private hands. In many cases the better-known have
been published, often in exhibition catalogues, frequently as postcards. The perspective plan, that
cross between picture and plan, will be considered
under the latter.

Photography can from our point of view be regarded as producing objective evidence. Recent
photographs can be valuable, but those taken before
c.1914 - most town collections have photographs
from the 1870s - are especially so, for much building then survived, often unaltered, from an earlier
time. (Fig.44) In the early days of photography
standards varied enormously, from something little
better than a grey or brown blur to pictures well-
defined and well-contrasted. All towns have considerable collections steadily increasing in quantity
now that members of the public have become conscious
of the historical value of such photographs. In
many cases they are in the form of negatives, which
have advantages, for photographs deteriorate more
readily with age. A difficulty at times is that the
subject has not been identified or the identification has been lost. Collections of photographs or
negatives are held by museums, reference libraries
and local societies. Photographs may be in the
form of postcards.

There is enough of this illustrative material
for most towns to provide reasonably comprehensive

cover for the eighteenth century, patchy cover for
the later seventeenth century and increasingly
scrappy cover as one moves further back. But even
where a building no longer stands and has left no
illustration it is frequently possible that there
is a written reference. And from general knowledge
of building styles combined with specific examples
from the locality it needs no great effort to envis-
age or even portray a "Tudor merchant's house" or
"seventeenth-century hovel" in general terms, although it must always be made clear where something
is based on conceptual reconstruction rather than
on evidence.

DESCRIPTION

Description can be verbal or written, but for the
period of our concern the former is of no assistance. Anyone working on aspects of the local past
is fed a steady supply of information reputedly
transmitted verbally down the generations. Usually
it can be identified in some work of local history;
where it cannot it is best disregarded. But this
is no real loss, for the quantity of official doc-
mentation for any town is very large and for many
it is enormous. Nor is relevant information limited to pre-1750 documents, for later ones frequently have some mention of an older building or feature. But comparatively few are in print and virtually none of the nineteenth century. So the topographer, lacking aid from indexes and ease of handling is best advised to leave later records and
concentrate on those of 1500 to, say c.1780 or even
1800. Documents, of course, provide much more than
topographical and architectual description: they can
mention infraction of building bylaws; they can de-

Fig. 44   St. Mary's Butts, Reading, facing south.
These two photographs are taken from virtually the
same spot, one in the 1870's, the other some ten
years later. The earlier shows the medieval and
seventeenth-century dwellings; the later the Jubilee
Fountain of 1887 with all old buildings gone. This
is a very good example of the value of really early
photographs, for a 10 year difference here shows a
very different scene. These come from the Taunt
collection of negatives in Reading Museum (copy-
right the Berkshire Archaeological Society and
Reading Museum).

Fig.44 St. Mary's
Butts, Reading,
facing south

Fig.44 St. Mary's
Butts, Reading,
facing south
/cont.

tail the actions of those defiling or damaging
streets and waterways; they can give the names and
backgrounds of property owners; and much more. And
information can occur in most unexpected places.(7)
Most documentation of this kind has some mention of
plots of land, buildings, building materials or
building accounts although it may be that the information given - such as annual statements of rent
paid for corporation property - is of little topographical interest. The main kinds of records that
carry what may be called this fringe-topographical
information are similar for all towns: there is a
record of corporation proceedings(8) which can vary
greatly in fullness between towns and at different times
in any one town; there are corporation accounts,
again full or slight, which can have separate building and maintenance accounts for corporation property, and there can at times be detailed accounts
relating to one specific project. Of course, borough records often give considerable information,
especially dates, when public buildings are involved. Unfortunately few corporation proceedings and
accounts are in print. There are also churchward-
ens' accounts that include building and maintenance
of parish property and church. Parishes also had
responsibility for highways although topographical
information given on these is normally very slight.
Wills, incidentally, are far more useful for information on fittings and furnishings than on buildings.
    The records described above usually have their
information on buildings and topography mixed up
with a miscellany of other topics, but there are
two kinds of documents which are concerned specifically with property. The first consists of a variety of property deeds - sales, conveyances, mort-
gages, leases etc. - and in any of these the location and dimensions of a plot of land may be given;
at times the overall dimensions of a building; and
a building lease will sometimes give considerable
detail of a projected building. Most deeds of this
kind owe their survival to the relevant property
coming into the hands of a corporate and permanent
organisation. The main such organisation in most
towns is the Corporation, but a cathedral town has
also the Dean and Chapter and a university town
the University and the colleges.(9) Thus in many
cases there are comprehensive dossiers, often covering centuries, concerning certain properties, and
it is normally possible to identify these. Unfortunately the documentation concerning property not

so transferred has frequently been lost(10), so the
situation in most towns is a patchwork of identified
properties separated and surrounded by uncertainty,
although for some towns the uncertainty is considerably less than in most others.(11) In the later
part of our period small plans can accompany property deeds: they are often more useful topographically than the deeds themselves, and will be mentioned under Plans. Accuracy of these deeds, which
are legal documents, can be assumed. However, they
deal with the very particular and their topographical value for our period is at present somewhat
limited, while most general work remains to be done;
doubtless they will later come into their own.(12)
They exist in very large numbers and very few are
in print.

The other of our two varieties concerned specifically with property consists of Rentals, or schedules of property, and Surveys. They can be done by
any individual or body owning property, or a Survey
can be done by an outside body. The various forms
taken by Rentals and Schedules need not concern the
topographer for as far as he is concerned they have
the common characteristic of being lists of properties with holders' names and rents paid. Where the
properties form a coherent block or where gaps can
be accounted for, it is possible - and worth while
for the earlier part of our period - to construct a
plan of plots, some of which may correspond with
something identifiable in a later and more cartographic time.(Fig.45) A plan so constructed can
make no pretence to accuracy in detail and in some
ways it is a schematic representation rather than
a plan. But it is certainly very much better than
nothing. A Survey is essentially a report on the
use and conditions of a building or group of buildings, possibly made by the Corporation or some other
internal body, possibly by an outside body, the
latter case covering buildings often unmentioned in
town records.(13)

Individuals can, of course, be involved with the
kinds of documentation mentioned above. But there
are other aspects of the written word that are much

Fig. 45 Plots and Owners in North Reading: 1552.
This plan has been constructed for the whole of
Reading, although only the main area of occupation
is shown here. It is founded on P.R.O. Misc. Books:
Land Rev; vol. 187 ff 314-47. It was compiled in
1919 and remains in manuscript.

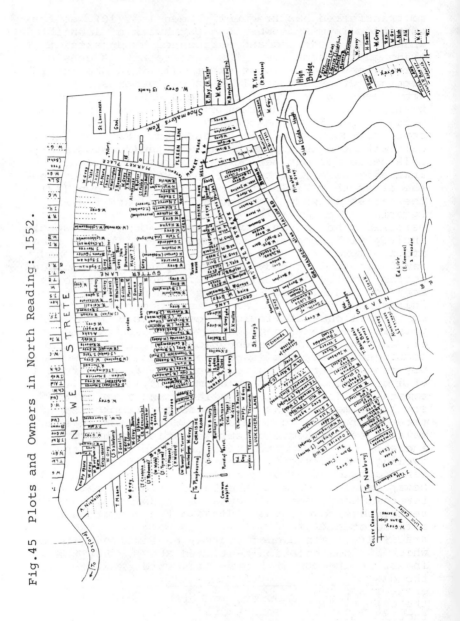

Fig. 45 Plots and Owners in North Reading: 1552.

more personal. Letters and diaries can mention topographical aspects amid the many other things with
which they are concerned. But they do not necessarily have a local basis, and the availability of
those outside local collections at present really
depends on whether they are in print.(14) There
are also a number of writers who have visited towns
with the idea of communicating their findings to a
wider public, normally by publication. Some were
concerned solely with antiquities, others with both
current and old, and among the better known are
Leland writing in the reign of Henry VIII, Camden
in Elizabeth I's reign, Celia Fiennes at the end of
the seventeenth century and Defoe and Stukeley in
the first half of the eighteenth century. The topographical information obtainable from any of these
personal records, whether local or wide-ranging, may
include detailed descriptions of buildings or alterations, but even these detailed descriptions are
rarely precise, and in any case most descriptions of
houses are in general terms, while those of streets
tend to be limited to such as "wide", "narrow",
"dirty", "pleasing" and so on. This is not to carp
at such descriptions, for general impressions are
valuable, especially those given by literate and
travelled contemporaries. Description can also
occur in newspapers. By the early nineteenth century this is becoming important, but the development
of local papers had not progressed far by 1750, and
even where they exist house advertisements are very
sparse. On the other hand, some properties mentioned later were in existence before 1750, although
sale advertisements are very chary about mentioning
age and even specific location.(15) The bulk of
dwellings, those housing the labouring poor, get no
mention until later, and then in editorial comment.
Newspapers also mention new public buildings, but
few of these came about before the late eighteenth
century. How credible is any of this personalised
information is difficult to say. There can be con-
tradictory comments and even descriptions, each of
which can be quite true to the individual making it.
In such cases all the topographer can do is to note
the discordant views. Comment can, of course, be
exaggerated for effect, but it is possible to detect
the core of truth. Detection is difficult where
fact is falsified, for the best solution, that of
finding evidence to the contrary, is impossible for
much of our period. It has to be assumed, in the
absence of evidence to the contrary, that published
work is factually correct; but there is no way,

except on grounds of probability, of giving a verdict on unique, personal manuscript information.
Finally in this section on description come
local studies both topographical and more general.
The classical age of town histories is the later
eighteenth and early nineteenth centuries, and their
contents can include original information, in that
they preserve documents and descriptions of buildings
no longer extant. This does not apply so much to
more recent writing on local history but this can
have information and references of interest to the
topographer. Pride of place here must go to the
Victoria County Histories. Standards have improved
greatly since the early volumes, but even these provide basic topographical information and, possibly
more important, copious footnote reference to original evidence and to secondary works in existence at
the time of writing.

PLAN

The fourth form of topographical information is the
plan, ranging from one of the smallest outbuilding
to one of an entire town.(16) Without doubt it can
be the most accurate evidence available to the urban
topographer, but it lacks the vertical - and often
the aesthetic - information of a drawing or painting,
and the in-depth information so often found in the
written word. The plans that concern us here are
not those, already mentioned, that can be constructed by the topographer from written evidence, but
those produced at the time as the result of contemporary survey. It would be a mistake, though, to
draw too sharp a line between the plan and the picture, for among the earliest plans are perspective
plans which have more in common with the picture
than they have with plans as identified today. A
few places have them for the sixteenth century but
the quality is very variable, and as very few places
have more than one, possibility of comparison is the
exception. This raises the problem of the accuracy
of such plans. From their nature they do not show
all sides of buildings, so even the best(17) cannot
really be translated into conventional plans. The
verdict for most must be that they give a fair impression of the town. They vary in accuracy over
numbers of houses shown and most do not significantly differentiate among houses.(18) But, to be fair,
there is no reason why we should expect cartographic accuracy in a perspective plan, for it was partly

an art form. Such doubts are present with the best-
known of these plans, those of John Speed of the
early seventeenth century who produced perspective
plans for 52 towns.(10) (Fig.46) His is an impressive achievement, but at times features may be
compressed to fit in available space. It is uncertain how far his houses are schematic, and his
streets often seem unexpectedly wide. But his work
is impressionalistically pleasing and without it
many a town would have no early plan. In fact, for
many places Speed's plan stands in isolation and it
can be a considerable number of years - often a century or more - before the next general plans appear.
Other places, better endowed, have a mixed phase of
plan and perspective plan.

Most towns have a definitive early plan in the
sense of one drawn up in some detail with features
to scale and relationships accurately established.
That most of these occur in the late eighteenth or
very early nineteenth century is no chance happening
for that is a time when improved standards of accuracy coincided with considerable interest in local
history, even if it was still largely on antiquarian
lines. In fact, it is unusual to find such key plans
done before 1750,(20) but that they usually occur
half a century or so beyond the end of our period
most certainly does not rule them out of court, for
they still occur before the great period of nineteenth century urban redevelopment and even, in most
cases, before the lesser improvement schemes of the
earlier part of that century.(Fig.47) The common
characteristic of almost all of these general plans
is that they were done for private purposes, and it
is some considerable time before plans by official
bodies, such as Boards of Health, become available.
It may well be that the "definitive" plan for a
particular town was produced in connection with a
work on local history, and many now existing as separate plans started life bound into volumes.

Fig. 46 Speed's Plan of Reading: 1610. Comparison
with Coates' Plan (Fig.47) shows that Speed's plan
is impressionistic rather than accurate in detail.
For the southern part of the town necessity to fit
into a given space has resulted in compression.

Fig.47 Coates' Plan of Reading: 1797. This plan
was 'surveyed,drawn and engraved' by Charles Tomkins
in 1797 and was published in the Rev. Charles Coates'
History and Antiquities of the Borough of Reading in
1802. It is the earliest accurate plan of Reading.

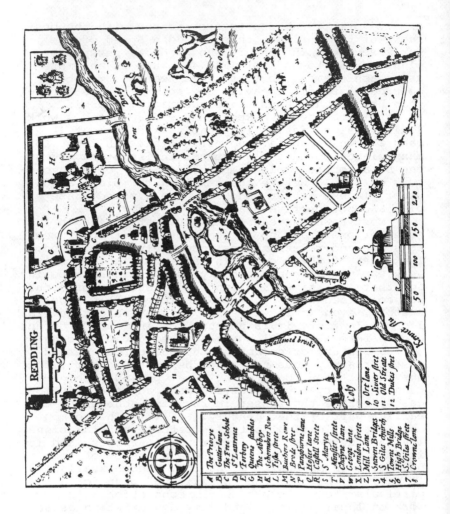

Fig.46 Speed's Plan
of Reading: 1610.

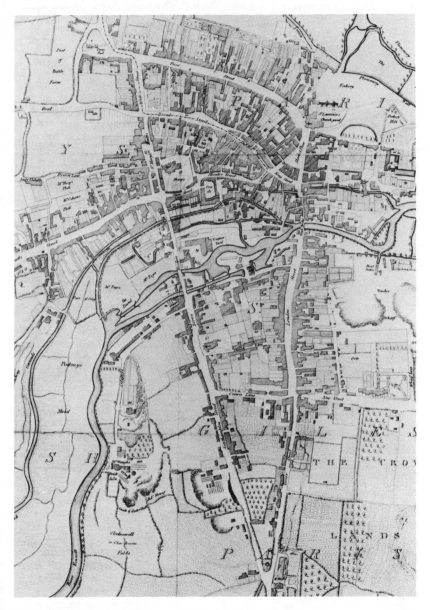

Fig.47   Coates' Plan of Reading: 1797.

In addition to plans like these every town can
show a number of small plans whose subjects include
individual buildings or features, groups of buildings, plots of land and so on. Their accuracy is
variable and reasons for their compilation are
usually matters of surmise, except, of course, where
they are in association with property deeds. They
belong to no one class of borough document and are
sometimes catalogued topographically. Their use,
even where their accuracy can be assumed, is very
limited where an overall plan of the town is concerned. They can be used to correct detail on more
general plans of about the same date and, obviously,
they can be used for spot-checks on the accuracy of
such plans. They are, of course, extremely important to the very local historian working on the subject covered by the small plan. Most towns possess
such things in quantity but as they spread over a
considerable time span and as they give a limited
coverage in space it is impossible to compile a general plan for them alone.

Accuracy of any plan, large or small, must concern the topographer, but often, and certainly for
the earlier part of our period, the verdict at
present - and possibly always - cannot be better
than "it must have looked something like this". But
even under the more favourable circumstances of the
later part of the period the establishing of accuracy is a matter that requires some thought, for even
where there are a couple of plans the correctness
of their mean is still an assumption, even if the
later published can be shown to be genuinely independent of the earlier. The reputations of plan-
maker and engraver obviously give some clue, but
reputation for reliability is frequently passed on
from one generation to the next, and at some stage
anyone seriously concerned will have to test reliability for him or her self. The limitations of
archaeology have already been mentioned: an additional one is the circular argument whereby the plan is
"proved" from the excavated building which is dated
from the plan. Buildings surviving from the time of
the compiler of the plan are few and decreasing,
and it is vital that details of any alterations to
such buildings be known if comparison is to be genuine: an unknown addition of even a porch or the
demolition of a wing in the intervening years casts
serious - if unfair - doubt on the credibility of
the plan whose accuracy can be presumed! This will
be considered further under the next section.

TOPOGRAPHY IN PRACTICE

To obtain a general impression of a particular town
at any time in this period is comparatively easy,
for the main shape is known and likewise the main
architectural characteristics, both local and national. For many purposes such may be enough. Certainly this imprecision is the inevitable characteristic of many other aspects of town life: the smells
of the streets, the thoughts and feelings of the
inhabitants and so on. Obviously the collection of
ever-more contemporary comments on the state of the
town has nothing, despite much popular belief, to do
with precision, for comment is subjective, and the
more refined and detailed so the more subjective.
This is not to deny the importance of collecting and
correlating such opinions, weighing up the in-depth
dimension to topographical study. But it can never
be a precise dimension. It could be said that great
precision in a couple of areas might unbalance the
overall picture. But these two areas, of elevation
and plan, differ from the others in being the only
ones susceptible to precise measurement. However,
there is a very practical difficulty for our period,
which is that every rise in the scale of precision
will increase the comparative imprecision for a growing number of buildings and features. And this situation steadily worsens as we move back towards our
starting-date, so that we end with a few very precise features in a sea of imprecision or even of
conjecture.
     For the accurate reconstruction of the eleva-
tion of a street frontage or of a group of buildings
at a particular date it is necessary to have architectural drawings and photographs as the base. (Fig.
48) There are a few of the former from even the
later part of our period and certainly none of the

Fig.48 North side of part of Broad Street, Reading:
c.1890. None of these buildings now survive and
this accurate reconstruction - in both features and
scale - is based on plans, photographs, postcards,
etc.   For earlier periods it is impossible to obtain
so complete a result, but this well illustrates the
techniques of reconstruction. It is the work of J.G.
Gafford, Hon. Treasurer of the Berkshire Archaeological Society, who over the years has compiled reconstructions for the main areas of Reading. It is
an excellent example of what can be accomplished by
the dedicated amateur. He has kindly permitted this
to be reproduced from his manuscript drawing.

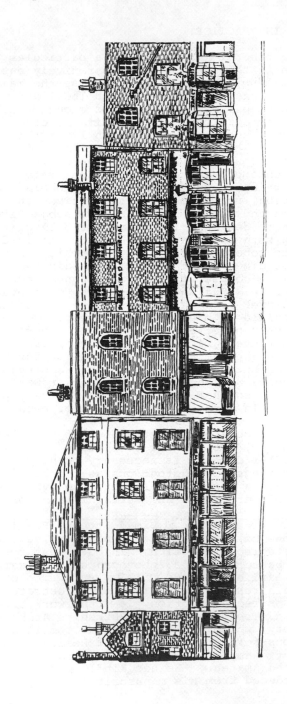

Fig. 48 North side of part of Broad St. Reading: c.1890.

latter, but as has already been mentioned there are
a large number of photographs taken in the later
nineteenth century which picture many buildings of
an earlier time. Starting with drawings and photographs that give the earliest comprehensive cover,
anything obviously built, or known to have been built,
after the desired date can be eliminated. At times a
drawing, an older photograph, written description,
a plan, or even an archaeological report will indicate, well or ill, what was there previously. If
the indication is clear the older feature can be
drawn in with some degree of precision, but the less
clear the greater the degree of conjecture, until
there may be some knowledge of the ground-plan but
none of the elevation, and eventually nothing but
likelihood. How far back one can take this exercise
depends partly on the former situation in the town,
for a prosperous eighteenth or nineteenth century
in the town's history has meant the disappearance of
many older and less fashionable dwellings and features in a spate of rebuilding both public and private. But although a surprising amount of information can be obtained for most towns it must be em-
phasized that precise, detailed reconstruction for
large parts of any town in the sixteenth century is
impossible, and largely so for much of the seventeenth century. This elevational reconstruction is
complicated by perspective problems, so that it is
necessary wherever possible to check against an
accurate plan. It can also be very difficult to reconstruct a street or group of buildings from a number of separate drawings or photographs - especially
if they are all of individual buildings - due to
differing scales, problems of exact location, and
uneven incidence, even apart from the considerable
time it takes.

So varying degrees of precision can be reached
for elevational reconstruction, and the end-product
can claim an accuracy whose acceptable limits vary
depending on the date involved. This, of course, is
what is normally produced, for there are few with
the powers of the late Alan Sorrell of making accurate reconstructions come alive in their context.
However, such comment does not apply to the production of plans which, inherently dehumanized, have
only one goal, that of increasing technical accuracy. The general principles of the exercise are
much as for elevational reconstruction. The first
thing is to start with a plan of known accuracy at a
satisfactory scale, and the earliest plans that meet
these criteria are the first edition Ordnance Survey

maps, produced in the later nineteenth century at
25 ins. to the mile.(21) It is then a matter of
proceeding back to the "definitive" early plan mentioned on p.208, where the question of reliability
was discussed. What is now needed is a number of
buildings, features and property boundaries (22)
that are known to have remained unaltered between
the times of the plans. It is comparatively easy
to get a scatter of these, and if there be good
agreement over them then the early plan can be presumed accurate elsewhere. Trouble arises when it
turns out to be inaccurate, and it is equally dis-
concerting when this happens for all or some of the
common features. It then becomes a matter of check-
ing back through any available plan - Board of
Health, local directory, estate and so on - to pick
up as many as possible of the buildings and features
no longer in existence when the Ordnance Survey map
was compiled. Inevitably there will be gaps that
have to be filled by using the information of the
unreliable plan. The extreme case is where there is
no plan compiled around 1800. Here procedures are
much the same except that gaps will have to be filled from the earliest suitable plans, which may not
occur until well into the nineteenth century. So
the end-product here will have even more uncertainty.
The problem is much the same where a plan exists
whose scale is too small to show significant detail.
     It has already been said that for almost all
towns these crucial base-plans will post-date the
end of our period. In some cases the post-dating
will be small, but to bring any of them to that end,
the mid-eighteenth century, is a matter of following
the techniques given above. And this is greatly
helped by the facts that the later eighteenth century was not in general a period of large-scale private rebuilding and that the interval is comparatively short. But times earlier give the plan-maker
major problems, and serious work on the subject is
very limited. Where plans, even perspective plans,
exist they can be used as revising points providing
the intervals between them are not too great. Where
such do not exist then, in theory, a space of not
more than about half a century should occur between
revisions. But on each occasion the revision will
be that much less precise, with surviving information becoming ever less accurate and gaps becoming
ever greater, until the situation resembles the one
mentioned under elevation, of a few fixed points
surrounded by conjecture. But whereas reconstruction in general terms can be allowed for elevation,

providing it is made clear that this is so - in fact,
artistic impression if architecturally valid can be
very acceptable - such cannot sensibly happen with a
plan; and at some point that varies for each town
the honest plan-drawer must call a halt. For many
towns it must be said that reasonably accurate planning of the whole cannot really be taken back much
before the mid-eighteenth century; for others the
limit comes in the early part of that century; for
a few there can be reasonably accurate work for the
later seventeenth century; but it needs a very unusual collection of records to enable accurate planning for any provincial town to be taken much further back.

A major attempt at the planning of towns has
been that carried out since 1965 under the auspices
of the Historic Towns Trust, and two volumes have so
far been issued.(23)   A plan that can be regarded as
definitive has been produced for each town for c.
1800 - obviously there is slight variation in date
depending on the availability of a reliable local
plan - and all towns are planned at the same scale.
The same plan is used for other aspects of a particular town's history with major relevant features
superimposed: for example the walls and ditches of
ninth to twelfth-century Nottingham or the Civil
War defences of Reading. This work was never intended to produce plans for earlier phases of the various towns, but what it has done for our period is
to produce for each town the plan that forms the
crucial starting-point for the appropriate work.
Further volumes in the series are planned, including
massive work on London.

Each town in the Atlas of Historic Towns has a
section of description so it is worth looking briefly at the relationship of the written word to a
town's topography. For the topographer this aspect
is in many ways both the easiest and the least rewarding side of his work, for the topographer as
such is concerned with description rather than cau-
sation, and where description is concerned words have
in most cases to compete with the much more precise
visual illustration. This, of course, is not an
attack on the written word, for words from the pen
of a master can produce a vivid picture, and written
description with or without comment is welcome to
the majority of recipients of the topographer's work
- in fact, it is usually the most popular part.
There is, as has already been said, a large body of
written evidence available to the topographer which
can give a considerable amount of information; and

information given on plans can likewise be translated into words. The end product can be a useful survey of the town's topography at a particular time. But care has to be taken not to transfer information to other periods, and there is a danger that unique description may be quoted as fact. Given that the written word has some place in the topographer's work, the point arises as to how far he should be concerned with comment. It is certainly hard to avoid comment on the design of a building, and it is easy to slip in some adjective before a street or a feature. Whether the topographer's task includes comment on the state of buildings or cleanliness standards in streets or any other such things is another matter. But as has been said the border between topography and local history is ill-defined, and it may be best to leave it so. However, most words carry some emotive content or at least are burdened with accumulated associations, both of which work against the objectivity and accuracy that form the topographer s ideal. And, of course, too much generalisation can disguise the local variation that is equally important in the urban topography of our period.

A few towns fall into quite a different class. These are the new towns that have arisen since 1750, some from nothing, some from the expansion of non-urban settlement; and they are mentioned here simply because present-day historians and topographers of such towns may have interest in their pre-urban roots. The only general point that can be made is that, as for any rural settlement, information may be copious or virtually non-existent depending largely on the survival and availability of estate records, enclosure maps and other official records, for there will rarely be mention - and that of the briefest - in letters, diaries and so on. To consider the nature of the evidence for village history would require a chapter on its own (see below, Chapter 7) but as far as the urban topographer is concerned he is only concerned with the immediate pre-urban situation of his subject, and this removes many from the period of our interest. A somewhat different problem is that of the small de facto towns that received official urban recognition in our period. All that can be said here is that information concerning them in their pre-charter days is usually slight and a mixture of urban and rural. Generally, once the modest new corporations had come into being they produced comparatively few records, and such places would not attract the plan-drawer

until much later. On the other hand, the more insignificant of such places avoided development until
very modern times, so that, as at Burfcrd, a dis-
proportionate number of older houses survive.

CONCLUSION

The mapping of the urban landscape in this period
involves plans, elevations and the written word.
Problems and possibilities differ from those of
periods before and after although each end shows
some overlap. For periods before there is the occasional precise detail with no hope of attaining
over-all precision; for later periods, certainly
after 1800 or so, there is evidence in abundance at
almost any point desired. For our period, however,
the task, except in the earliest phase, can usually
be accomplished satisfactorily, albeit with some
effort. But although most towns have received considerable attention in writing - even if some is
incidental to historical pursuits - this has not
been associated with any systematic work on the visual aspects, systematic, that is, in the sense of
the construction of plans and elevations for a particular town at regular intervals. Such work, properly done, is very time-consuming and this is certainly the reason for the comparatively modest output,
for the work is good to do, is challenging without
being overdifficult and the endproduct is very sat-
isfying. It is a field eminently suited to the dedicated amateur - in the sense of one making time
for the pursuit but not depending on it for a living
- who has a real regard for the past of his or her
town and who wishes to make a real contribution to
urban studies.
        It has doubtless been noticed that many exam-
ples here and all the illustrations are taken from
Reading. This has been done deliberately where the
illustrations are concerned to give some cohesion
and common theme and to allow comparison of plans.
There is also the personal side: for some time I
have been concerned with original material for
Reading whereas knowledge of other towns is based
on the work - often admirable - of others. But by
every test Reading proves to be a good average town
in the amount and quality of its plans and documentation.

REFERENCES

1. Topography is conveniently defined in The
Shorter Oxford Dictionary as "detailed description,
representation on map etc., of natural and artificial features of town, district, etc., such features". It will be used in both these senses in the
following pages, being clarified only when there is
chance of ambiguity.
2. This is certainly a possibility in Norwich,
for example. See J. Campbell, 'Norwich', in M.D.
Lobel, (ed.), The Atlas of Historic Towns, 2 (1975),
p.17.
3. For example in 1628 about a third of Banbury was consumed, see P.D.A. Harvey, 'Banbury', in
M.D. Lobel, (ed.), Historic Towns, 1 (1969), p.7,
and in 1724/5 138 houses in the centre of Buckingham
were burned down. (D.I. Elliott, Buckingham: the
Loyal and Ancient Borough (1976), p.48). A fire in
1731 destroyed the centre of Blandford Forum. See
J. Newman and N. Pevsner, The Buildings of England:
Dorset (1972), p.95. See generally, S. Porter,
'Fires and Pre-Industrial Towns, Local Historian, 10
(1972-3), pp.395-397.
4. The bad storm at Bedford in 1672, for
example, was described in a broadside "A True Relation of What Hapned at Bedford', V.C.H. Bedfordshire
III, p.4.
5. Royal Commission on Historical Monuments,
England, The Town of Stamford (1977). The three
volumes concerned with York (The City of York Vol.3
1972, Vol.4 1975, Vol.5 1981) are also very satisfactory. Towns covered earlier, such as Hereford,
get thinner treatment. The volumes on Oxford and
Cambridge are largely concerned with colleges. Be-
sides line-drawings and plans there are many photographs.
6. W. Stukeley, Itinerarium Curiosum (1724).
A good example of later work are the many architectural drawings of the late eighteenth and early
nineteenth centuries by J. and J.C. Buckler. Other
noteworthy work was done by the Bucks in the eighteenth century. General information on illustrations is given in M.W. Barley, A Guide to British
Topographical Collections (1974).
7. A typical example is the earliest known
references to the division of large houses in Reading into tenements, which occurs in the charter from
Charles I. See. C. Fleetwood Pritchard, (ed.),
Reading Charters, Acts and Ordinances, 1253-1911
(1913), p.68.

8. For example the Town Book of Liverpool,
the Corporation Book of Buckingham and the Corporation Diary of Reading.
9. It should be remembered that before 1836
England had only two universities.
10. A certain amount survives in lawyers'
offices, but it is largely inaccessible. That vast
untapped archives survive there is a myth.
11. Good examples are Oxford (collegiate),Exe-
ter,(dean and chapter) and Coventry (corporation).
12. For periods earlier than ours such deeds
are of basic topographical importance. A good example is the chapter 'The Geography of Medieval Oxford', in H.E. Salter, ed., 'Medieval Oxford', Oxford
Historical Society, 100 (1936). His monumental
posthumous work, 'Survey of Oxford', W.A. Pantin,
ed., Oxford Historical Society, New Series 14 (1960)
and 20 (1969) incorporates information from a number
of post-medieval deeds.
13. A good example of this is the Parliamentary
Survey of that part of Reading Abbey that had remained in royal hands.
14. If not, it is usually a matter of chance
whether information is picked up. Nor, at present,
does it greatly help if they are in local collections other than those of the student's own town,
for it is not necessarily the nearer ones that are
the most useful.
15. Up to 1750 the local Reading Journal aver-
ages two or less house advertisements per week,
most for properties outside the town. A good example of house-advertisement, although slightly later
is: "To be lett and entered uppon immediately.
A genteel DWELLING-HOUSE situate on the south side
of Fryer Street, consisting of two parlours, a good
dining room, kitchen and pantry, four bed-chambers,
convenient closets, good cellars, wash-house and
garden. The premises were late in the occupation
of Mr. Mayhew, Attorney". (Reading Mercury and
Oxford Gazette, 2 May 1785). The Times has large
numbers of such advertisements, both for London and
the Home Counties, although few for any one particular place outside the capital.
16. There is an interesting discussion of these,
at greater length than is possible here, in H.
Carter, 'The Geographical Approach', in M.W. Barley,
ed., The Plans and Topography of Medieval Towns in
England and Wales, Council for British Archaeology
Research Report No.14 (1975).
17. A good example is Hamond's 1592 Perspective
of Cambridge, see. M.D. Lobel, 'Cambridge', in her

ed., The Atlas of Historic Towns 2 (1975), p.19.
   18. The difficulties are well expressed by
James Campbell in discussing Cunningham's Perspective View of Norwich of 1558: "it gives an impression (though by no means an accurate impression) of
most of the houses in the city... Granted the considerable size of most of the houses which Cunningham depicts one is left... to wonder where the poor
lived". J. Campbell, 'Norwich' in M.D. Lobel, ed.,
The Atlas of Historic Towns, 2 (1975), p.16.
   19. Published in his Theatre of the Empire of
Great Britain in 1611.
   20. Ogilby's map of Ipswich, published in 1674,
for example, is untypically early.
   21. Other Ordnance Suvey maps produced around
this time are the 6" to the mile County Series of
the later 1880s and the 1:500 series produced between 1855 and 1895. Neither of these is as satisfactory for our purpose as the 25 inch.
   22. These are, from their conservatism, extremely useful for our purpose. Unfortunately they frequently are not shown on late-eighteenth/early nineteenth century plans.
   23. The towns covered are Banbury, Caernarvon,
Glasgow, Gloucester, Hereford, Nottingham, Reading
and Salisbury in Volume 1; Bristol, Cambridge, Coventry and Norwich in Volume 2.

Chapter Seven

MEDIEVAL SETTLEMENTS: TOPOGRAPHY AND DOCUMENTS

B.K. Roberts

Britain is a land of greatly varied environments
and these undoubtedly gave rise to diverse medieval
landscapes. Only archaeology can reveal with clarity the physical traces of these scenes, but some
documents do provide topographical information.
They are rarely easy to interpret and must be
brought together with two other important sources
first, the landscape, which contains within itself
the physical remains of many medieval structures,
not only castles, great churches and other buildings,
but also boundaries and routeways, settlements and
farms, place-names and administrative territories.
Second, there is always a need to use post-medieval
documentary sources and landscapes to create a
framework for retrogressive analysis, a context
within which to evaluate the earlier written evidence with its many ambiguities and uncertainties.
This is a technique fraught with problems and it
should always be stressed that medieval documents
should be approached with a willingness to consider
a wide range of possibilities. As Mackie said of
archaeological evidence 'the existence of at least
two alternative explanations for a given set of data
is essential if the true scientific spirit of enquiry is to flourish' and this is equally valid for
the many problems encountered in the topographic
interpretation of medieval documentary sources.(1)
It is not proposed to study the sources used as historical documents: one can only regret the absence
of wide-ranging studies of, for example, the post-
Conquest land charter, inquisitions post mortem,
or of the evolution of the manorial survey, although
Harvey's work is casting light on the critical movement towards the representation of the English landscape in local maps. There are challenges here for
the historian. Nevertheless, fundamental problems

problems of document interpretation cannot merely
be set aside, for what a document can reveal of
topographical detail is inevitably filtered through
the rigidities of convention and common form.(2)

> In reading early medieval land charters, it
> must not be forgotten how vague is their use
> of areal names: the different manors, tenements
> and hamlets, which now lie in a modern eccles-
> iastical parish... might either form a compact
> area with a ditch and dyke as boundary, or
> might have their strips of arable intermingled
> in the open fields. In either case the app-
> lication of an areal name was of the vaguest.
>
> G. Herbert Fowler, The Cartulary of the Cist-
> ercian Abbey of Old Warden, Bedfordshire
> (Manchester, 1931), p.9.

PATTERNS, TERRITORIES AND ESTATES

Writing in the Cambridge Medieval History of Europe,
Eileen Power made a fundamental point when she
stated that the peasant lived within two frameworks,
one physical, involving the varied terrains of the
continent which offered diverse opportunities for
tillage and pasturage, and the second administrative,
the organisational frameworks of kingdom and barony,
diocese and parish, manor and vill.(3) Terrain and
soils form an essential backcloth to all topographical reconstructions. Nevertheless it is at once
easy to overemphasise their importance, for many
powerful social and economic forces were also at
work, and yet to undervalue them, for the modern observer is set at a distance from their harsher real-
ities: there are sharp contrasts between the lands
of the north and west of Europe, where rocks had to
be torn from the earth and decades of husbandry and
manure invested to establish yielding arable fields
on obdurate virgin land, and the fertile river lowlands and drift terrains of the Paris basin, the
Danish archipelago and the Thames valley, the core
areas of nation states, where equally hard labour
was more generously rewarded.(4) On the other hand
small-scale more subtle variations were of vital importance to peasants living by relatively primitive
mixed subsistence farming and having small amounts
of manure relative to the area of their tillage, the
variations to be seen in the gentler scarp and vale
topography of southern England, the open vales and

drift-covered ridges and flats of the English midlands, the rolling red hills of west Somerset or the
varied scenes around the Milfield Plain of Northumberland.(5) Stern necessity ensured the creation of
a mosaic of fine adjustments between medieval communities and the lands supporting them, for the uncertainty of the harvests created an ultimate bondage more complete than that envisaged by lawyers.(6)
Peter Sawyer touched the core of the problem
involved in reconstructing medieval settlements,
territories and estates when he wrote 'Episcopus
tenet Ferneham may dispose of some 25,000 acres of
land'(7); medieval documents often conceal as much
as they reveal of the man-land relationships they
describe. In attempting reconstructions the initial
geographical problem is one of establishing known
points or localities, then defining likely limiting
lines, boundaries, thus obtaining a picture of the
areas, or territories involved. Where a single
place-name can dispose of a large area questions of
name-territory relationships loom large; an awareness of scale is crucial.(8) The general problems
of all reconstructions using charters, chronicles
and surveys can be illustrated with particular reference to a small portion of a history of St. Cuthbert's lands in County Durham:(9)

(a) The first concerns lands leased by Bishop
Alduhun to three earls:

> *Hae sunt terrae quas Alduhun episcopus (c.990-*
> *1019) et tota congregatio Sancti Cuthberti*
> *praestit his tribus, Ethred eorle, et Northman*
> *eorle, et Uhtred eorle, Gegenford, Queornington,*
> *Sliddewesse, Bereford, Stretford, Lyrtingtun,*
> *Marawuda, Stantun, Stretlea, Cletlinga, Langa-*
> *dun, Mortun, Persebrigce, Alclit ij, Copland,*
> *Weardseatle, Bynceastre, Cuthbertestun, Thicc-*
> *elea, Ediscum, Wudutun, Hunewic, Newatun,*
> *Healme......*

(b) The second concerns a grant from King Canute
(1017-1035) to the dead but undecayed saint:

> *Item Cnut rex dedit Sancto Cuthberto tempore*
> *Eadmundi episcopi, sicut ipsemet tenuit, cum*
> *saca et socna, villam quae vocatur Standropa*
> *cum suis appenditiis, Cnapatun, Scottun, Raby,*
> *Wacarfeld, Efenwuda, Alclit, Luteringtun,*
> *Elledun, Ingeltun, Thiccelea, et Middletun.*

From this text, deliberately quoted in Latin
and readable with a little imagination, three inter-
related problems emerge: one, the context, is historical and will not be considered further here, but
the second and third concern the identification of
the places listed and an analysis of their distribution.(10) If the second problem is successfully
resolved then, using the pattern of points so established, the way is open to reconstruct the real
territories involved and relate them to the terrains
beneath. This case does indeed illustrate the more
general problems of topographic reconstruction underlying all studies based on documents such as
Domesday Book, Lay Subsidy rolls and ecclesiastical
taxations.(11) It will be appreciated as the argument develops that no mere parochial scale is involved, and in mapping at a local regional scale -
that of a hundred or wapentake - it is often sufficient to see the locational evidence in terms of the
statement 'at or near the place X', so that the
inherent limitation of the detail which can possibly
be shown on a map of such a territory can be used to
mask deficiencies or uncertainties in the record.
It is worth noting that only in the last decade has
it become possible to map the detail of contemporary
census data, or some of it, on the fine mesh created
by the kilometre squares of the National Grid.(12)
The local authority areas formerly used would invariably contain both settled and unsettled zones but
this was inevitably concealed in, for example, a map
generalising the population per square kilometre:
such data, of course, only has meaning when compared
with other adjacent but equally imprecise measures.
In short, the approximations which reconstructions
of medieval circumstances represent are often not
vastly different from those of maps derived from
modern data.

To begin analysis of the texts cited above
certain assumptions must be made, namely that the
places appearing on nineteenth century maps of County
Durham are likely to bear some relationship, however
this be eventually defined, to those in the list,
and that the places can be initially analysed as a
series of points. They may of course be villages,
hamlets or farms, but settled locations may be assumed. Figure 49 is a basic map of the distribution,
and the data is tabulated in Table 5. Several
points emerge:

      (i)   Although they appear as separate trans-
            actions some of the names are common to

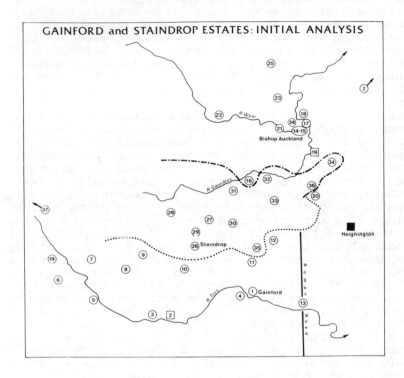

Fig.49 Gainford and Staindrop Estates: Initial
Analysis

Table 4   The Gainford and Staindrop Estates

Name in Document	Nineteenth Century Identification	Parish/County	Revised Identification and Notes
LIST A			
1 Gegenford	Gainford	Gainford	
2 Queorningtun	Quarrington	Quarrington	
3 Sliddewesse	Sledwich	}	Whorlton, Co. Durham
4 Bereford	Barford	} Yorkshire	
5 Stretford	Startforth	} (North Riding)	
6 Lyrtingtun	Lartington	}	
7 Marawuda	Marwood	} Chapelry of	
8 Stantun	Stainton	} Barnard	
9 Stretlea	Streatlam	} Castle	
10 Cletlinga	Cleatlam	}	
11 Langadum	Langton	} Gainford	
12 Mortun	Morton	} Parish	
13 Persebridge	Piercebridge	}	
14 Alclit (1)	Auckland (?)	}	North Auckland and
15 Alclit (2)	Auckland (?)	} Auckland	St. Helen's Auckland
16 Copland	Copeland Farm	} St. Andrew	
17 Weardseatle	?	} Parish	Bishop's Palace, Auckland
18 Bynceastre	Binchester	}	

229

Table 4 (continued)   The Gainford and Staindrop Estates

Name in Document	Nineteenth Century Identification	Parish/County	Revised Identification and Notes
19 Cuthbertestun	Cotherstone	Yorkshire (NR)	?South Church, Auckland
20 Thiccelea	Thickley		
21 Ediscum	Escomb		
22 Wuduntun	Wittan le Wear	Auckland	
23 Hunewic	Hunwick	St. Andrew	
24 Newatun	Newtan Cap		
25 Healme	Hemlington		
LIST B			
26 Staindropa	Staindrop	Staindrop	Keverston or Snotterton
27 Cnaptun	Keverston/?	Parish	
28 Scottun	Shotton		
29 Raby	Rably		
30 Wacarfeld	Wackerfeld		
31 Efenwuda	Evenwood	Auckland	
32 Alclit	Auckland	St. Andrew	
33 Luteringtun	Lutterington	Parish	West. Auckland
34 Elledun	Eldon		
35 Ingletun	Ingleton	Staindrop Pa.	
36 Thiccelea	Thickley	Auck.St.A.Pa.	
37 Middletun	?		Middleton in Teesdale?

the two lists. This could, of course, be explained by the different dates, with places 'leased' to the earls being restored to the church by Canute.

(ii)   However, list A clearly involves two components: items A1-A13 and items A14-A25 for the map shows these to be spatially discrete, indeed they are separated by the items of list B.

(iii) Several places either cannot be identified - i.e. they cannot be traced on later map sources (e.g. item 17, Weardseatle) or are notably separate of the remaining places of the group (item 19, Cuthbertestun and item 2, Queorningtun). Such discontinuities may either result from the fortuitous addition of extraneous items to what were once spatially coherent groups, as errors in transcription at any stage in the history of the document, or as simple errors in identification: thus Queorningtun is not the modern Quarrington in central Durham but Whorlton, a coherent part of list A, and Cuthbertestun is not the modern Cotherston. It cannot be certainly identified.(13)

The pattern of points plotted reveals the members, dependent portions, of an estate or estates granted to Saint Cuthbert, probably in the ninth century, and at that time described as 'Gainford and that which pertains to it, from the river Tees to the Wear and from the road called Deorestrete to the hills in the west', a wording which gives substance to the boundaries and territories involved and confirms that the two lists A and B involve subsequent transactions concerning this same land.(14) The evidence, of course, begs the question whether the original Gainford estate when granted involved these sub-units: the fact that the name of the northern third (Fig.50) Alclit is of Celtic origin hints that this may have been so.(15) Such boundary descriptions, some merely sketched in, other perambulated in great detail, are characteristic of pre-Conquest documents, post Conquest charters and post medieval surveys, and provide vital structural frameworks for more detailed topographical work.(16) (See Chapter 8 below).

The lines sketched in on Figure 49, based on

the grouping of localities, do in fact suggest three
linear subdivisions of the earliest Gainford grant,
subdivisions which echo the phrase 'from the road
called Deorestrete to the hills in the west' and
the rational subdivision of arable lowland and upland
grazing lands which it implies. The river Gaunless
has been added and allows sense to be of certain
minor textual problems. Why does Alclit (Auckland)
appear in both list A and B? Only one settlement
bearing this name lies south of the Gaunless, West
Auckland, and this must surely be the Alclit of list
B (item 32). Significantly, in the late fourteenth
century it still retained a portion of Staindrop
glebe, reflecting the situation recorded in Canute's
charter. This hypothesis is supported by the name
Copland (Copeland) of list A: lying south of the
Gaunless it is derived from an Old Norse root, kaupa
-land meaning the 'purchased land', suggesting that
by 990-1019 the northern Auckland estate was in process of acquiring land south of the river, a conclusion confirmed by a survey of 1183 which shows
that West Auckland (item 32), Evenwood (item 31) and
Lutterington (item 33) were then part of the Auckland estate (Fig. 50).(17) At this point in the
argument, of course, the fact that these named localities emerge into the full light of history as
townships (parts of larger parishes) and parishes
cannot be ignored, and the boundaries of these,
finally documented on mid-nineteenth century maps,
must reflect medieval antecedents.(18) Detailed
arguments based upon such data sets are notoriously
difficult to read and follow, but it is nevertheless
upon such frameworks that sound topographic reconstructions are founded. Even the ambiguous Thiccelea
(item 20 and item 36) has a place, for a later survey
assigns it to yet another estate, Heighingtonshire
(Fig. 50), and it is clear that this 'dense wood'
and the clearings within it lay on the march between
three estates: thus each could have a portion.(19)
     This analysis demonstrates the technique of
moving from points to lines, to areas, and eventually to the substance of estates, a common procedure
in topographic analysis. Nevertheless, it is remarkable how many classic historical studies of estates fail to develop fully their spatial and topographical aspects, even when this is firmly within
an author's mind. Much has indeed been written on
landed estates, but studies tend to concentrate
upon administration, income, internal heterogeneity,
economic structure and origins, together with some
degree of comparison.(20) Little has been put for-

ward concerning their spatial characteristics and on
the processes involved in their geographical evolution. All estates are constructed on the basic
functional entities of townships or vills, the local
communities and the lands which support them, across
which are imposed the structures of manors, parishes
and fees.(21) Any primary classification must involve a measure of size, with subsets defined on the
basis of spatial structure and origin. An initial
classification might usefully recognise four size
levels, in descending order:

(i) <u>Realms and principalities</u>, involving England, Scotland and Wales.

(ii) <u>Great estates</u>, landed inheritances extending over vast tracts of land, conglomera-
tions of territories built up by great
magnates, for example the Earls of Cornwall, the Earls of Norfolk, the estates of
the Bishops of Winchester and the Palati-
nates of Lancaster and Durham.(22)

(iii) These great estates were normally made up
of smaller estates of varied types, but
such smaller estates could of course emerge
in the hands of lesser lords and the term
<u>mediate estates</u> can usefully be applied to
these diverse intermediate entities.(23)

(iv) <u>Small estates and manors</u> constitute the
lowest level in the hierarchy, the holdings of knights and freemen.(24)

Geographically all of these, excluding the
special cases of kingdom and principality, tended to
be either compact, with lands forming a continuous
area, or discrete, with lands widely scattered, indeed held together by administrative pressures only.
The range of sub-types this implies closely reflects
origins, for some estates originated as coherent
unitary blocks while others reflect a long process
of aggregation - processes which are neither irrev-
ersible nor mutually exclusive, for the estates so
assembled may prove to be temporally ephemeral or
they may retain a coherence for many centuries.(25)
This digression into questions of classification is
more relevant than might at first appear for there
is a body of literature concerned with the stability
of estate structures over very long-time periods and
these, the author would argue, are primarily con-

cerned with certain types, and only certain types, of mediate state. Jones and Barrow have emphasised the elements of continuity present upon certain royal and ecclesiastical estates, mediate estates which form part of aggregate larger entities, the Canterbury estates, the estates of the Honour of Denbigh, and the estates of the Bishops of Durham. These 'multiple estates' to use a term adapted by Jones, vary considerably in size, and Winchester has commented upon this; Islandshire and Norhamshire, Northumberland, account for 10,854 ha and 7,612 ha respectively, Allerdale and Copeland (Cumberland) for 68,960 ha and 111,685 ha, and Aucklandshire, County Durham approximately one third of the Gainford estate, comprised 273,000 ha. As Winchester concludes 'such wide variations in the scale of territorial groupings with common features suggests that a careful study of contrasting shires (or multiple estates) is called for'. Above all else the 'common features' need careful definition so that comparative work can be placed on a secure foundation.(26)

The case study already examined can illustrate much of this argument: County Durham originated in grants to St. Cuthbert of blocks and pieces of land which were part of the Earldom of Northumbria, itself once a separate kingdom.(27) Amongst other items these grants included a type of mediate estate, often what Jolliffe calls a 'mediatised hundred' and Jones a 'multiple estate', comprising a central place with its dependencies. The case of Staindrop, cum suis appenditiis, is very clear. These lands were aggregated to create a great estate, County Durham, which in effect survived until 1972! The Gainford estate shows that the mediate units may themselves have contained smaller units above or near the level of what could normally be seen as a single manor, but all authors stress that in time the individual component townships of each estate suffered varied fortunes, either being retained in the hands of the tenant in chief or subinfeudated to individuals of lesser status.(28) Of the three estates visible in Figure 50 the southern two, following the post conquest division of the Cutherbertine lands, were granted to lay landowners, passed through the lands of various great magnates (the Earls of Warwick, the Earls of Westmorland) and are still present, indeed visible, in the landscape because of the current Raby estate practice of painting farms and cottages white - a condition of the leases.(29) Of course, in different circumstances such early

Fig.50 South-west Durham c.1050, the Gainsford and Staindrop Estates.

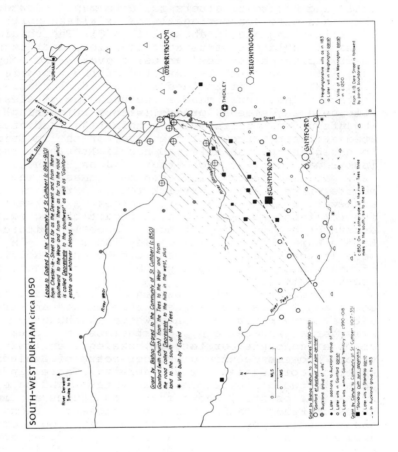

entities could be submerged without trace beneath
a tide of later land transactions.

Durham, of course, is not in all respects typical, and Figure 51 alters scale to map landownership in a more conventionally manorialised portion
of midland England in about 1315.(30) The shading
shows the holdings of tenants in chief, and, unash-
amedly using parish boundaries, converts the complex
manorial accounts characteristic of the Victoria
County Histories of England into a visual spatial
pattern. Individual manors are shown as circles -
some held in demesne, others (with a thick ring)
subinfeudated, others (with a thin ring) subinfeudated at least twice. At the level of the individual
township and parish this map has limitations, and
individual holdings, note that of John Pecche (no.
32), have a complex relationship to these. The
manors of the Earl of Warwick found in this small
area were of course part of a larger Warwickshire
estate (inset to Fig.51), itself part of a great
estate of national importance. Concealed within the
Earl's Warwickshire holdings lay lands which in 1086
were in the hands of two men, pre-Conquest holdings
of unknown origin, probably subdivisions of ancient
sub-kingdoms.(31)

The general picture presented here suggests, as
Jones and Barrow have argued, that within any great
estate there may be elements which, although part of
a larger aggregate, can, nevertheless, be survivals
of older coherent, or largely coherent, entities,
stable elements within a broader pattern of often
kaleidoscopic change. These survivals normally
occur in two contexts, on royal estates and on ecclesiastical estates, where the vicissitudes and inci-
dents of Feudal landholding were missing. Such
stable mediate estates can provide a window to more
ancient arrangements and, as Jones has repeatedly
demonstrated, their relationship to underlying terrain conditions is often rational and explicable,
with the careful inclusion of complementary economic
resources; thus the Gainford estate runs from the
good lands of the Tees valley to the Pennine terra
montana. Of course, such ancient units need not be
coherent blocks. As Ford and many others have shown,
detached sections could be created to give access to
specialised localised resources, an arrangement long-
recognised in the Weald but also apparent in the
Midlands and many other regions,(32)

There are, nevertheless, some fundamental problems, not least the criteria for identifying these
ancient stable units. Jones argues that there are

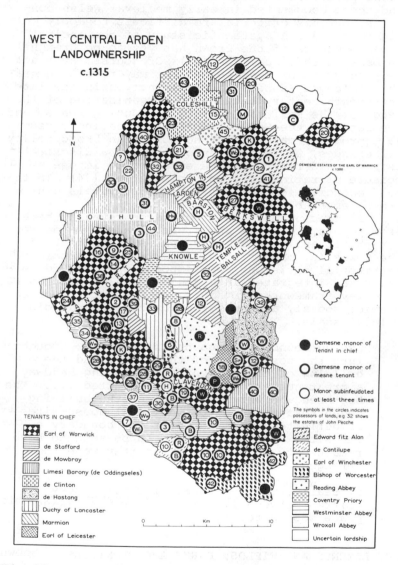

Fig.51   West Central Arden: landownership c.1315.

close parallels between their rents and services and those documented in early medieval Welsh contexts, but his criteria are difficult to apply rigorously and a systematic study of the ancient demesne manors of the crown has yet to be brought to bear on this question.(33) Of course, even aggregated great or mediate estates may reveal geographical 'common-sense': the distinction in the late thirteenth century between the organisation of the lands of the Earl of Cornwall, producing rents, and the lands of the Earl of Norfolk, creating consumable produce, may reflect no more than broad policy differences, while any landowner with a discrete estate could reasonably be expected to impose a measure of rationality in exploitation.(34) In this cold economic searchlight ancient survivals can prove remarkably elusive.

In conclusion, the progression revealed here, from points, to lines and areas, leads towards topographical analyses at many scales above that of the township, manor, or village. In the mosaic of territorial divisions superimposed upon varied terrains and integrated into a hierarchy of estates we have key frameworks within which the details of economic, social, and topographic phenomena unfold at a local scale.

> The surrounding leuga having been.... brought into the possession of the abbey, and the building of the church by now making headway, a great number of men were recruited..... The brethren who were in charge of the building began to apportion to individual house-sites of definite dimensions near the boundary of the site. These, ... can be seen to have remained to this day just as they were then arranged.
>
> E. Searle, The Chronicle of Battle Abbey written between 1175-1200 of events taking place soon after 1070.

SETTLEMENTS AND FIELDS, FARMS AND FRONTIERS

'Wood 4 leagues long and half a league broad is worth 12 shillings when it bears.' This laconic entry from Domesday Book, relating to the Warwickshire manor of Ulverley, demonstrates how minimal information can, given the right circumstances, be topographically interpretable.(35) Writing in 1905

P.E. Martineau pointed out that this curious dimension, six miles by three quarters of a mile, probably refers to the great pan-handle extension of what
later became Solihull parish.(36) This flash of insight is in practical terms unverifiable, indeed we
can have no certain indication that the linear measurements of Domesday woodland can be so interpreted,
but, nevertheless, this reflects the possibilities,
inherent in a change of scale, for investigation
within the bounded frameworks of township and parish. Figures provided by Winchester of a sample of
over 400 township acreages from southern counties
and over 380 from northern counties yield average
values of 2019 acres (817 ha) and 2320 acres (938 ha)
respectively and suggest relatively little difference in the spatial extent of the typical township
in different parts of the country, although northern
areas have significantly larger numbers of very
large townships in excess of 8000 acres (3240 ha).
Nevertheless, 75% of all the townships sampled contain less than 300 acres (1200 ha).(37) Although
not without problems, topographical reconstruction
within such limited territories allows a logical
process of identification and elimination, so that
reconstruction can be likened to land-surveying,
where a series of known points, lines and hence
areas are identified and their relative locations
established. This means that further detail can
then be fitted in.

In practice local topographical reconstructions
depend upon several types of evidence. Post-medieval
documentary materials include maps, written surveys
and more limited materials, charters and other documents relating to or referring to individual holdings. Ordnance Survey maps, Tithe maps, Enclosure
maps and private estate maps, with their rich harvest of detail concerning topography, place-names,
landownership and land use, form foundation stones
for the process of retrogressive analysis, arguing
backwards in time from the known to the uncertain and
the unknown.(38) Maps form a vital interface between all other documentation and the landscape, a
basis for a classification which locates individual
records in space, a dimension as important as locating them in time. Even the most detailed written
survey is a poor substitute for a good map and while
maps, like all other documents, are created by human
hands and minds, and can therefore be inaccurate as
a result of error, dishonesty or lack of skill (and
should be critically evaluated as carefully as other
sources) they can also be taken to landscapes and

assessed in the context of surviving details. Of
course, no reconstruction of the medieval landscape
can ignore the effects of processes of landscape
change operating at all times, for these constitute
a filter through which the remoter past must be
viewed: at worst, earlier landscapes can be lost
beneath the sprawling estates of twentieth century
suburbia or nineteenth century industrial conglom-
erations, but in contrast, as Beresford and St.
Joseph have demonstrated, the tangible medieval
scene can simply be there, visible on maps, air photographs and the ground, subtly integrated within
landscapes enclosed, farms consolidated, hedges
replanted, meadows drained and water-courses straigh-
tened, farmsteads rebuilt and fields ploughed, reploughed and reploughed.(39)

Medieval sources can be used as a basis for reconstruction: here there is a paradox, for it is
often easier to create a reconstruction with a relatively little material, and a modern map, for a
mass of detail can overwhelm and inconsistencies become more evident. While in general detailed surveys and charters are the most used in topographical
reconstructions, for these are concerned with the
intricacies of the countryside, few if any classes
of medieval document fail to provide at least some
crumbs for the persistant researcher. When used in
combination with maps, and the third source, the
ground itself, even the most unpromising items can
be recognised as part of a wider jig-saw of data.

Landscapes themselves can produce remarkable returns
as the quarter century of work at Wharram Percy,
East Riding, Yorkshire, demonstrates.(40) Careful
excavation linked with the persistent recording of
surface indications has built up a picture and posed
questions whose repercussions reverberate through
many fields of enquiry. This work began as the
study of a single deserted village and is now treat-
ing the evolution of the landscape within a small
region between the Mesolithic period and the present
day, although from the beginning the study gained
strength from the fact that it was part of a wider
pattern of enquiry into deserted medieval villages
initiated by Beresford and others.(41)

In practice this study has a close relationship
to a less ambitious programme of work by James Bond.
Beginning with a known estate he examines the landscapes in the field, systematically discovering and
recording the visible evidence for barns and fish-
ponds, fulling mills, dovecots and vineyards, chapels and warrens, using the relevant documents both

as a source of guidance and elucidation and of questions.(42) At first sight his method of enquiry has
much in common with the landscape catalogues produced by the Royal Commission on Historical Monuments,
an uncomplimentary description for these splendid
records which must necessarily concentrate on description rather than on analysis and explanation.
(43) Bond's work, putting the field monuments into
their correct administrative context, leads towards
an appraisal of the extent to which topographical
details reflect diverse estate policies. It is, of
course, theoretically possible to recover a lost
topography from medieval sources alone, by welding
together a multitude of minute fragments of information to establish a more general picture. It is
normal in such documentation for the surveyor or
clerk to describe pieces of land, enclosed crofts,
meadow doles, furlongs of individual strips, <u>rela-
tive</u> to their immediate surroundings, giving two,
three, four or even five <u>abuttal</u> references:

> *Know all men present and future that I ....*
> *have given, granted etc. .... to .... nine*
> *acres and half a rood of land .... of which*
> *five and a half acres extend in length from*
> *the land of Roger de Bordesley as far as le*
> *Causey and in breadth from the land formerly*
> *belonging to Richard Clerc on the one hand and*
> *the highway leading from Beoley to Warwick on*
> *the other; and three and a half acres ...*
> *extending from le Causey as far as*
> *Hauekesschaweslade .....* (44)

If every piece so described in a cartulary or survey
were contiguous, and if every piece were delimited
by four abuttals, then reconstruction would be relatively easy, but this is rarely the case. In a remarkable paper, a statistician with historical
interests, David Kendall, discussed his attempts to
use a computer to reconstruct the fields of Whixley,
East Riding, Yorkshire. In spite of his skills his
success, using largely medieval evidence, was limited.(45) The present author attempted a similar
reconstruction exercise, with manual card-index
techniques, to reassemble the information for a
single parish of about 3804 ha. using some seven
hundred charters falling before 1350. Some success
was achieved, but it has to be admitted that a vital
break-through was provided by the discovery of a
detailed survey of about half the parish in <u>circa</u>
1500 which, almost literally, did list every field

of this enclosed woodland landscape. This, with the
Tithe map and other materials, allowed detailed topographic reconstruction.(46)   In contrast, in the
Durham township of Burn Tofts two of the author's
colleagues have been able to collect dozens of medieval place-names relating to the minute details
of field topography: however, the Tithe map helps
not at all, and in the absence of any evidence of
intermediate date no medieval reconstruction is
possible because the abuttal details are too scanty.
      Figure 52 illustrates the simplest type of re-
construction which is often feasible: the base tracing is from the Tithe map of about 1843 and on this
have been superimposed three types of point symbol
and two lines using the evidence of a small collection of medieval deeds and place-names recorded in
the Warwickshire volume of the English Place-Name
Society.(47)   In itself this superimposed evidence
would mean little, but set against the field-trace
(which includes an eighteenth century canal!) an
interpretable pattern emerges: (l) close to the
church hamlet lay a small area of common, subdivided field, once in open strips; (2) the body of
the parish contains a mass of small hedged fields,
assarted from waste and woodland during the twelfth
and thirteenth centuries; (3) to the east, where
late-enclosed waste can be documented, what seems
to be a fossilised frontier is detectable, while
(4) in the south-west a small park, with associated
fishpond complex and moated site, is visible. Although lacking detail this picture accords well with
the entry in Domesday Book:

          The same (Hugh) holds in Lapeford (Lapworth -
          a commonly agreed identification) half a hide.
          There is land for one plough. There are three
          villans. Woodland two leagues long and one
          league broad. It was worth l0 shillings; now
          20 shillings. Baldwin held it freely.'(48)

This, however, begs many questions: were the peasant
farms scattered through the landscape as Hoskins
argued for Devon, boldly moving between Domesday
Book and the Land Tax records of the nineteenth
century.(49)   Must we see them as clustered around
what was to become the parish church, for there was
no priest mentioned in l086 and Lapworth was an outlying member of an estate further south in the
county? When did the communal fields develop? Were
they based on the single ploughland of l086? If so,
why did the three villans have no plough working?

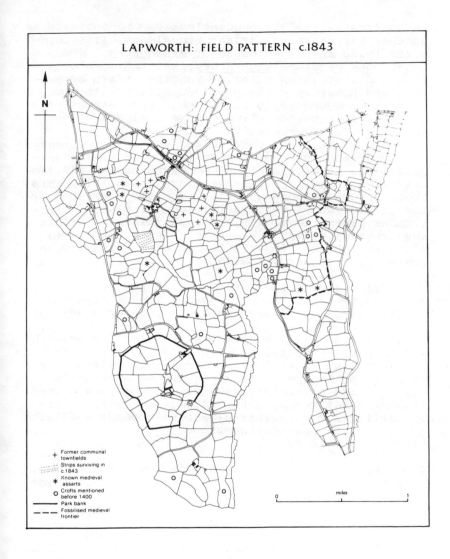

Fig.52   Lapworth c.1843 with added medieval data.

In contrast, these same questions can be answered in
another Warwickshire parish, Stoneleigh, like Lapworth lying in the woodland or Arden zone. The
Leger Book of Stoneleigh Abbey, written in about
1392 and containing material ranging in date between
then and Domesday Book, provided Hilton with the
evidence for schematic topographic reconstructions.
The material awaits retrogressive analysis using
post-medieval sources.(50)

Such work of reconstruction can all too easily
become an end in itself, time-consuming, utterly
absorbing, magnifying the importance of the minute
details of topographical discovery. Discipline must
be exercised through a series of basic questions in
the resolution of which detail can be placed in a
broader perspective. In a normal rural context, for
the urban situation presents particular problems,
six questions are important when attempting topographical reconstruction.(51)

(i) What was the extent and character of the
territory supporting a given settlement?
(ii) What settlement patterns and forms were
present?
(iii) What field systems existed and how were
they spatially organised?
(iv) What system of farming was practised?
(v) What tenemental structure was present and
can any relationship to topographic
features be detected?
(vi) Did any industrial activity occur and did
this lead to the presence of specialist
premises?

There are other questions, of course, concerning
specialist land use such as parks, warrens or fisheries, but a final question permeates all others,
for none of the features examined under the six
headings need be stable and the question 'What processes either generating or retarding change occur?'
gives a dynamic dimension to every problem.

SETTLEMENT TERRITORIES: TOWNSHIP AND PARISH

The basic territorial unit of medieval England was
the township or vill (rendered villa in medieval
Latin). 'The township' says Helen Cam 'was an en-
tity both older and longer lived than the lordship,
and even in the heyday of feudalism, the township,
the villata, the community of the vill, imposes it-

self on our attention.'(52) Bracton was more specific, 'if a person should build a single edifice in
the field, there will not be there a vill (<u>villa</u>),
but when in the process of time several edifices
have begun to be built adjoining to or neighbouring
to one another there begins a vill.'(53) In the
southern counties and Midlands there is a tendency
for townships to be co-terminous with the ecclesiastical parish, but in the north parishes are chara-
cteristically formed of groupings of townships.
These are the basic cells, comprising either a nucleated cluster or a more dispersed pattern, together
with associated arable, meadows, woods, waters and
normally some grazing lands. Winchester found them
to be the same order of size in regions as far apart
as Dorset and Durham, Cumberland and Leicestershire.
This is not the place to review the complex relationships between townships and parishes but it must
be stressed that the establishment of this relationship and the boundaries involved is a vital preliminary to topographic interpretation. To complicate
this picture manors, units of lordship, are superimposed on township and parish in many ways, sometimes conformably, sometimes at discord. Numerous
studies demonstrate the antiquity of elements within
this trichotomy of township, parish and manor:
boundaries portrayed on nineteenth and eighteenth
century maps can be confirmed or modified using post-
medieval perambulations, while medieval and Anglo-
Saxon charters reveal both stability and change, and
logic and insight have achieved retrogressive proj-
ections towards Romano-British and prehistoric antecedents. Such arguments cannot of course be divorced
from the evolution of the entire hierarchical framework of territorial government touched upon in the
first section of this essay.(54)

SETTLEMENT PATTERNS AND FORMS

The disposition of farmsteads within a single township is rarely directly revealed by medieval documents, be they scattered to create a dispersed
pattern of single farms and/or hamlets or concentrated within a single village cluster. It is of
course possible to attempt to locate all messuages,
the dwelling houses and adjacent land in a piecemeal
reconstruction, or schematically by locating them
generally within named sections of a territory.
Davenport, using an Elizabethan survey of 1565 attempted the former for the Norfolk manor of Forncett,

245

and argued retrogressively from this datum towards
her earlier sources, while in Cornwall Beresford,
using fourteenth century taxation records and Acces-
sion rolls of the Duchy, has been able to demonstrate the presence of both dispersed and grouped
settlements - with two-farm groups being more frequent than single farms - and hint at complex patterns of change.(55) In fact this work, in spite of
just criticism of less cautious attempts, is nevertheless dependent upon the earliest Ordnance Survey
and Tithe maps for the vital place-names which
create a framework for imaginative reconstruction
from intractable medieval sources. In Cumberland
retrogressive analysis has revealed the dispersed
character of medieval settlement, while in Devon
Hoskins has demonstrated that the dispersed patterns
there are concealed within the text of Domesday Book.
In Wales Jones and others have shown the complex relationships between dispersed farms and hamlets,
territorial arrangements and agnatic lineages.(56)
     Reconstructions of the topography of individual
villages derive from two roots; first, some medieval
sources are formulated in a manner which reveals
something of settlement form, allowing a direct
correlation with surviving plans, while a second
approach uses retrogressive methods. A most remarkable example of the former is noted by Searle in her
work on Battle Abbey, a portion of which is cited
above. In an account of the founding of the abbey
written between 1175 and 1200, nearly one hundred
years after the event, the chronicler notes the
existence of carefully measured plots and then follows by citing a rental (c. 1102-1107) which describes the tenements in precise geographical order,
allowing the reconstruction of the villa de Bello,
the modern town of Battle.(57)   Hilton refers to
Peterborough abbey rentals of c.1400 which 'describe
the tenants' houses as they lay along the village
streets' while a Guisborough Priory rent roll dated
before 1300 actually describes the disposition of
properties along streets.(58)   In Durham, the present
author has used a rental of pre-1200 (possibly as
early as 1130) to argue that the regular village
plans visible today in the county originate before
the date of the rental. The terminology used, which
appears in many thirteenth century documents from
the region, designates locations by reference to
cardinal orientations, East row, North row, etc. and
in every case where a village survives these correspond with what is to be seen on the ground.(59)   The
basic structures, the rows, are of medieval origin,

a conclusion which of course in no way excludes a
variety of subsequent changes. One can only speculate how commonly such locational descriptions lie
concealed within the texts of many rentals and surveys, both published and unpublished.

In a classic study of village morphology, June
Sheppard in her reconstruction of Wheldrake, East
Riding, Yorkshire, used an assumption of a measure
of plan continuity together with retrogressive arguments to reconstruct a regular planned settlement
present by the twelfth century if not somewhat earlier.(60) Paul Harvey created a reconstruction of
Cuxham, Oxfordshire, carefully described as 'conjectural', as a by-product of a more extensive investigation of the whole manor. He drew upon an estate
map of 1767, the Hundred Rolls of 1279, tax assessments, court roll entries, account rolls and charters, paying careful attention to the order in which
tenants were listed, and created a reconstruction
which has a group of villein tenements in an orderly
row adjacent to a manor house-church complex, a
cottage row facing these across a small green with
later tenements inserted into open spaces along a
green lane leading out of one end of the village -
the hall-marks in fact of careful planning which was
then adapted to changes. Similar reconstructions of
village layouts appear in Ravensdale's study of the
Fenland villages of Cottenham, Landbeach and Water-
beach. Noting in Cottenham the visible morphologi-
cal contrasts between a roughly rectangular core,
with no consistent internal pattern, and the linear
extensions to the north and south, whose toft boundaries clearly reflect their origin as arable strips,
he concluded that the rectangular core was the oldest focus and that the two extensions are likely to
be of Norman origin. (61) In a study of Kibworth
Harcourt, unfortunately unpublished, Cecily Howells
based a retrogressive analysis on a splendid series
of college maps and rentals and concluded that the
present village plan evolved from a regular antece-
dent present, and reconstructable, in 1086.(62)

Figures 53 and 54 are useful in drawing this
section to a close because they can be used to illustrate the actual process of reconstruction. Figure
53 records the documented history of the plan of
Acklington, Northumberland: that of 1864 is the
village on the earliest Ordnance Survey 1:2500 maps;
the plan of 1800-1820 appears in the appropriate
drawer in the muniment room at Alnwick, as does the
pre-reorganisation plan of c. 1800. This latter is
clearly the outline seen on a map of 1616 and the

Fig.53 Acklington, Northumberland, 1616-1864:
the documented village plan.

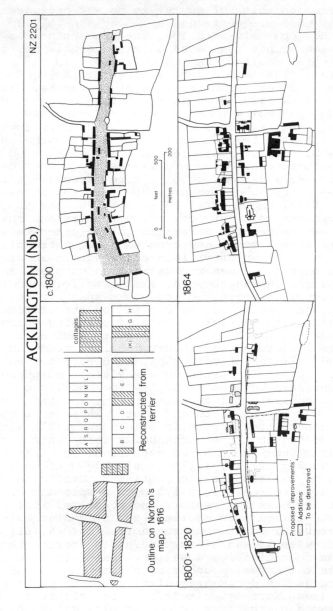

ACKLINGTON (Nb.)

NZ 2201

c.1800

1864

cottages

A S R Q P O N M L J I

B C D E F

K J G H

Reconstructed from terrier

Outline on Norton's map, 1616

1800 - 1820

Proposed improvements
Additions
To be destroyed

terrier accompanying this allows a schematic reconstruction. Figure 54 carries the argument backwards,
from a simplified reconstruction in 1616, to two
surveys of 1585 and 1567 (in village order) and thence
to earlier surveys, schematically represented on the
assumption of broad continuity, for even the major
reorganisation of 1472 appears merely to have involved the amalgamation of pairs of earlier farms -
perceived in terms of husbandland units. The use
of the earlier evidence involves an imaginative
leap, relating the figures in Inquisitions <u>post mor-
tem</u> to known later evidence, and the 'conjectural
reconstruction' of 1248 hints at the presence of a
regular two-row green village, quartered, with each
quarter being socially distinct - a similar conclusion in fact, to that reached by Paul Harvey. The
detailed arguments for this series of steps would
be tedious, and the reconstruction remains to be
tested against other archival material, but three
further points should be noted, namely the change
in status of the manor house toft (hall-garth) and
the incidental evidence for destroyed tofts in that
quarter provided by the 1616 survey (the presence
of a prison on the site excludes field investigation!), where some of the extra tofts of 1309 may
have been located, and the change from 30 acre holdings to 16 acre holdings of the bondage husbandlands
between 1248 and 1352.(63)   Ordered fields are apt
to go with ordered settlements, but each can change
independently of the other.

LAND USE, FRONTIERS AND FIELD SYSTEMS

The essence of the township lay in its economic
heart, the potential arable, meadow, woodland, water
and grazing resources encompassed by its boundary:
initial frameworks for all medieval reconstructions
are to be sought in retrogressive analysis from the
recorded disposition of these basic land use types
in later sources, even when radical transpositions
appear, with woodland encroaching on former arable.
A broader context for local interpretations must be
sought in the contrasts between champion mixed farming regions, wood pasture areas and open pasture
zones recognised by Joan Thirsk, but at the level of
the township the topographic problem can be seen
in terms of reconstructing a series of critical
boundaries or frontiers.(64)   First, there will be
those boundaries between arable, meadow and pasture-
land, be the latter mountain pasture, lowland heath

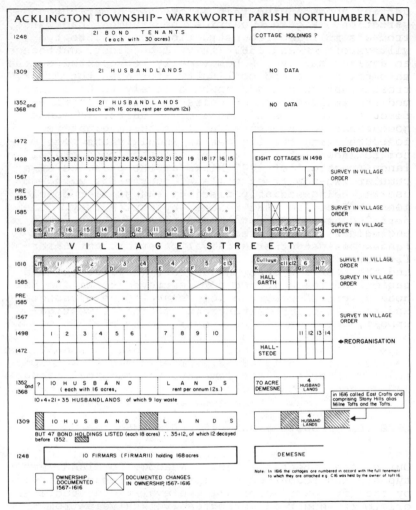

Fig.54 Acklington township, Northumberland, the pre-1616 analysis.

or fen, and these will normally closely reflect
variations in land quality touched upon in the introduction to this chapter. The true meadowlands
will almost invariably be bottomland, but while in
an area dominated by intermediate and poor land
this division will reflect the arable-pasture contrast, in a township dominated by good and intermediate lands the land-quality distinctions will reflect the same distinction, the arable being on the
good lands and the intermediate lands being relegated
to rough grazing. Of course, these frontiers are
not immutable, they advance and retreat according to
land improvement or adverse economic or social circumstances, but in general land evaluation and land
use will closely reflect the character of the regional environment.(65)
     Second, there will be frontiers between land
enclosed in some manner by a physical boundary and
land wholly unenclosed, distinctions which will reflect management practices, conditions of ownership
and the tenurial arrangements superimposed upon the
basic land-usage patterns. In practice, within the
head-dyke - the outer boundary of improved pasture
and tillage - three types of field arrangements
appear;

    (i) a form of open fields, subdivided, held
       and cultivated in common, usually involving
       arable and meadow with fallow grazings;(66)
   (ii) a form of enclosed fields, hedged, dyked,
       embanked or fenced, arable or pasture
       closes; (67)
  (iii) a pattern involving both open fields and
       closes.(68)

Our perception of the varied combinations of these
types which can be expected is strongly conditioned
by the concept of regional types of field system
originally outlined by Gray but given recent form
by Baker and Butlin.(69) There has been an inevitable tendency to interpret earlier, more tenuous
sources, in the context of models based on post-
medieval evidence and the writings of Dodgshon are
a stimulating and cautionary reminder of the inter-
pretational problems.(70)
     The reconstruction of medieval field systems
follows the same principles enunciated earlier in
this chapter, but the work is necessarily structured
around boundaries rather than points; routeways,
stream lines and more particularly the boundaries
of furlongs and their headlands. These latter often

outline blocks whose forms may be substantially
older than the strip systems superimposed within
them.(71) Following leads given by Homans, Goransson
demonstrated that many English open field systems
must be very carefully planned and recent work by
David Hall, linking detailed landscape work with
both post-medieval surveys, medieval fragmentary
evidence and, more rarely, medieval terriers (or
land surveys, sometimes termed dragg books) has
shown that both field structures and the tenurial
cycles or partition units - recurrent sequences of
strips in regular order - can be reconstructed.(72)
Figure 54 provides a late example of this to illustrate the possiblities. In the early seventeenth
century some of Acklington's furlongs were clearly
recent and peripheral additions to the system. In
some of these a regular sequence of strips is found,
ABCD and so on, to QRS, an order reflecting the sequence of village tofts. In other furlongs, however,
the introduction of a random element complicates
interpretation: thus the strip sequence in one of
the village's furlongs, Danes Flat, runs

MNOPQRSABCDEFGHIJCDEFGHIJLMNOPQRSABCDEFGHIJMONPQRSA-
BCDEFGHIJLMNOP

At first sight this is nonsense, but when it is analysed, using a simple contiguity matrix, a strictly
regular order appears:

MNOPQRSABCDEFGHIJ,   CDEFGHIJLMNOPSRSAB,

BCDEFGHIJMNOPSRSA,   ARSABCDEFGHIJLMNOP.

There are four cyles here; each begins randomly but
is complete within itself; H is missing because it
was a former hall-garth (manor house) site and was
rated a cottage, while L, technically a half farm,
has only one strip in every other partition unit.
Elsewhere in the fields there is evidence of the
sequence tenurial cycle/cottage strip/tenurial cycle/
cottage strip. Such explanations are in their
infancy, but the variations found in Acklington suggest that we may be dealing with several phases of
imposed regularity followed by a process of devolu-
tion, creating irregularity. The possibilities for
further research in this area appear tremendous,
and the implications, in terms of what it tells us
about the organisation of agrarian communities, are
quite fundamental.(73)

RETROSPECT

One hitherto unemphasised thread runs through every
theme examined in this essay - place-names. In the
absence of place-name survival, or the evidence to
provide critical through-time linkages when names
change or mutate, then topographical reconstruction
using documentary sources is virtually impossible.
As Gelling has emphasised, since about 1965 work on
the historical context of much of the place-name
material has been undergoing re-evaluation and its
interpretation demands greater expertise than is
generally appreciated. Use must be tempered with
caution.(74) Nevertheless, the volumes of the English Place-Name Society provide a sound basis for
beginning the interpretation of names to the township level, and many volumes deal with field names
although they provide no locational guidance. Place-
names are truly 'signposts to the past', and the
'trig-points' of topographic reconstruction, and the
EPNS volumes, in addition to giving an authoritative
etymological analysis (varying somewhat in quality
according to their date) also provide vital clues
to the availability of disparate record materials,
although tracing some of these can prove unreward-
ing. Why names survive, mutate or alter completely
remains one of the most intractable problems,(75)
but one of the most powerful and lasting impressions
deriving from the examination of medieval local
documents is their richness in locational terminology: field names, place-names and area names (attached to a particular position of a township or parish) proliferate.(76) Our problem is not merely to
relocate or use these names; it is to interpret cor-
rectly what they do tell us, free of our own intel-
lectual luggage of preconceptions, misinterpreta-
tions, objectives, prejudices and models. As Sauer
wrote, this 'needs the ability to see the land with
the eyes of its former inhabitants', a most difficult but wholly rewarding task.(77)

REFERENCES

    1. E. Mackie, Science and Society in Prehisto-
ric Britain (1977), p.5; A.R.H. Baker, 'A Note on
the Retrogressive and Retrospective Approaches in
Historical Geography', Erdkunde, 22 (Bonn 1968),
pp.243-4.
    2. A.R.H. Baker, J.D. Hamshere and J. Langton,
(eds.), Geographical Interpretations of Historical

Sources (1970), A.R.H. Baker, (ed.), Progress in
Historical Geography (1972).
    3. E.E. Power, 'Peasant Life and Rural Condi-
tions', Cambridge Medieval History, VII (1932), pp.
716-19.
    4. N.J.G. Pounds and S.S. Ball, 'Core-Areas
and the Development of the European States System',
Annals of the Association of American Geographers,
51 No.1 (March 1964), pp.24-40, E.E. Evans, 'The
Ecology of Peasant Life in Western Europe', in W.L.
Thomas, (ed.), Man's Role in Changing the Face of
the Earth (Chicago 1956), pp.217-239, H. Clout,
The Regional Problem in Western Europe (1976),
Chapter 1.
    5. B.H. Slicher van Bath, The Agrarian History
of Western Europe (1963), pp.7-25.
    6. P. Vinogradoff, Villeinage in England
(1892), pp.43-88, Van Bath, Agrarian History, W.
Abel, Agricultural Fluctuations in Europe (1980).
    7. P. Sawyer, (ed.), Medieval Settlement
(1976), p.4.
    8. P. Haggett, A.D. Cliff, A. Frey, Locational
Models (1977), pp.1-24, particularly pp.6-10,
Rennell of Rodd, 'The Land of Lene', in I.Ll.
Foster and L. Alcock (eds), Culture and Environment
(1963) pp.303-326.
    9. J.H. Hinde, (ed.), 'Symeonis Dunelmensis
Opera et Collectanea', Surtees Society, 51 (1868),
pp.151-2.
    10. E. Craster, 'The Patrimony of St. Cuthbert'
English Historical Review, 69 (April 1954), pp.177-
199, P.A.G.Clack and B.H. Gill, 'The Land Divisions
of County Durham in the Early Medieval Period',
Medieval Village Research Group, Annual Report, 28
(1980), pp.30-34.
    11. H.C. Darby and G.R. Versey, Domesday Gaze-
tteer (1975), R.E. Glasscock, The Lay Subsidy of
1334 (1975), A.R.H. Baker, 'Evidence in the Nonarum
Inquisitions of Contracting Arable Lands in England
during the Fourteenth Century', Economic History
Review, 2nd Ser. 19 (1966), pp.518-32.
    12. J.C. Dewdney and D.W. Rhind, People in Dur-
ham (1975), pp.4-16, see also A.R.H. Baker, J.D.
Hamshere and J. Langton, (eds.), Geographical Interpretation of Historical Sources (1970).
    13. E. Ekwall, The Concise Oxford Dictionary of
English Place-Names (4th edition, 1970), under
Cotherston: one likely location is adjacent to the
mother church of the great parish of St. Andrew
Auckland, a place now simply called South Church.
    14. Hinde, 'Symeonis Dunelmensis', p.142.

Medieval Settlements

15. V. Watts, 'Place-Names' in J.C. Dewdney,
(ed.), Durham County and City with Teesside (1970),
p.252.
16. W.G. Hoskins, Fieldwork in Local History
(1967), pp.34-40, H.P.R. Finberg, Lucerna (1964),
pp.116-130, Ibid, West-County Historical Studies
(1969), pp.11-69, M. Gelling, Signposts to the Past
(1978), pp.191-214, P. Sawyer, Anglo-Saxon Charters
(1968) provides a bibliography.
17. W. Greenwell, 'Bishop Hatfield's Survey',
Surtees Society (1857), p.31, B.K. Roberts, The
Green Villages of County Durham, Durham County Local
History Publications, No.12 (1977), pp.13-18, Watts,
Place-Names, p.260-1.
18. A.J.L. Winchester, Territorial Structure
and Agrarian Organisation in medieval and Sixteenth
Century Copeland, Cumberland, unpublished Ph.D.
thesis, University of Durham (1978), pp.27-52, D.
Bonney, 'Early Boundaries and Estates in Southern
England' in Sawyer, Medieval Settlement, pp.72-82.
19. Roberts, Green Villages, p.10, Greenwell,
'Hatfield Survey', pp.26-7, where it is clearly part of
Heighington, W. Greenwell, 'Bolden Buke', Surtees
Society, 25 (1852), pp.22-23, 60-61 reveals the
same link.
20. E. Miller, The Abbey and Bishopric of Ely
(1951), J.A. Taftis, The Estates of Ramsey Abbey
(Toronto 1957), E. King, Peterborough Abbey 1086-
1310 (1973), F.R.H. Du Boulay, The Lordship of Canterbury (1966), M. Morgan, The English Lands of the
Abbey of Bec (1946), G.A. Holmes, The Estates of the
Higher Nobility in Fourteenth Century England (1957).
21. E. Miller and J. Hatcher, Medieval England
(1978), Chs. 7-8, M.M. Postan, The Medieval Economy
and Society (1972), Chs. 5-6, Van Bath, Agrarian
History, pp.40-53.
22. Holmes, Estates of Higher Nobility, W.E.
Wightman, The Lacy Family in England and Normandy
(1966), C. Ross, The Estates and Finances of Richard
Beauchamp, Earl of Warwick Dugdale Society Occasional Papers, No.12 (1956), J. Hatcher, Rural Economy
and Society in the Duchy of Cornwall 1300-1500
(1970), Craster, 'Patrimony of St. Cuthbert'.
23. Few of the references cited in footnotes
20-22 fail to demonstrate the composite qualities of
great estates; see also R.H. Hilton, The Economic
Development of Some Leicestershire Estates at the
End of the Fourteenth Century (1947), B. English,
the Lords of Holderness 1086-1260 (1979), H.P.R.
Finberg, Tavistock Abbey (1951).
24. E.A. Kosminsky, Studies in the Agrarian

255

History of England in the Thirteenth Century (1956)
pp.68-151.
    25. Holmes, Estates of Higher Nobility, G.W.S.
Barrow, The Kingdom of the Scots (1973), pp.7-68,
G.R.J. Jones, 'The Multiple Estate as a Model Frame-
work for Tracing Early Stages in the Evolution of
Rural Settlement', in F. Dussart, (ed.), L'Habitat
et les paysages ruraux d'Europe (Liege 1971), 251-67,
Ibid, 'Multiple Estates and Early Settlements' in
Sawyer, Medieval Settlement, pp.15-40.
    26. Winchester, Territorial Structure, p.48,
Roberts, Green Villages p.15, G.W.S. Barrow, 'The
Pattern of Lordship and Feudal Settlement in Cumbria',
Journal of Medieval History, 1 (1975), pp.117-138,
Jones, 'Multiple Estates as a Model'.
    27. G.W.S. Barrow, 'Northern English Society in
the Twelfth and Thirteenth Centuries', Northern
History, 4 (1969), pp.1-28, P.H. Blair, 'The Origins
of Northumbria', Archaeologia Aeliana, 4th Ser., 25
(1947), pp.1-51, Craster, 'Patrimony of St. Cuthbert', W.E. Kapell, The Norman Conquest of the North
(1979).
    28. J.E.A. Joliffe, 'Northumbrian Institutions',
English Historical Review, 41 (1926), pp.1-42,
Jones, 'Multiple Estates and Early Settlement'.
    29. B.K. Roberts, 'Man and Land in Upper Tees-
dale' in A.R. Clapham, (ed.), Upper Teesdale (1978),
pp.141-159, Dewdney, Durham County, pp.184-5, 220-
226, Deputy Keeper of Public Records, Forty Fourth
and Forty Fifth Reports (1883 and 1884), Appendices,
pp.525-535, 279-281, Holmes, Estates of the Higher
Nobility, p.48
    30. B.K. Roberts, 'The Historical Geography
of Moated Homesteads: The Forest of Arden Warwickshire', Transactions Birmingham and Warwickshire
Arcaeological Society, 88 (1976-7), pp.62-70, B.K.
Roberts, The Forest of Arden 1086-1350, unpublished
Ph.D., thesis, University of Birmingham (1965),
Fig.10.
    31. Ross, Estates of the Earl of Warwick, pp.
20-22, J.B. Harley, 'The Settlement Geography of
Early Medieval Warwickshire', Transactions Institute
of British Geographers, 34 (1964), pp.115-130, W.J.
Ford, 'Settlement Patterns in the Central Region of
the Warwickshire Avon', in Sawyer, Medieval Settle-
ment, pp.274-288.
    32. Sawyer, Medieval Settlement, pp.1-7, 277-
288.
    33. R.S. Hoyt, The Royal Demesne in English
History (1971), R.H. Hilton (ed.), 'Stoneleigh Leger
Book', Dugdale Society Publications, 24 (1960).

34. Miller and Hatcher, Medieval England,p.181.
35. Victoria County History, Warwickshire, I (1904), p.340-1.
36. R. Pemberton, Solihull and its Church (1905), Introduction.
37. Winchester, Territorial Structure, p.22.
38. J.B. Harley, The Historian's Guide to Ordnance Survey Maps, National Council for Social Service (1964), Ibid., Maps for the Local Historian, National Council for Social Service (1972), J. West, Village Records (1962), F.G. Emmison, Archives and Local History (1966).
39. M.W. Beresford and J.K.S. St. Joseph, Medieval England, an Aerial Survey (2nd ed. 1979).
40. Sawyer, Medieval Settlement, pp.114-144 contains a summary; see also M.W. Beresford and J.G. Hurst, (eds.), Deserted Medieval Villages (1971).
41. Beresford and Hurst, Deserted Medieval Villages.
42. J. Bond, 'The Estates of Evesham Abbey', Vale of Evesham Historical Society Research Paper, 4 (1973), pp.1-62, Ibid., 'The Estates of Abingdon Abbey', Landscape History 1 (1979), pp.59-75.
43. Royal Commission on Historical Monuments, Northamptonshire, 2 vols. (H.M.S.O., 1975 and 1979), see also M. Aston and T. Rowley, Landscape Archae-ology (1974).
44. Roberts, The Forest of Arden, vol. II, Appendix I, a charter of c. 1268-98.
45. D.G. Kendall, 'The Recovery of Structure from Fragmentary Information', Philosophical Transactions of the Royal Society, Series A Vol.279 No.1291, (1975), 547-582.
46. Roberts, The Forest of Arden, Ibid., 'A Study of Medieval Colonisation in the Forest of Arden, Warwickshire', Agricultural History Review, 16 (1968) pp.101-113, Ibid., 'An Early Tudor Sketch Map', History Studies, 1 No.1 (1968), pp.33-38.
47. Deeds of the Lapworth Charity Trustees, c. 1190 to 1520, Calendar in Birmingham Reference Library, MSS. 184962; Lapworth Title Map, c. 1843, Warwick County Record Office, J.E.B. Gover, A. Mawer and F.M. Stenton, 'The Place-Names of Warwickshire' English Place-Name Society, 13 (1936), pp.288-290, 377-8, Roberts, The Forest of Arden, provides a context.
48. V.C.H. Warwick, I, 326a; Roberts, The Forest of Arden, p.116, Fig. 24.
49. W.G. Hoskins, Provincial England (1963), pp.15-52.

50. Hilton, 'Stoneleigh Leger Book', map, R.H. Hilton, 'Old Enclosure in the West Midlands' Annales de L'Est, 21 (Nancy, 1959) pp.272-283.
51. M.R.G. Conzen, 'The Use of Town Plans', in H.J. Dyos (ed.) The Study of Urban History (1968), pp.113-130, M.W. Barley, The Plans and Topography of Medieval Towns in England and Wales, Council for British Archaeology, Research Report No.14, (1975).
52. H.M. Cam, 'The Community of the Vill' in V. Ruffer and A.J. Taylor (eds.), Medieval Studies Presented to Rose Graham (1950), pp.1-14,Winchester, Territorial Structure, pp.21-26, 32-43.
53. Winchester, Territorial Organisation, p.37.
54. C. Taylor, Dorset: The Making of the English Landscape (1970), pp.49-78.
55. F.G. Davenport, The Economic History of a Norfolk Manor 1086-1565 (1906), pp.1-19 and map, M.W. Beresford, 'Dispersed and Group Settlement in Medieval Cornwall', Agricultural History Review, 12, pt. 1 (1964),pp.13-27, W.J. Corbett, 'Elizabethan Village Surveys', Transactions of the Royal Historical Society, New Series, 11 (1897), pp.67-87, L.C. Coombes, 'The Survey of Langley Barony 1608', Archaeologia Aeliana, 4th Ser. 43 (1965), pp.261-273.
56. Hoskins, Provincial England, W.G. Hoskins, Devon (1954), 30-68, G.R.J. Jones, 'The Distribution of Medieval Settlement in Anglesey 'Transactions Anglesey Antiquarian Society (1955), 27-96, T. Jones Pierce, Medieval Welsh Society (1972), pp.251-287.
57. E. Searle, Lordship and Community: Battle Abbey and its Banlieu (Toronto 1974), p.69, Ibid., The Chronicle of Battle Abbey (1980), pp.51-59.
58. R.H. Hilton, A Medieval Society (1966), p. 92, W. Brown, (ed.), Cartularium Prioratus de Gyseburne', I-II, Surtees Society, 86 (1889) and 89 pp.412-450.
59. B.K. Roberts, 'Village Plans in County Durham', Medieval Archaeology, 17 (1972), pp.33-56.
60. J. Sheppard, 'Pre-Enclosure Field and Settlement Patterns in an English Township', Geografiska Annaler, 48, Ser. B (1966), pp.59-77, P.D.A. Harvey, A Medieval Oxfordshire Village (1965), pp. 25-29, 122, 172-3.
61. J.R. Ravensdale, Liable to Floods (1974), pp.121-150.
62. C. Howell, The Social and Economic Condition of the Peasantry in South-East Leicestershire, A.D. 1300-1700, Oxford University D.Phil. thesis, 1974; ex inf. the author.
63. J.C. Hodgson (ed.), History of Northumber-

land, V (18))), pp.362-376. The maps used as the basis for Figure 53 were consulted by kind permission of His Grace the Duke of Northumberland.
64. J. Thirsk, (ed.), The Agrarian History of England and Wales, IV, 1500-1640 (1967), pp.1-160, H.C. Darby, The Domesday Geography of England; Eastern England; Midland England; South-East England; Northern England; South-West England (various editions 1962-1971) contain a clear record of local regional divisions in 1086. A challenging, if at times controversial, view of the medieval scene is to be found in H.E. Hallam, Rural England 1066-1348 (1981).
65. H.E. Hallam, Settlement and Society: A Study of the Early Agrarian History of South Lincolnshire (1965), M.L. Parry, 'Secular Climatic Change and Marginal Agriculture', Transactions of the Institute of British Geographers, 64 (1975), pp.1-13.
66. A.C. Chibnall, Sherington, Fiefs and Fields of a Buckinghamshire Village (1965), C.P. Hall and J.R. Ravensdale, 'The West Fields of Cambridge', Cambridge Antiquarian Records Society, 3, for 1974-5 (1976).
67. Roberts, Medieval Colonisation.
68. J. Yelling, Common Field and Enclosure in England 1450-1850 (1977).
69. A.R.H. Baker and R.A. Butline, (eds.) Studies of Field Systems in the British Isles (1973) contains numerous examples of retrogressive analysis.
70. R.A. Dodgshon, The Origin of British Field Systems (1980), especially p.127; T. Rowley (ed.), The Origins of Open-Field Agriculture (1981).
71. Ford, 'Settlement Patterns' in Sawyer, Medieval Settlement pp.292-94.
72. G.C. Homans, English Villagers of the Thirteenth Century (New York 1960, pp.83-106, S. Goransson, 'Regular Open-field Pattern in England and Scandinavian Solskifte', Geografiska Annaler, 43, Nos.1-2, (1961), pp.80-104, D. Hall 'The Origins of Open-field Agriculture - The Archaeological Fieldwork Evidence', in T. Rowley (ed.), The Origins of Open-field Agriculture (1981), pp.22-38. Work by Tony Brown on Daventry, Northamptonshire, is suggesting remarkable degrees of spatial organisation, which may extend back to 1086.
73. These comments are based upon Mason's survey of the Northumberland estates consulted by kind permission of the Duke; Alnwick Castle MSSc. AI, Ip, A.V.6; see also A.R.H. Baker and R.A. Butlin (eds.), Studies of Field Systems in the British Isles, pp.

111-120, Hodgson, History of Northumberland, V.
pp.362-376, B.K. Roberts, 'The Regulated Village
in Northern England', Geographia Polonica 38 (1978),
pp.245-252.
    74. M. Gelling, Signposts to the Past, (1978).
    75. W.F.H. Nicholaisen, Scottish Place-Names
(1976). The Introduction contains a particularly
useful analysis of name-changes for two places.
    76. The English Place-Name Society was founded
in 1923 and has now produced 53 volumes.
    77. J. Leighley, (ed.), Land and Life; A
Selection from the Writings of C.O. Sauer (Califor-
nia, 1963), p.362. See also E. Ekwall, 'Variation
and Change in English Place-names', Vetenskaps -
Societeten i Lund, Arsbok (1962), pp.3-49.

Chapter 8

ANGLO-SAXON CHARTER BOUNDARIES*

Michael Reed

The period between the traditional date for the end
of Roman Britain, namely 410 A.D., and the Norman
Conquest in 1066, is almost as long as the period
covered by all of the other Chapters in this book
put together. It is a period of the most fundamental importance in the evolution of the English
landscape in that it sees the first stages of the
formation of 90 percent of its place-names and the
establishment of those administrative units - shire,
hundred and parish - whose boundaries have over the
course of subsequent centuries become etched into
the landscape, and into the hearts, minds and affec-
tions of men to an extent which it is almost impossible to exaggerate. Historians can write, for example, of Neolithic Wiltshire or Roman Buckinghamshire with no apparent sense of incongruity.
    We have seen in the first two Chapters of this
book historians of the nineteenth century rural landscape able to exploit fully the mountains of documents before them only by calling in the computer to
their aid. If it is the wealth of documentation
that is the problem for the nineteenth century historian, then it is the paucity of documentation that
is the chief problem facing the historian of the
evolution of the Anglo-Saxon landscape. Leaving on
one side such literary and narrative sources as
The Anglo-Saxon Chronicle and Bede's Historia Eccle-
siastica, there are less than 2000 documents surviving for the six hundred years of this period,(1) of
which 272 are lost or incomplete, and the great
majority in any case date only from the last century

* I am most grateful to Dr. Margaret Gelling for her
comments on successive drafts of this Chapter. She
has saved me from many errors. I alone can be held
responsible for those that remain.

and a half. The problem is exacerbated by the fact
that only a few have been edited and published in
reliable texts.(2) Although steps have been taken
to remedy this, and two volumes of accurate texts
with fully scholarly apparatus have now appeared,
(3) it will be many years before this project is
completed.

The documents loosely known as Anglo-Saxon
charters have attracted the attention of generations
of scholars and students, and for many periods and
aspects of the history of the Anglo-Saxon centuries
they are our only source of information.(4) Nevertheless, few though they are it would seem that they
have still not yet been wrung dry.(5) Indeed in
many respects their proper exploitation has scarcely begun.

Almost all of these documents are concerned
with the ownership, possession and transfer of land,
and most are in the form of a diploma, the most
solemn and formal of the written methods of making
their wishes known which the Anglo-Saxon kings had
at their disposal. Many diplomas and some less
formal documents such as leases contain a written
description of the bounds of the landed estate being
conveyed. There are in addition a further 63 boundary perambulations which are not, formally at any
rate, part of a diploma.

We are not here concerned with the history of
the diploma itself, about which there is still uncertainty, but with the boundary perambulations.
They have in their own right fascinated successive
generations of historians by the wealth of minute,
although all-too-frequently elusive, detail about a
particular locality which they so often contain.
Much of this fascination undoubtedly lies in the
opportunities which attempts at their reconstruction
present for the exploration of some of the most
tranquil and least changed parts of rural England.
If to this is added the occasion to revisit scenes
of childhood then the spell they cast is complete.
J.Y. Akerman, after studying the bounds of possessions of Malmesbury abbey in Wiltshire, could write
movingly in 1857:

> I have perambulated the greater part of these
> possessions, and visited districts which,
> though lying in the very heart of England, are
> little known to the topographer, and still less
> to the tourist. In some instances I have succ-
> eeded in identifying obscure localities, which
> still bear names by which they were known long

before the Norman Conquest. While thus engaged
I have wandered again into the track and reviv-
ed the recollections of my boyhood.(6)

In all some 710 documents, almost all of them
diplomas but including two wills (7) and a number of
leases, survive with at least one set of bounds, together with a further 63 sets on the face of it unrelated to any other document.(8) Several of these
documents contain two or more sets of bounds, (9) so
that in fact there are well over 800 sets of boundary perambulations. Unfortunately however, not only
are they very unevenly distributed chronologically,
they are also very unevenly distributed geographically.(10) There are for example 74 for Berkshire,
of which 61 are attached to charters to be dated
between 930 and 985, but only six for Buckinghamshire, four for the whole of Yorkshire, only one
each for Lincolnshire (Barrow upon Humber), and
Lancashire (Amounderness), and none for Norfolk and
the four northern counties. Further, the texts of
a number which are traditionally included in the
corpus must, in their present form, date from after
the Norman Conquest.(11)
     This total of some 800 boundary perambulations
can be misleading however, since for some estates
there are two or more sets of bounds. Perhaps the
most fortunate in this respect is Moredon in Rod-
bourne Cheney, Wiltshire, for which there are at
least four, and probably five.(12) On the other
hand some sets of bounds, ostensibly relating to
the same estate, in fact are concerned with only a
part of it, and thus illustrate most vividly that
process of estate subdivision which, it has been
claimed, was the main development in the settlement
history of Anglo-Saxon England.(13) Thus, again
from Wiltshire, there are at least five charters
referring simply to Eblesburnan, but it is clear
from the boundary perambulations themselves that in
fact they refer to separate portions of an estate
which are strung out along the valley of the river
Ebble and is now divided into parishes of Odstock,
Homington, Coombe Bissett, Stratford Tony and
Bishopstone.(14)   (See Fig.55)
     The great majority of boundary perambulations
are to be found in, or attached to, diplomas or
analogous private documents. Some may well embody
an oral tradition that was old when it was first
written down. Others may be comparatively new in
that they record the subdivision of an ancient
estate. There are yet others which may have been

Fig.55 Anglo-Saxon Charter
Boundaries in Wiltshire.
A number of estates are
too small to show on
a map of this scale.
Dotted lines mark
later subdivisions.
For estates lettered
A (Brinkworth),
B (Grittenham),
C (Dauntsey),
D (Christian Malford)
and E (Bremhill),
see Fig.56.
Estates lettered
F-K are all called
Eblesburnan. The
estate called
Chalke in a charter
of 955 (BCS 917)
included six
subdivisions and a
detached portion.

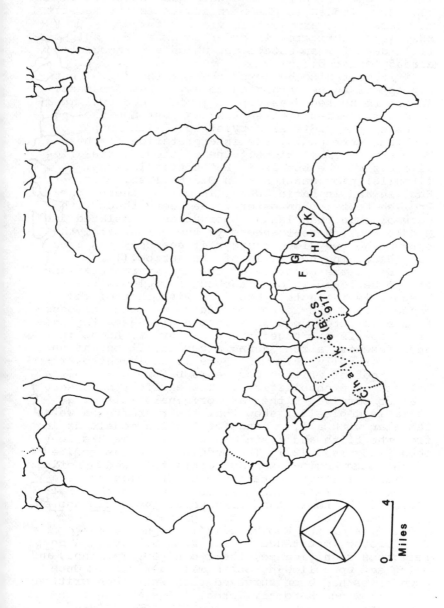

written out for purposes other than inclusion in a
charter. Indeed it has been suggested for several
charters which are quite obviously forgeries that
they were fabricated in order to provide a suitable
title deed for an estate for which a perambulation
already existed.(15)

It must also be noted that of the 63 which today appear to be unrelated to any other document,
42 are to be found as copies in four medieval monastic cartularies,(16) so that we must add the vag-
aries of the medieval copyist to all the other
problems surrounding the interpretation of these
boundary perambulations. One of these cartularies
(17) has all the bounds in Latin translations. A
fifth(18) provides texts in Old English, Middle
English and in Latin. When, in one of these, the Old
English text thonan oster thone beorh thaet lith
betweol than twan langan beorgan is translated into
Middle English as thanne ovyr the borw that lyth
bytwen the twey long bryggys it scarcely inspires
confidence in the skills of the scribe.(19)

Since the majority of boundary perambulations
are to be found in or attached to diplomas their
history is intimately bound up with that of this
document. There is no certainty over the introduction of written documents into Anglo-Saxon England.
Dr. Chaplais has urged the case for St. Augustine
and presents a convincing argument,(2) but as he
himself readily admitted 'there is no incontrovert-
ible proof of written documents before 669, only a
balance of probabilities'. The earliest documents
that do survive, either as 'originals'(21) or as
reliable copies(22) show that their draftsmen were
familiar with a wide range of Italian models dating
from the fifth and sixth centuries. This has long
been recognised.(23) The models which the scribes
of the first Anglo-Saxon documents followed but did not
slavishly imitate contained boundary clauses as a
matter of course. These clauses reflect the practices of the Roman land surveyors, the agrimensores,
practices which in their turn go back to the earliest days of the Republic.(24) Boundary marks were
of profound importance to the Romans, having a deep
religious significance, their own god, Terminus, and
being set up following an animal sacrifice. Once
boundaries had been surveyed they were then written
out following customary formulae, which could include compass points. The boundary points used
could include rivers, hills, roads and the names of
neighbouring estate owners. The use of such boundary points can be illustrated ad nauseam from pub-

lished collections of fifth and sixth century private deeds. From a collection of such documents
relating to estates in what is now Tunisia may be
noted the   following:(25)

No.3, of 493
inter adfines eiusdem agri ab oriente felix
fortuni ab occidente quintianus a coro leporius
benditor inter adfines eisdem loci supra
scripti ab africo bia qui ducit ad magula a
meridie et a marino quintus a coro lateretis
et bergentisque suis.

No.6, of 493
inter adfines eiusdem agri a coro martialis
benditor et ianuarius fortuni ab aquilo
supradictus martialis benditor a meridie
quintianus ab africo supradictus quintianus et
victor sibe quibus adfinibus.

No.12, of 494
inter adfines a meridie gibba de buresa ab
africo victorinus benditor a coro aquariis et
uergentibusque suis a marino bia de buresa.

From a collection of private deeds relating to
estates around Ravenna in the mid and late sixth
century:(26)

No.118, of about 540
cum finibus omnibus terminisque earum campis

No.120, of 572, being a sale of a farm called
Curtinis lying in territorio Ariminensi inter
affines fundum Varianum et fundum Titianum
atque fundun Quadrantula.

It is possible today to locate the estates
mentioned in such documents only in the most general
terms,(27) and yet they relate to parts of the Roman
world which were neither deserted nor thinly settled
at the time when the documents were drafted.
Such phrases are echoed in the earliest English
documents:

BCS. 67, of 686
quae terra determinatur ex una parte habet
vadum quod appellatur Fordstreta publica
indirectum et a parte alia flumen quod nomina-
tur Stur.

BCS. 97, of 697
iuxta notissimos terminos id est bereueg et
meguines paed et stretleg

BCS. 121, of 663-693
terra autem haec site est in monte et circa
montem qui dicitur Brente habens ab occidente
Sabrinam ab aquilone Axam ab oriente Termic ab
austro Siger.

In other words, in boundary clauses as in the
other clauses of the earliest diplomas, English
scribes were following their Continental models, and
so it would appear to be unwise to argue from the
very brief nature of the earliest English boundary
clauses either that the boundaries themselves were
vague and lacking in precision or that they reflected a thinly settled and largely pioneering landscape.(28)

Nevertheless, even if the boundary perambulations were modelled upon late Roman deeds, they
were quite quickly adapted to needs and conditions
in England, so that the form in which these perambulations were written out has its own history, its
own diplomatic, quite distinctive from that of the
main body of the charter, a diplomatic which enables
a perambulation to be dated within very broad
limits. If a chronology of boundary perambulations,
as opposed to that of their charters, can be established this means that when we come to study the
landscape of Anglo-Saxon England through their re-
fracted imagery then it may be possible to avoid
some of the more glaring anachronisms, since it is
clear that some very early charters, such as that
for Chertsey of 672-4 (BCS.34) have appended to
them some very late boundary surveys. The surveys
may well relate to the estates mentioned in the
charter, but they could have been drawn up as much
as three hundred years later, and so incorporate
features of the landscape which were not in existence at the time of the charter. It is for this
reason that it is worth while spending some time
trying to establish, at least in broad terms, a
chronology for the boundary surveys themselves.

In order to establish this chronology we must
begin with those charters which survive in copies
generally considered to be genuine, authentic, contemporary, and perhaps even original.(29) It must
of course be stated clearly that not every genuine,
authentic and contemporary charter has a boundary
perambulation. The earliest to survive, a grant of

land in Thanet made in 679 by Hlothhere, king of
Kent, to abbot Brihtwold,(30) states merely that
the estate is marked by its well-known bounds -
notissimos terminos. This phrase, or variations on
it, occurs again and again, both in boundary clauses and in those charters without them, until well
into the tenth century. As yet no simple explanation can be offered as to why some grants needed a
more or less detailed boundary survey and others
did not, but there is evidence to show that in several cases an estate was being divided by the grant,
and so the new boundaries would need to be recorded.
(31)
    The charters with boundary surveys surviving
in genuine, authentic, contemporary copies from
before 899 may be arranged as follows:

Table 5: Boundary Surveys in Contemporary Copies
from before 899

	(a)	(b)	(c)	(d)
	before 700	701-800	801-899	totals
Bucks.			1	1
Devonshire			1	1
Essex		1		1
Gloucs.		2		2
Kent	1	3	15	19
Middx.			1	1
Sussex		1		1
Wilts.		1		1
Worcs		2		2
	1	10	18	29

    Of these twenty-nine charters only three have
boundary surveys in Old English. The first is that
for South Hams, in Devonshire, dated 847.(32) Here
lengthy bounds in Old English, introduced simply by
the word Aerest, are to be found in the text of the
charter, between the dating clause and the anathema.
The second is that for Wotton Underwood, Buckinghamshire,(33) and in many ways this document is unique.
It is written entirely in Old English. The boundary clause is no more than a list of five points,
with neither introductory nor directional material.
It has no date but may be assigned to the period
843-855. The third is a grant made in 889 by the
bishop and community at Rochester of land at Frinds-
bury in Kent, and so it is strictly not a royal

diploma at all. The boundary survey is introduced by a Latin clause which leads straight into an Old English account of the bounds.(34)

We must now turn to the very much larger group of documents which survive only in later copies, but in copies which appear to be sound and reliable:(35)

Table 6: Pre-899 Boundary Surveys Surviving only in Later Copies

| | (a) | (b) | (c) | (d) |
	before 700	701-800	801-899	totals
Berkshire			3	3
Devon		1		1
Dorset			3	3
Gloucs.		7	1	8
Hampshire			3	3
Kent	1	7	10	18
Middlesex		3		3
Oxfordshire			1	1
Somerset	1	3	1	5
Surrey	2			2
Isle of Wight			1	1
Wiltshire			1	1
Worcestershire		3	6	9
	4	24	30	58

Of these 58 charters, 32 have bounds in Old English. It is clear, however, from a closer examination of individual documents, that many of these boundary surveys are in fact very much later than the date of the document to which they are ostensibly attached. Many of the reasons for this are due to factors unique to individual documents,(36) but the single most important factor at work is the nature of the Anglo-Saxon diploma itself. Written on one side of a single sheet of parchment with no unimpeachable marks of authenticity - it had neither autograph signature nor seals - it was all too easy to copy and recopy, each scribe introducing his own textual alterations, inserting and removing paragraphs, modernising phrasing, terms and language. Some of this alteration was done innocently, but there was nothing to prevent it being done fraudulently, even though the motives may on occasion have been unexceptionable. Further, the 'original' text of the diploma did not always entirely fill the sheet of parchment, and there was in any case the

reverse, clean, unsoiled, unmarked, crying out for
someone to write something on it. In 770 Uhtred,
regulus of the Hwicce, granted land at Aston in
Stoke Prior, Worcestershire, to Aethelmund, his
minister.(37) The names of the witnesses spilled
over on to the reverse of the parchment, but there
was still room for a scribe to squash in at the
foot of the sheet the briefest boundary survey:
hii sunt termini donationis istius saluuerpae
cymedes halh huitan stan readan solo. In 778 Egc-
bert, king of Kent, gave land to the bishop of
Rochester lying at Bromhey, in Kent. The grant survives in a copy which is contemporary. In the text
it states merely that the land is granted cum
notissimis terminis omnibusque utilitatibus ad eam
rite pertinentibus. On the back, written in a later
hand, are the bounds of the attached meadowland.(38)

Since the charters listed in Table 7 survive in
much later copies and so are subject to all the
perils in their transmission just described, we must
be prepared for many of them to have boundary surveys which are later interpolations, additions or
modernisations. We may begin the process of distinguishing later additions from contemporary surveys by making a statement: Old English boundary
surveys attached to documents prima facie to be
dated from before 899 are unlikely to be contemporary with the document unless they are in the text,
have some clause or sentence in Latin by way of
introduction, and begin with the Old English word
Aerest.

Those Old English boundary clauses which are
to be found at the end of a document would be particularly easy to add later, and so all of these,
fifteen of them, must be suspect.(39) Interestingly,
this also elminates all save four(40) of those documents in which the Old English survey is introduced
by this synt tha land gemaeru. Of these four, one
is incomplete in that it lacks witnesses and so the
boundary survey could easily be a later addition.
(41) Two(42) belong to a small group in which there
is both a Latin and an Old English introduction to
the boundary survey.(43) Even in documents in which
prolixity is the rule rather than the exception, to
say the same thing twice, even if it is in two different languages, must in itself arouse suspicion.
In the fourth, BCS. 525, whatever its relationship
with BCS. 526,(44) the bounds as they stand cannot
have descended unaltered from the last half of the
ninth century. It would therefore seem that boundary surveys introduced by this synt tha land

gemaeru are unlikely in their present form to date
from before the beginning of the tenth century.
This is not to suggest, however, either that the
boundaries themselves did not exist or that there
was no written survey of them before that time. It
is merely to suggest that they did not reach their
present form before the beginning of the tenth century, with the corollary that it may be misleading
to project back much further than the middle years
of the ninth century any view of the Anglo-Saxon
landscape that may emerge from the study of such
documents.

The argument so far has also succeeded in elim-
inating from the 31 charters with Old English bounds
in Table 6 all save two from before 833. The first
of these is BCS 346, a Kentish charter with the
bounds in West Saxon, something very unusual for its
date of 814. The second is BCS.1331, relating to
Crediton, in Devonshire. This appears to be a post-
Conquest copy of what is probably an authentic document, but with the bounds, which also survive in an
independent document of the tenth century, (BCS.
1332), interpolated.(45)

If we now look at the documents included in
Tables 5 and 6 together then certain very interesting conclusions emerge. The earliest boundary
surveys are simple, short, in Latin and to be found
in the text of the document. They make frequent
use of obvious, prominent boundary marks - woods,
hills, roads, streams and valleys. They usually
give a directional bearing. They are almost always
introduced by a Latin clause or sentence in which
the commonest word for boundary is terminus. Other
words, confinium and limes, are used only very rarely indeed. The influence of their late Roman exam-
plars is obvious. There is however no slavish copy-
ing of these exemplars, and it is clear from the
wording of those surveys that survive from the early
years of the eighth century that they are describing
genuine boundaries and that as a consequence their
phrasing is being adapted to meet individual, local
conditions. It is from these years too that the
earliest boundary surveys survive that can with some
certainty be identified with ancient parish boundaries. The oldest parish boundary survey seems to
be that for Woodchester, in Gloucestershire, dating
716 x 745, in BCS. 164.

Although comparatively simple and short boundary surveys continue to be found into the last
quarter of the ninth century, the middle years of
the eighth century seem to be marked by a distinct

272

change in practice. This change seems to take place
in Wessex and to be signalled by two charters of
Cynewulf. The first is a grant of lands in Somerset
to the minster in Wells,(46) dating somewhere between 766 and 774. It has a lengthy perambulation,
in Latin, although the actual boundary points themselves are in Old English, and there appears to be
only one attempt to give a Latin translation, when
one sector runs in viam publicam usque sambucin
quam vocitant Ellentrow. The second is a grant of
lands at Little Bedwyn, Wiltshire, made in 778.
Again there is a lengthy perambulation in Latin,
with the boundary points themselves in Old English.
Unfortunately part of the document is illegible,
including the phrases that introduce the bounds, but
the directions, east, south and west, are quite
clear.(47)

The next lengthy survey appears to be BCS. 282,
relating to lands at Crux Easton, in Hampshire, and
probably to be dated to about 801. At about this
time the use of a phrase such as cum antiquis term-
inibus to describe an estate but giving no further
details of its bounds seems to come to an end. The
last time this phrase is used on its own would
appear to be in BCS. 343, of 814.

The next document with a long boundary survey
would appear to be that relating to lands at Wolland, in Dorset, dating from 833.(48) This survey
is entirely in Old English, although it is possible
that it is later than the ninth century. It is
followed by the South Hams charter of 847,(49) and
one entirely in Old English concerning lands at
Wotton Underwood, in Buckinghamshire.(50) By the
time king Aethelberht comes to grant land at Dinton,
in Wiltshire, to his minister Osmund in 860,(51) the
practice of using Old English bounds seems to be
well-established, being found not only in royal documents but also in a lease made by Ealhhun, bishop
of Worcester, of lands in Worcestershire and Warwickshire in 849,(52) making a group of Kentish
charters to be dated between 839 and 859,(53) in
which brief Latin bounds continue to be used, look
slightly old-fashioned. Only with a charter of 862
is the practice of using Old English bounds introduced into Kent, and even then the preliminary
phrases are still in Latin.(54)

We may perhaps summarise the discussion so far.
Boundary surveys were introduced into Anglo-Saxon
England with the use of written documents, either
with St. Augustine in 597 or else in 669, when
Theodore of Tarsus arrived in England to become

273

archbishop of Canterbury. The first surveys were
modelled on those to be found as a matter of course
in late Roman private deeds, and hence on Roman
surveying practice, but they were quite quickly
adapted to English curcumstances. The first really
lengthy ones date from the reign of Cynewulf, king
of Wessex between 757 and 786, and the first unob-
jectionable one wholly in Old English dates from
833. From this time on Old English is widely and
rapidly adopted, so that by the end of the ninth
century the use of Latin has all but disappeared.

A close examination of the surviving documents
reveals that there are only 29 boundary surveys that
survive in contemporary authentic copies from before
899, with a further 31 represented by later but
acceptable copies. We can look at two hundred years
of landscape history through no more than 60 documents, and 32 of these relate to Kent. The others
are scattered over 14 other counties of southern
England from Devon and Worcestershire to Middlesex
and Surrey.

These faint pinpoints of light in the darkness
that veils the early Anglo-Saxon landscape reveal
one thing with quite startling clarity, and that is
that boundaries themselves were a normal, accepted
feature of the landscape. In other words Anglo-
Saxon England by the end of the seventh century was
divided up and parcelled out into blocks of land
that for want of a better word may be called estates
and, if such phrases as hunc agrum intra terminos ab
antiquis possessoribus constitutos mean anything at
all, it had been so divided for a very long time.

It is equally clear that these territorial
units varied enormously in size and contained their
own internal subdivisions, so that it is possible
to speak of a hierarchy of such units. Thus in 780
Offa, king of the Mercians, gave an estate of 35
tributarii in the province of the Hwicce.(55) The
estate itself was divided into four separate
villulas, these containing in their turn five
manentes, 10 cassati, 10 mansiones and finally another ten manentes. Whether there was any significant difference between manentes, cassatos and
mensiones is a nice point to which at present there
can be no certain answer. The complexity of the
territorial organisation cannot however be in doubt.

A similar hierarchy becomes apparent in a grant
of 761(56) in which Eadbert, king of Kent, gave to
St. Peter's abbey in Canterbury terram aratrorum
sex in australi parte vici antiqui qui appelatur
Mundelingeham. The boundaries were not however

written out because they were known to the inhabitants sine dubitationis scrupulo. An aratrum, a
ploughland, may perhaps have been a basic territorial unit, and larger estates may have been built up
of two or more ploughlands. But this unit could itself be subdivided. Thus in 732 Aethelberht, king
of Kent, granted away quarta pars aratri unius, and
another grant made in 778 comprised half a ploughland. (57)

If, as seems likely, territorial divisions and
subdivisions were well-established long before documents survive to bear witness to their existence,
and these boundaries were sufficiently well-known
to the local inhabitants not to need to be written
out, then the development of increasingly detailed
boundary perambulations calls for some explanation.
It seems most likely that one explanation is to be
found in the further subdivisions of existing territorial units, and another explanation in their regrouping. Thus if one ploughland had its own boundaries and was a recognisable unit, then if three or
four ploughlands were granted away from a large
estate then a new territorial unit could emerge that
would develop a life of its own and call for the
perambulation of its boundaries. We may perhaps see
this taking palce in BCS. 213, a grant dated 774
made by king Offa of aliquam partem terrae in loco
qui dicitur Hehham. This piece of land contained by
estimation five ploughlands. Its boundaries were
then set out, including sic per viam quae ducit ad
eohinga burh in terram sancti Andreae, in which
perhaps we may see the adoption of a Roman road as
a boundary mark, something which is a noticeable
feature of many parish boundaries. The boundary
then goes on per confinia mersc tunes, by the bounds
of mersc tun. This perambulation has every appearance of being a combination of new and old bounds,
especially if we may take confinia as perhaps still
retaining at least something of its original meaning
of common bounds.

Does this evidence of a complex hierarchy of
territorial units contribute to the debate on the
antiquity of such boundaries?(58) Probably only in
a general sense in that it draws attention to the
complexity of such territorial units even as the
first documents appear, with the implication that
such complexity is unlikely to have been of recent
development.

In some fourteen documents(59) including one of
929 (BCS. 666) the word vicus is used as the name
for the territorial unit, although in one document

it appears only as an endorsement.(BCS. 97) This
was the name given to the lowest unit of administration in Roman Britain. The word itself was adopted
into Old English as wīc, and in due course it acquired a variety of meanings, including 'dairy farm'
and 'centre for the production of salt'. It has
been suggested that in the earliest period of the
English settlement it may have been used by the
English to refer to existing Romano-British settlements or administrative units, more especially when
used in the compound wīchām.(60) It would therefore
appear to be not unreasonable to suggest that vicus
in these fifteen documents may reflect some atten-
uated memory of Romano-British settlements or administrative units in the eighth century. A word of
caution is however necessary. Ten of the documents
in which vicus is used are preserved in copies in
one monastic cartulary (BL. Cotton Tiberius A.xiii)
and an eleventh is a nearly contemporary copy at
Worcester. The use of vicus may therefore reflect
nothing more than scribal practice at Worcester.
Nevertheless two other documents from the fifteen
relate to land in Kent. One, (BCS. 190, of 761),
already quoted, refers to 'the ancient vicus which
is called Mundelingeham'. The second (BCS. 248 of
786), surviving in a nearly contemporary copy,
refers to 'the vicus which is called Currington in
the city which is called Canterbury'. In these two
instances certainly, further investigation may well
produce a balance of probabilities in favour of some
kind of continuity of territorial units from Roman
Britain.

    The actual boundary surveys in these early docu-
ments are often too concise for us to be able to
identify exactly the land in question, and in any
case it is clear that they frequently concern territorial units which have long been dismembered or
absorbed into others. It seems likely for example
that the estate at Brent, in Somerset, granted at
the end of the seventh century to Glastonbury and
bounded by the Severn, the Axe, the Termic, which is
probably the Tarnock and the Siger, for which no
identification can be offered, comprised the block
of land now made up of the parishes of Lympsham,
Brean, Berrow and Burnham, as well as Brent Knoll and
East Brent.(61) In this respect that survey relating to Woodchester in Gloucestershire and already
mentioned is of particular interest in that it would
appear that it is the earliest survey for which it
is now possible to identify fairly precisely the
area of land involved.(62)

The one feature of the landscape that comes through most clearly from these early boundary surveys is the existence of boundaries themselves. They are mentioned in the earliest documents in so matter-of-fact a manner as to suggest that their existence was accepted as normal, so that references to them gave no cause for comment, with the further implication that, although some areas, such as woods, heaths and marshes, where the intensity of land use may have been low, were exploited in common, there was no part of England which was not in a clearly defined territorial unit.

Other features of the landscape find only scattered and isolated references in these earliest documents. There are several hints to suggest that woods and marshes were being exploited. Woods were being used as sources of timber for fuel. Their boundaries were known, and there is in 839 a reference to a common wood. The detached swine pastures of the Weald were in existence by 788 (BCS. 253). Among the appurtenances granted in the charters there is a mention of hunting rights in BCS. 260 of 765-785, after which it is quite commonly mentioned, together with fishing and fowling rights. Salt boiling was being practised at Lyminge by 732 (BCS. 148) and there was a watermill near Chart Sutton in Kent, in 814 (BCS. 343). The market place in Canterbury is mentioned in 762. These however are but disjecta membra from which it is impossible to construct any coherent spatial pattern or to suggest any chronology of change or development.

We have been concerned so far first of all to establish a chronology, within broad terms, for Anglo-Saxon charter boundary surveys, and secondly to look a little more closely at those which certainly date from before 899. The great majority of surveys from before this date are brief and in Latin. However we have seen two important changes take place in their form and structure. First of all, from the middle years of the eighth century they become increasingly lengthy. Secondly, by the middle years of the ninth century the use of Old English instead of Latin has become established practice. There was a long period of transition rather than a clean break, and 899, apart from being the year of the death of king Alfred, has little real significance in the evolution of the boundary survey save that it is probably true to say that by this time the transition from the old form to the new had been fully completed.

By the middle years of the ninth century the

detailed boundary survey in Old English seems to
have become an established feature of Anglo-Saxon
administrative machinery, and there is evidence to
suggest that it was compiled after a careful walking, or riding, of the bounds themselves. It is
very likely that many were drawn up for purposes
unrelated to the transfer of land. They certainly
lie at the beginning of a very long tradition, since
boundary surveys continue to be compiled for a wide
range of purposes concerned with the management of
landed estates generally until well into the nineteenth century, and the annual beating of the
bounds at Rogationtide continues in some parishes
down to the present day. The likelihood that boundary surveys were drawn up for purposes other than
inclusion in a diploma is strengthened if we remember that written documents were not strictly necessary for the transfer of land. They were merely
evidentiary.(63) Some symbolic act indicating transfer was much more important. Indeed it is not
until the Statute of Frauds of 1677 that written
evidence becomes essential for the transfer of land.
     Even if one adopts a liberal attitude towards
those suspicious or spurious documents that claim
to date from before 899,(64) there are still less
than a hundred boundary surveys from before the
tenth century, and the great majority are in the old
form, brief and in Latin. This means that there are
about 700 fully developed, detailed, Old English
boundary surveys, almost all of them from the tenth
and eleventh centuries. This has several important
implications. First of all, the landscape that
emerges from a study of these documents is essentially that of these two centuries. Secondly, the
search for Roman material of whatever kind, either
to support a suggested reconstruction or else to
provide evidence of continuity from Roman Britain
to Anglo-Saxon England, is a work of supererogation,
and this on two counts: first of all the explosion
in archaeological knowledge over the past twenty
years has made it abundantly clear that Romano-
British occupation sites were to be found everywhere,
and that the English could not have avoided them
even if they had wished to do so: secondly it fails
to take account of the passage of some five hundred
years of change, growth and movement, and some of
the changes during this very long period of time
were undoubtedly significant and far-reaching,
those brought about by the Viking invasions for
example.
     It is the identification on the ground of the

boundaries described in these detailed Old English
surveys that has exercised the skill, learning and
ingenuity of antiquaries and topographers. Their
solution calls for much patient searching of old
maps and documents, something which generates its
own excitement, whilst success brings a sense of
achievement that is its own reward.

The two centuries of scholarship which have
been lavished on the solution of these boundary surveys means that there is now much accumulated experience on the best methods and approaches to employ
when attempting what on the face of it would seem to
be the impossible task of identifying on the ground
in the late twentieth century an estate described in
a thousand-year old document.(65) It is first of
all important to establish an accurate text. Those
that appear in Birch's Cartularium Saxonicum are
usually quite reliable but those in Kemble's Codex
Diplomaticus are often inaccurate and misleading,
and they need to be checked against surviving manuscripts. The publication of Professor Sawyer's
bibliography in 1968, in which all important manuscripts are listed, means that this is now a comparatively easy task, although it can be expensive
in time and in travelling costs if there are a large
number to be checked in this way.

The text must then be translated into modern
English. This translation is important since for
the modern reader it can re-create vividly a little,
hard facet of a remote landscape, as when the boundary survey of Christian Malford, in Wiltshire, begins at cristemalforde, or the ford by a crucifix,
thus bringing the verisimilitude of a concrete example to the vague generalisation that it was common
practice to mark boundaries by means of crosses.
Similarly, the befer ige, or beaver island, of
Brimpton, in Berkshire, recalls a wild animal that
has long disappeared from English streams and pools.
(66)

Old English is a remarkably subtle and complex
language, with its own history of change and development, and a number of local and regional dialects.
This means that a comparatively simple-looking word
such as aecer can have a variety of meanings, and
only the most careful scrutiny of each word in its
context can reveal what particular meaning should be
attached to it in a given text. Thus aecer can mean
both a plot of arable land and a measure of land,
not only arable but also meadow and woodland. It is
also clear that in many boundary surveys it is referring to the pre-enclosure strip of land in the

open fields, and this is something which could vary
considerably in area. Evidence of this kind is of
the first importance if there is to be any real
progress in one of the most vexed areas of English
historiography, namely the origins of the open
field system in this country.(67) Evidence from
charters as a whole has been examined, but usage in
boundary surveys may differ in important respects.
The careful and critical study of this evidence in
its own right has been attempted on a systematic
basis only for Berkshire(68) and for Warwickshire,
Worcestershire and Gloucestershire.(69) Similar
detailed studies for other counties which have large
numbers of boundary surveys, such as Somerset, Wiltshire, Dorset and Hampshire, promise to be very rewarding.

The implication of the immediately preceding
paragraphs for the historian or geographer approaching Anglo-Saxon boundary surveys for the first time
is that he should have his translation checked by
an expert in Old English. This translation, when
complete, may well assist in the reconstruction of
many features of past landscapes. It cannot however, in itself directly assist in the solution of
the boundary survey on the ground, since those
boundary marks which have survived into the present
as place-names will have been transformed by recognised processes of linguistic change. They will
not have been translated. Thus the ford by a crucifix, cristemalforde, has become Christian Malford,
and the rugan hlawe of the Chetwode-Hillesden boundary survey has become Rowley, not rough burial
mound.(70)

The establishment of an accurate text and then
its translation into modern English are but preliminaries to the location upon the ground of the
estate being described in the boundary survey.
There are now comparatively few, perhaps less than
a dozen, for which no location at all can at present
be suggested. The Upthrop of BCS. 524 for example,
together with Wudetune (BCS 969), Hamstede (BCS.
1075) and Cealuadune (BCS. 1198), cannot be identified, but they are quite exceptional, whilst the
Madanlieg of BCS.1312, which could not be identified
in 1968, is now known to be Madeley in Staffs.(71)
There are however others for which the identification is still controversial or uncertain. The Cern
of BCS. 1035 probably relates to an estate in Berkshire, and the Gamelanwyrthe of BCS. 813 lies in
Kent, probably near Folkestone, but neither can as
yet be more certainly located. Reasons for the

disappearance of these estates and their names are
obvious. We have seen already that one of the
purposes for the compilation of boundary surveys in
the first place may have been the need to record
the subdivision of an estate, something which may
lead to the disappearance of an old name and the
emergence of new ones. This occurred at Aescesbyrig,
in Berkshire. A narrow strip of land was detached
from this estate in 856, and was acquired in 944 by
the thegn Wulfric. He was given an adjacent strip,
also taken from Aescesbyrig, in 958. These two
pieces of land when amalgamated became known as
Woolstone, Wulfric's estate. The remaining third
of Aescesbyrig in due course was renamed Uffa's
estate, or Uffington, and the name Aescesbyrig then
dropped out of use.(72) This example also serves to
illustrate a further reason for the loss of estate
names, namely the practice of changing the name of
an estate when it came into the hands of a new lord.
This can also be illustrated from the history of an
estate in Kent. In 788 an estate called Duningcland
in the regio of Eastry was granted to the thegn
Osberht. In 824-30 another grant of land in the
Eastry district records that Osberhting lond lay on
its southern boundary. It seems very likely that
Osberht gave his name to his estate, and in turn his
name has also been superseded, since Osberhting lond
cannot now be identified.(73) Yet other names have
been lost for reasons which cannot now be established. Readanora became Pyrton, in Oxfordshire, some
time between 887 and 987, Sherborne was once Lan-
probi, and Evesham was formerly Cronuchomme.(74)
Indeed, what is so astonishing is not so much the
fact that a small number of estates covered by
Anglo-Saxon boundary surveys remain unidentified,
and probably unidentifiable, but rather that, coming
as they do from a long period of considerable insta-
bility and change in place-names generally, so many
can still be identified and worked out on the ground
today, a thousand years later.
 Once the general location of an estate has been
established then work on the location of individual
boundary points can begin. The actual points themselves are either fixed points, such as a tree, a
stump, a stone or some similar, isolated object, or
else they are a linear feature, a stream, a road, a
hedge or the boundary of an adjoining estate. The
boundary of Monks Risborough, in Buckinghamshire,
described in a survey of 903.(75) makes use of both
of these kinds of boundary features, linear: the
black hedge and roe deer hedge, Eadric's boundary

and the boundary of the people of Kimble, and fixed
points: ash tree on the river bank, heathen burials
and hay clearing. Clear and unequivocal evidence is
needed before the identification of these boundary
marks can be said to be certain, and this will be a
combination of toponymic and topographical evidence.
The actual name itself must survive in a form which
can be accepted. It will be a transformation, not
a translation. Thus the hay clearing of Monks
Risborough, heg leage, survives as Green Hailey.
Secondly the point must be identifiable on the
ground, and this means that it must be recorded on a
map or else in local oral tradition as being attached to a particular feature, perhaps a field name or
the name of a lane.

The search for toponymic evidence means combing
documents of every kind for developing and changing
forms of the name. Although post-medieval documents
such as glebe terriers cannot be ignored it is early
medieval ones which are of particular importance.
Deeds, rentals, surveys, extents, court rolls, taxation records, the entire repertoire, both national
and local, needs to be searched, something which it
is impossible to do thoroughly for each boundary
point of each boundary survey, not least because it
is after all a boundary point that is being sought,
which means that it may occur in documents relating
to neighbouring estates, vastly increasing the bulk
of the documents which ought to be searched. Even
if an exhaustive search is rewarded with a collection of place-name forms they still remain to be
identified topographically. This can only be done
from maps, which do not survive in any numbers from
before the last decades of the sixteenth century.
It is most important that the student who is attempting to relate an Anglo-Saxon boundary survey to a
parish boundary should use a map of the parish that
is as old as possible. In this context the Ordnance
Survey maps can be dangerously misleading, since
they are concerned to record only contemporary civil
parish boundaries, and these, by the end of the
nineteenth century, can differ considerably from
ancient ecclesiastical parish boundaries. Eighteenth and early nineteenth century county maps are
the best source for ancient parish boundaries, but
even these are not always entirely reliable. Unfortunately the maps which accompany volumes of the
English Place-Name Society are based upon contemporary Ordnance Survey maps and not upon early maps.
This makes them unsuitable for even simple exercises
such as the study of the relationship of adjacent or

neighbouring boundary surveys.

Pre-enclosure estate maps can be especially rewarding. It was for example from a series of mid-eighteenth century estate maps that several points in a boundary survey of <u>Bedintun</u>, now Pillaton, in Staffordshire, were identified.(76) Post-enclosure maps are generally less useful, since it was one of the minor calamities of Parliamentary enclosure that old field and furlong names were swept into oblivion by the enclosure commissioners and replaced by modern, more prosaic ones, although it must be said that it is from the enclosure map that the worth of the Barrow upon Humber boundary survey has been identified.(77) It should also be remembered that Parliamentary enclosure commissioners had the power, which occasionally they exercised, to change parish boundaries, and such changes may be recorded only in the Enclosure Award.

Tithe maps are particularly important since they record the boundaries of parishes, tithings and townships before the extensive boundary changes of the nineteenth century really got under way. These boundaries often have a very long history but appear on tithe maps for the first, and all too frequently for the last, time. Thus the 1840 tithe map of the parish of Merstham, in Surrey, shows a parish twice as large as that of today, and it is this ancient parish which is surveyed in a charter of 947.(78) Similarly it is from the tithe map that the ancient parish boundary of Minster in Thanet has been reconstructed. Since the date of this map only a short section of the boundary has remained unchanged. The ancient boundary is recorded in a map of 1410-1411, and if the identification of <u>Uuestanae</u> of BCS. 45 as the western half of the Isle of Thanet is indeed correct, then this ancient boundary of Minster, which lies in the eastern half of Thanet, may well be the notissimos terminos of that grant, and hence the earliest parish boundary of which there is record.(79)

In spite of the hazards of a thousand years of accelerating change a surprising number of boundary features can still be positively identified in the landscape today. It must be one of the landscape historian's greatest pleasures when, after months of unrewarded search, a name stares up at him from some eighteenth century estate map or nineteenth century tithe map in a form which has scarcely changed for a millenium. Its location upon the ground is then a comparatively simple matter. The accompanying sense of achievement can be fully appreciated only by those who have themselves made a similar journey.

Even with the most diligent search, however, it is unlikely that all the boundary points in any one survey will be firmly identified on both toponymic and topographical grounds. Indeed for a number of proposed solutions there are no firm identifications of this kind at all, and if is added to this the impossibility of locating the estate at all precisely, perhaps because it has a common name, such as Aston, then any solution must be conjectural, and remain so until further evidence comes to light. (80) For those points for which there is no toponymic evidence then it is necessary to fall back upon purely topographical evidence, the presence of a stream at a suitable point, or a bend in a parish boundary which could conceivably have been marked by a boundary stone. Evidence of this kind, however plausible, must always remain less than satisfactory.

When a boundary survey has finally been worked out it should of course be mapped. It is one of the weaknesses of the work of one of the great pioneers in the study of Anglo-Saxon boundary surveys, G.B. Grundy, that he failed to present his conclusions cartographically, and his published solutions cry out for maps.(81) Fortunately more recent work has recognised the importance of maps for the presentation of the results of research and they are now included in published work almost as a matter of course.(82) Whether, once a solution has been mapped, it is then worth walking round a boundary is a nice question to which there can be no firm answer. Certainly older scholars have insisted upon the importance of walking the bounds, and as many times as possible,(83) and such walking can on occasion be rewarded with the discovery of boundary marks, such as banks and ditches, still present in the landscape today.(84) More recently doubts have been cast upon the value of this. 'Perambulation of charter boundaries is always illuminating to the person who undertakes it, but it is not certain that it contributes to the solution of problems proportionately to the time and energy, and in recent years the expense, which it involves'.(85)

The solution of boundary permabulations has until quite recently been very much an end in itself. It is as if the effort to solve them has exhausted the inventiveness of the historian,(86) and many solutions have been published almost naked of comment. They have, of course, more especially in conjunction with their associated charters, long been

quarries for historians of specialised aspects of
Anglo-Saxon England,(87) but it is only quite recently that attempts have been made to exploit systematically and on a large scale the mass of detail
concerning the landscape of Anglo-Saxon England that
is contained in these eight hundred or so boundary
perambulations.(88)   There are however very real
problems.

    First of all, we must not expect too much of
boundary perambulations. They are essentially
linear, (see Fig.55) and so we cannot look for any
areal survey or spatial description. This applies
equally as well to the immensely, and hence decept-
ively, detailed tenth century surveys as it does to
the simple, laconic five or six word surveys from
the end of the seventh. It is a boundary that is
being described and it is the very existence of
these boundaries that is the single most important
contribution that these documents can make to our
understanding of the Anglo-Saxon landscape. The
very earliest documents reveal an ordered, regulated,
landscape, one in which boundaries are almost taken
for granted. When, in very early surveys, boundary
points are actually mentioned, we must probably
think of them as boundary sectors rather than points,
with the distinguishing feature which is named re-
presenting the name of an estate. Thus, when in
788 king Offa granted land at Trottiscliffe, Kent,
to St. Andrew's, Rochester, the boundary survey
names only three points: <u>Boerlingas</u>, <u>Uurotaham</u> and
<u>Meapaham</u>, to be identified as Birling, Wrotham and
Meopham. These three points must be seen as existing estates with their own fixed boundaries. It
was sufficient merely to name them for the extent
of the estate being granted to be known. The same
remarks apply when the boundary point named is a
topographical feature. Thus two charters of the
end of the eighth and the beginning of the ninth
centuries (BCS. 203, 357), for lands in Worcestershire use the Salwarpe as a boundary mark, and yet
Salwarpe by the same date was also an estate with
its own boundaries (BCS. 360, 362). This is not to
imply that <u>all</u> topographical features are invariably
to be interpreted as the names of estates, even in
the earliest surveys, but merely to suggest that
many of the topographical features that do occur in
the earliest perambulations should be seen in this
way.

    Secondly, these documents reveal, not only that
the landscape is regulated, but also that it was
divided up into a complex hierarchy of administra-

tive units, many of which have now been lost. It is
often now almost impossible to recover the exact
boundaries of many of the estates covered in these
surveys, and the older the survey the less chance
there is of being able to do this. We have perhaps
been too pre-occupied with parish boundaries and
the fact that so many tenth century surveys fit
very closely ancient parish boundaries that can be
walked today, to appreciate fully the astonishing
variety of territorial units revealed in these documents and the equally astonishing extent to which
they could be, and were, changed during the course
of the Anglo-Saxon centuries. The estates which
eventually became parishes were in many cases the
result of the late subdivision or regrouping of very
much older territorial units.

Thirdly, the essentially linear nature of the
bounds can be subtly misleading. It is possible for
one boundary sector to take up many miles of a total
boundary, only to be followed by several boundary
points in quick succession. The black hedge of the
Monks Risborough boundary survey, for example,
covers more than three miles, and the boundary of
the people of Kimble almost as much.(89) There is
nothing at all to indicate what topographical features, man-made or natural, lay along these lengths
of boundary. To argue from silence is extremely
dangerous: whether it is to suggest that long boundaries of this kind were passing through featureless
or thinly exploited areas, or else through districts
void of settlement. After all, the boundaries of
the two Woolstone estates in Berkshire appear to
have passed right through the middle of what is now
Woolstone village without making any mention of it.
(90) Only when two boundary surveys of approximately the same date are found to describe a common
boundary can what is fundamentally a line start to
take on any depth, and even then, as the Woolstone
example, shows there can be no certainty that important features have not been omitted, either by
chance or by design.

The essentially linear nature of boundary surveys has a further corollary. It means that too
much significance should not be attached to distribution maps plotting features named in boundary surveys. Certainly such maps are very interesting for
the detail that they reveal about the Anglo-Saxon
landscape, but such detail is arbitrarily selected
and upon a lineal dimension. The items used in a
boundary survey must of necessity form a unknown but
very probably a small proportion of the total popula-

tion of such items within the area whose boundaries
are being delineated. That some items are mentioned
is in itself of the greatest interest. That others
are not in itself proves nothing. When all the
texts have been published accurately, when all the
boundary points have been identified and their meanings fully explained, and when all this information
has been computerised, it may then be possible to
detect if there is any statistical significance in
the frequency with which trees, ditches or stones
are used as boundary marks, but even when this has
been done it will still not tell us what lay between
and beyond these points.

Distribution maps have another weakness. They
lack a chronological dimension. Boundary surveys
do have a chronology of their own, as earlier paragraphs in this Chapter have been at pains to show.
To plot every item from every boundary survey without further comment on the probable date of the survey, even within broad limits, is to fudge the likelihood of being able to detect change within the
Anglo-Saxon landscape, and it is one of the themes
underlying all the Chapters of this book that change
in the landscape is a continuing process, even
though its pace may vary over time and space.

The mapping of two boundary surveys from Wiltshire may serve to illustrate in detail the problems
surrounding the interpretation of these documents
outlined in general terms in the preceding paragraphs. (Fig.56) The first is for Christian Malford. In 940 king Edmund granted to Dunstan, then
abbot of Glastonbury, twenty mansae At Cristemalford
juxta derivativis fluencium successibus Be Afene,
in a quite unexceptionable charter (BCS. 752), which
contains a lengthy and detailed boundary clause.
The charter and its boundary survey survive in two
fourteenth century cartularies for the abbey (91)
and by the time the document reached the cartulary
the survey had been 'modernised' to a certain extent
so that as it stands it is post-Conquest rather than
Anglo-Saxon. Nevertheless there is no reason to
believe that it is not based upon a survey contemporary, or almost contemporary, with the charter.
The survey is as follows, the numbers referring to
the points on the map:

1. Erest on Christemalford first to the ford by a
                             cross

2. endlang Afne   along Avon

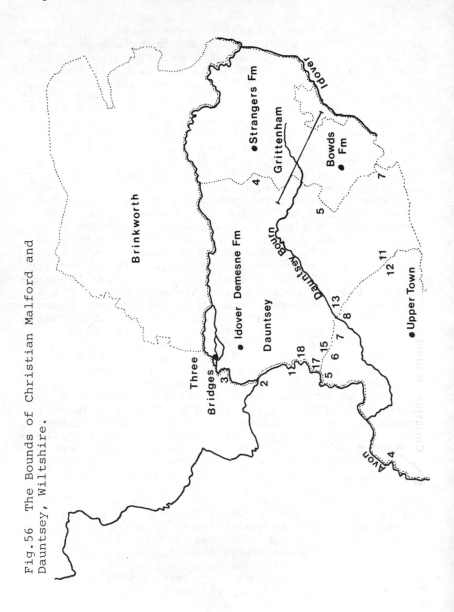

Fig.56 The Bounds of Christian Malford and Dauntsey, Wiltshire.

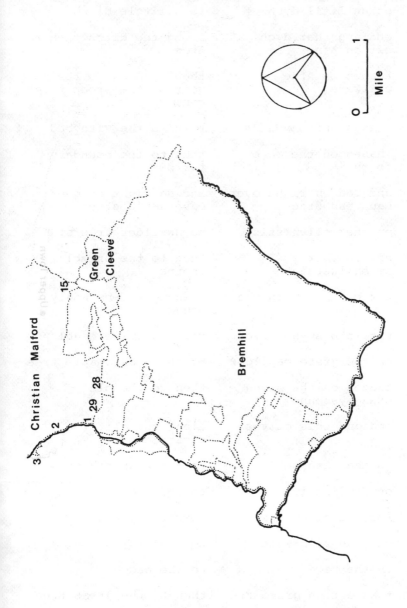

3.	on an litil dych	to a little ditch
4.	endlang thar dych eft on Afne	along the ditch then to Avon
5.	thanen by Afne on clifwere	then by Avon to the weir by the steep river bank
6.	thanen on the wythibed	then to the withybed
7.	thanen on the mere fourh	then to the boundary furrow
8.	and soa on right over Dauntesbourne	and so right on over Dauntsey's stream
9.	on ther ellenistib	to the elder tree stub
10.	eft on ther brimbilwernan	then to the bramble thorns
11.	eft on ther merhawyn	then to the boundary hedges
12.	eft into swynesheved	then to swine headland
13.	on the grete mapildor	to the great maple tree
14.	thanen on tha olden oden myssenne	then to the old ?
15.	endland this clives	along the cliff/ escarpment
16.	on then henash	to the high ash tree
17.	on Hoddisclive	to Hod's cliff
18.	foryerd bi wyrtwalen	forward by edge ?
19.	on sand riddryate	to sand ?
20.	on the hege	to the hedge
21.	thar eft on grete tre	then to the great tree
22.	endlangis hawyn	along the hedge
23.	on the elde strete	to the old street

24.	eft on teonescanen southwerd	then to the south side of thieves' shaw
25.	thanne endlanges thar brodefurtigh	then along the broad furrow
26.	on the hegeberghes	to the hedge barrow/ burial mound
27.	in on the toun northward	in to the north of the farm
28.	endlangthar forerthe	along the projecting piece of ploughland
29.	be thar akerheved	by the acre headland
30.	thar eft on Criste malford	then to the cross by the ford.

The second boundary survey to be considered is that for Dauntsey, the parish immediately to the north of Christian Malford. The survey is undated. It occurs in the Malmesbury abbey cartulary, which dates from the end of the thirteenth century. Like the other boundary surveys in this cartulary it is in Latin. A document, (BCS. 457) possibly based upon authentic materials, records the grant in 850 of ten mansiones to Malmesbury, and the abbey held ten hides in Dauntsey in Domesday Book. It is very likely that the survey relates to this estate, although as it stands it cannot be contemporary with the charter of 850 and is instead most likely to be a late twelfth century redaction of a tenth century Old English text. The survey is as follows:

1.	primo a loco qui vocatur Dameteseye	first from the place which is called Dom-geat's island (92)
2.	directe per Auene	directly by Avon
3.	usque Woddebrigge	as far as wood bridge
4.	et ab eodem loco usque strengesburieles	and from that place as far as Strenges burials place

5. et ab eodem loco directe per fossatum quod appellatur holdedyche usque Budezet

and from that place directly by the ditch which is called oled ditch as far as Bude's gate

6. et ab eodem loco usque ad locum quod appellatur hetheneburieles

and from that place to the place which is called heathen burial

7. et ab eodem loco usque ad Grutehames suth hele

and from that place as far as Grittenham south corner

8. et ab eodem usque ad quoddam lignum quod appellatur Grete trewe

and from there as far as a certain tree called Great Tree

9. et sic ultra clytescombe usque le Staneclyf

and thus over Clytescombe as far as the stone cliff/escarpment

10. et ab eodem loco directe per quendam locum qui appellatur le Egge usque ad locum qui dicitur Scufanborwe

and from that place directly by a certain place which is called the Edge to a place which is called Scufa's burial mound

11. et ab eodem loco usque ad fontem qui appellature Swyneswelle

and from that place as far as the spring which is called swine's well

12. et ab eodem fonte usque hayeleyezate

and from that spring as far as hay clearing gate

13. et ab eodem loco directe in Dameteseye bornebuye

and from that place directly to Dauntsey bourn bend

14. et ab eodem loco usque le Rigweye videlicet super le hetheneburieles

and from that place as far as the ridgeway that is to say above the heathen burials

15. et ab eodem loco usque ad le Wythybed videlicet ad eundem locum qui appellatur

and from that place as far as the withybed that is to say at the same place which is

heuedakerhende	called acreheadland end
16. et sic ab eodem loco usque le apeldorestob	and so from that place as far as the apple tree stub
17. et ab eodem loco usque Auene videlicet ad locum qui dicitur le Syche	and from that place as far as Avon that is to say at the place which is called the sike
18. et ab eodem loco directe per Auene circa locum primo nominatum videlicet Dameteseye	and from that place directly by Avon round to the place first named that is to say Domgeat's island

This survey then goes on to give the bounds of the meadow that belongs to Dauntsey. They are as follows:

1. primo a quodam loco qui vocatur torre qui jacet in parte occidentali ejusdem prati	first from the place which is called torre (stone) which lies in the western part of the meadow
2. usque ad spinam que appellatur Haythorne a midewarde	as far as the middle of the thornbush which is called Haythorn
3. et ab eadem spina usque ad rivulum qui dicitur ydouere vide-licet contra le holde garanne	and from the same thorn-bush as far as the river which is called Idover that is to say opposite the old gore
4. et sic directe per ydouere usque le Blakepole	and thus directly by Idover as far as the black pool
5. et ab eodem loco usque ad quandam petram recte contra le ellerne	and from that place as far as a certain stone right opposite the elder tree
6. et sic ab eadem petra directe per viam usque ad locum primo nominatum videlicet	and thus from the same stone directly by the road as far as the first named place that

la torre   is to say the torre (stone)

To these two surveys should be added three more, although there is no space here to consider them in detail. To the south of Christian Malford lies Bremhill (BCS. 717) again a 'modernised' Latin survey from the Malmesbury cartulary, whilst to the north of Dauntsey lie Brinkworth (S.1576) and Grittenham (S.1583), again both 'modernised' Latin surveys in the Malmesbury cartulary. Grittenham is now only a township in the parish of Brinkworth.

The survey of Christian Malford begins in the southwestern corner of the estate at a point which must once literally have been a ford over the Avon distinguished by a crucifix. The same boundary point also occurs in the Bremhill perambulation. The boundary then goes north along the Avon, turns into a ditch or side channel, rejoins the Avon and then follows it until it comes to a weir by a steep river bank. The location of this weir is uncertain but it is likely to have been at the point where the boundary leaves the Avon because the next point, the withybed, is also noted in the Dauntsey boundary before it reaches the Avon. The Christian Malford boundary then follows a boundary furrow, crosses the Dauntsey bourn, also mentioned in the Dauntsey survey, and, passing by an elder tree, bramble thorns and boundary hedges, reaches a swine headland, which may well have some relationship with the swine's well of the Dauntsey survey. Up to this point it seems very likely that the survey coincides with the ancient parish boundary. From here on however it is almost impossible to locate the exact line of the boundary recorded in the survey, and it seems very likely that the complexities of the ancient parish boundary, with no less than four detached portions, are the result of later changes, perhaps the consequence of estate management practices in use before these estates became fossilised as parishes.

There is however some correspondence with the Bremhill survey:

	15.	16.	17.	18.	19.	20.	21.
Christian Malford direction ——>	cliff	henash	Hod's cliff	wyrtwalen	sand	hedge	great tree
Bremhill <—— direction	cliff				sand seteth		great tree

The various 'cliffs' and the 'wyrtwalen' seem
to mark the line of the steep scarp of hills, rising
to 513 feet above sea level just about where the
Christan Malford and Bremhill boundaries meet, and
over-looking the Avon valley to the west. They are
perhaps recalled in the place-name Green Cleeve (see
Fig.56). The tun of point 27 could be any of the
hamlets and farms in the southern part of Christian
Malford, and there is still an Upper Town. The next
point which can be identified with some degree of
certainty is 28, the projecting piece of ploughland.
The rectangular shape of the boundary here has every
appearance of having been drawn round a furlong of
arable land. The boundary then returns to the starting point via the acre headland.
    The Dauntsey survey begins at the islet in the
Avon which has given its name to the entire estate.
From here it follows the course of the Avon to the
point where it joins the Brinkworth brook and Three
Bridges may still commemorate the wooden bridge.
The next points cannot be certainly identified but
strengesburieles may be reflected in Stranges or
Strangers Farm, and Budezet in Bowd's Farm, whilst
Grittenham south corner is probably the southernmost
point of Grittenham township. There are no points
in the Grittenham survey corresponding with any in
the Dauntsey survey. Clytescombe, Staneclyf and
the Edge reflect the northern extension of the escarpment referred to in the Christian Malford and
Bremhill surveys. The remaining length of the
Dauntsey boundary corresponds with that recorded
in the Christian Malford survey, and there are three
points, swine's well, Dauntsey bourn and the withybed which would appear to match exactly.
    The detached portion of meadowland remains to
be identified. Grundy was mistaken when he wrote
that Dauntsey parish had no detached portions.(93)
The map accompanying Akerman's edition of the text
of these surveys, published in 1857,(94) shows quite
clearly a detached portion of the parish lying to
the east (see Fig.56). He was perhaps misled by the
reference to the Idover. This stream does indeed
form part of the boundary to the meadow, but the
meadow lay much further up the stream than Grundy
thought. The Idover flows in a north-easterly direction before making a sweep to the west to flow
into the Avon. It forms the whole of the southern
boundary of Brinkworth, and is mentioned as such in
the Brinkworth survey. Its name is still preserved
in Idover Demesne Farm.
    This detached meadow land of Dauntsey is but

one of a score or more of detached portions of parishes lying in the rich meadowlands of the Avon
valley. Their survival may well reflect estate
management practices on the part of the abbeys of
Glastonbury and Malmesbury in providing meadowland
for their estates before these estates became fossilised as parishes. Such practices are hinted at
in Domesday Book, where it is recorded that the
abbot of Glastonbury had granted away six acres of
meadow in Stanton St. Quintin and four in Littleton
Drew which had once been part of Christian Malford.
Similar management practices have been suggested as
a possible explanation for the detached portions of
parishes to be found in the neighbourhood of Worcester.(95)

These two boundary surveys illustrate all the
points which have been made during the course of this
Chapter: the importance of dating the survey, the
significance of identifying the archive in which the
survey is preserved and the fact that some are not
attached to a charter at all, the difficulties of
identifying individual points on the ground and of
establishing the exact meaning of the words used,
the fact that some parts of a perambulation relate
to a length of boundary and others refer to isolated points, the importance of using old maps when
attempting to identify them, the remarkable persis-
tence in the landscape of some lengths of boundary
against which must be set the very real likelihood
of boundary change after the survey was drawn up.

They also serve to illustrate both the strengths
and the weaknesses of these surveys as records of
the Anglo-Saxon landscape. It is the existence of
boundaries themselves, and all that this implies of
a regulated, ordered landscape of interlocking estates allowing room neither for an advancing frontier
nor for an untamed wilderness, that comes through
most clearly. Apart from this they provide only
isolated, disjointed fragments of the landscape,
although they are fragments from a remote landscape
of which we would otherwise know nothing. Such
fragments are of necessity concerned only with the
boundaries or peripheries of estates. They can
therefore do no more than hint indirectly at the
landscape of the interior of the estate. Thus points
28 and 29 of the Christian Malford survey, by referring to ploughland and acre headlands, would seem
to suggest that cultivation had reached the boundary
of this particular estate at this particular point.
Absence of similar references on other boundaries
cannot however support any suggestion that cultiva-

tion had not reached the boundary elsewhere in the estate, or that it was absent from other estates. Similarly, references to streets, roads and bridges would seem to hint at a communications network, without however providing any clue as to its density. Sand pits and withybeds point to the exploitation of natural resources, as does the reference to the weir on the river Avon. These are, nonetheless, no more than references of the most oblique kind. Boundary surveys were not intended to provide systematic or areal surveys of the landscape. They tell us almost nothing, for example, of settlement patterns. The reference to the tun or farmstead in point 27 of the perambulation of Christian Malford is most unusual, and it is even more uncommon to find any reference to churches.(96) There was far more in the Anglo-Saxon landscape than ever finds mention in boundary perambulations.

It must be clear from the preceding discussion that the proper exploitation of Anglo-Saxon boundary surveys has scarcely begun, and that a great deal of preparatory work must be done before this exploitation can be attempted. First of all the publication of reliable texts has only just started and this in itself will take many years to complete. Secondly research at microscopic level will undoubtedly contribute to the solution of those boundary surveys which still have not yet been fully worked out on the ground, and will at the same time add further precision to those for which there are already acceptable solutions. Thirdly the publication of accurate texts will permit closer scrutiny of the language of the surveys and the subtle shades of meaning to be attached to each word, the importance of local and regional linguistic usage and the practice of scribes in the monastic scriptoria in which so many surveys were copied out. Much effort has gone into the study of these surveys upon a geographical basis - parish, region, county - with the result that archival influences have been largely overlooked, and this is an area in which future research may well prove very rewarding. The publication of The Dictionary of Old English and its associated microfiche concordance from the University of Toronto, based upon an entirely fresh examination of the whole corpus of Old English texts put into computer readable form and thus replacing the less than satisfactory Bosworth and Toller dictionary, now nearly a hundred and fifty years old, will be of incalculable value in every aspect of this work.(97) There is clearly employment here for several

generations of scholars still to come. It is very
unlikely however that they will be able to overcome
to any marked degree the very severe limitations
inherent in the documents themselves. Nevertheless,
in spite of these limitations, and the problems and
difficulties surrounding their interpretation, Anglo-
Saxon charter boundary surveys must always remain
documents of the first importance for the understanding of one of the most formative periods in English
history. The spell they have cast, and continue to
cast, over generations of antiquarians and topographers is perhaps understandable, since it is they
which give to a scene such as that in Fig.57 its
extraordinarily rich historical density.

ABBREVIATIONS USED IN THIS CHAPTER

BCS   W.de Gray Birch, ed., Cartularium Saxonicum,
      3 vols., 1885-1899, reprinted 1964.

K   J.M. Kemble, Codex Diplomaticus Aevi Saxonici,
      6 vols., 1839-1848.

S.   P.H. Sawyer, ed., Anglo-Saxon Charters: An
      Annotated List and Bibliography, Royal
      Historical Society, Guides and Handbooks
      No.8, 1968.

I have used Birch and Kemble numbers in preference
to those of Sawyer since these were the actual
texts that I consulted.

REFERENCES

      1. P.H. Sawyer, (ed.), Anglo-Saxon Charters:
An Annotated List and Bibliography, Royal Historical
Society, Guides and Handbooks No.8, (1968) lists
1875 documents but some others have been omitted,
see his Preface, p.vii.
      2. see N. Brooks, 'Anglo-Saxon Charters; the
work of the last twenty years', in P. Clemoes, (ed.),
Anglo-Saxon England, 3 (1974), pp.211-231.
      3. A. Campbell, (ed.), Anglo-Saxon Charters I:
Charters of Rochester (1973), and P.H. Sawyer, (ed.),
Anglo-Saxon Charters II: Charters of Burton Abbey,
(1979).
      4. see, generally, F.M. Stenton, The Latin
Charters of the Anglo-Saxon Period (1955), and
D. Whitelock, (ed.), English Historical Documents
Vol.1, c.500-1042, (2nd ed. 1979), esp. Part 2.

Fig.57 This very ordinary hedgerow, in the depths of the Buckinghamshire countryside, in fact marks the boundary between the parishes of Upper and Lower Winchendon. The boundary is described in a charter of 1004 (K 709, and see M. Reed, 'Buckinghamshire Anglo-Saxon Charter Boundaries', in M. Gelling, (ed.), The Early Charters of the Thames Valley (1979), pp.181-184) although the hedge as such is not mentioned. This photograph was taken at the point in the boundary perambulation called 'the dirty pit' (fulan pitte) looking northwest.

5. see S. Keynes, The Diplomas of Aethelred the Unready, 978-1016 (1980), and D. Hooke, Anglo-Saxon Landscapes of the West Midlands: The Charter Evidence, British Archaeological Reports, British Series, 95, (1981).
6. J.Y. Akerman, 'Some Account of the Possessions of the Abbey of Malmesbury, in North Wiltshire, in the days of the Anglo-Saxon Kings: with Remarks on the Ancient Limits of the Forest of Braden', Archaeologia, 37 (1857), p.271, and see too H.P.R. Finberg, (ed.), The Early Charters of Wessex (1964), p.11.
7. S.1486 and S.1513.
8. These figures are based upon Sawyer, Anglo-Saxon Charters, but his listing of bounds is not always entirely accurate. He does not for example mention the bounds to the Amounderness charter, (S.407), and there are not in fact bounds to his S.452. (See M. Gelling, (ed.), The Early Charters of the Thames Valley (1979), No.204).
9. e.g. BCS.1282, K.709.
10. see D. Hill, An Atlas of Anglo-Saxon England (1981), fig.35 on p.24, a map which omits the Amounderness, Lancashire, boundary and two of the six for Buckinghamshire.
11. e.g. BCS.279A-458, 500, 717, 922, 1215. S.1559 appears to date from the time of Richard I, see D. Austin and D. Hill, 'The Boundaries of Itchell and Crondall', Proceedings of the Hampshire Field Club, 27 (1970), pp.63-64.
12. BCS.788, 1093, 1217, K.1305 and possibly BCS. 1093.
13. P.H. Sawyer, 'Anglo-Saxon Settlement: the Documentary Evidence', in T. Rowley,(ed.), Anglo-Saxon Settlement and Landscape,British Archaeological Reports, 6, (1974), p.108.
14. BCS.832, 1004, 962, 1071, K.655, and see G.B. Grundy, 'The Saxon Land Charters of Wiltshire', Archaeological Journal, 76 (1919), pp.143-301.
15. see, e.g. M. Gelling, (ed.), Early Charters of the Thames Valley (1979), Nos. 260, 263, 268.
16. British Library, Cotton Claudius C.ix (10), Cotton Tiberius A.xiii (12), Additional MS.15350, (7) and Additional MS.15667, (13).
17. British Library, Additional MS.15667.
18. E. Edwards, (ed.), Liber Monasterii de Hyda, Rolls Series, (1866).
19. BCS.604.
20. P. Chaplais, 'Who Introduced Charters into England? The Case for Augustine', Journal of the Society of Archivists, 3 (October 1969), pp.526-542.

21. BCS.45, 81, 97.
22. BCS.34, 35, 36, 40, 41, 57, 67 and 73.
23. W.H. Stevenson, 'Trinoda Necessitas', English Historical Review, 29 (1914), pp.689-703.
24. O.A.W. Dilke, The Roman Land Surveyors, (1971).
25. C. Courtois, L. Leschi, C. Perrat and C. Saumagne, (eds.), Tablettes Albertini (Paris 1952), pp.218, 233, 256.
26. C. Marini, (ed.), I Papiri Diplomatici (Rome 1805), pp.179, 183.
27. C. Courtois, etc., (eds.), p.193.
28. cf. F.M. Stenton, Anglo-Saxon England (2nd ed., 1947), pp.282-283.
29. BCS.81 (the Barking charter, Essex, to be dated 687. The bounds however were added about a century later. Brooks, op.cit., p.216. It is for this reason that it has been grouped under Column (b) in Table 1, and not Column (a)). 97, 148, 154, 187, 203, 213, 225, 227, 230, 261, 326, 339, 341, 348, 353, 370, 373, 380, 400, 426, 442, 451, 452, 467, 497, 507, 539, 562.
30. BCS.45.
31. BCS.148, 213.
32. BCS.451. see H.P.R. Finberg, West Country Historical Studies (1969), pp.11-28, and D. Whitelock, (ed.), op.cit., pp.522-524.
33. BCS.452 see M. Gelling, (op.cit), No.146, and Appendix, pp.184-187.
34. BCS.562.
35. BCS.34, 67, 82, 111, 121, 139, 147, 163, 164, 166, 182, 192, 193, 200, 209, 210, 214, 219, 223, 232, 236, 246, 253, 255, 257, 260, 282, 317, 327, 346, 349, 356, 357, 378, 392, 396, 410, 438, 455, 491, 496, 499, 502, 504/5, 506, 513, 518, 525, 526, 543, 544, 547, 551, 552, 581, 852, 855, 1331, together with S.119, on which see M. Gelling, ed., Early Charters of the Thames Valley (1979), No.203 and below, r.39.
36. see H.P.R. Finberg's account of the Hallow/Hawling charter (BCS.356) in his (ed.), Early Charters of the West Midlands (1961), pp.184-196.
37. BCS.203. S.59 does not mention bounds.
38. BCS.227. A. Campbell, op.cit., No.9.
39. BCS.34, 82, 166, 246, 327, 349, 356 378 (strictly an endorsement), 396, 502, 543, 551, 552, 581 and S.119, a document with Middle English boundaries which probably date from the time when the charter itself was copied out. see above r.35.
40. BCS.219, 392, 491, 525.
41. BCS.219.

42. BCS.392, and 491.
43. BCS.82, 392, 438, 491, 513.
44. see A.J. Robertson, Anglo-Saxon Charters
(2nd ed., 1956), pp.281-283.
45. D. Whitelock, (ed.), op.cit. pp.495-496,
and H.P.R. Finberg, West Country Historical Studies
(1969), pp.29-69.
46. BCS.200.
47. BCS.225.
48. B.410, see C.R. Hart, 'Some Dorset Charter
Boundaries', Proceedings of the Dorset Natural
History and Archaeological Society, 86 (1964-1965),
pp.158-163.
49. BCS.451.
50. BCS.452. see M. Gelling, (ed.), Early
Charters of the Thames Valley (1979), No.146.
51. BCS.499.
52. BCS.455.
53. BCS.426, 442, 467, 496 and 497.
54. BCS.506, and see Campbell, ed., op.cit.
No.25.
55. BCS.236.
56. BCS.190.
57. BCS.148, 227. BCS.497 grants half a tūn.
58. for a recent discussion see D. Hooke,
Anglo-Saxon Landscapes of the West Midlands: the
Charter Evidence (1981), pp.82-118.
59. BCS.77, 97, 183, 190, 202/3, 204, 209/210,
240, 246, 248, 350/351, 357, 492, 666.
60. see M. Gelling, Signposts to the Past
(1978), pp.67-74.
61. BCS.121. G.B. Grundy, 'The Saxon Charters
of Somerset', Proceedings of the Somersetshire Archaeological and Natural History Society, 77 (1931),
p.150.
62. BCS.164, and see G.B. Grundy, 'Saxon
Charters and Field Names of Gloucestershire',
Bristol and Gloucestershire Archaeological Society,
(1935-1936), p.9.
63. D. Whitelock, (ed.), English Historical
Documents, c.500-1042, (2nd ed. 1979), pp.375-376.
64. The very brief Latin bounds in such
charters as BCS.240, 296, 328 may well be in favour
of their authenticity, whilst the lengthy Latin ones
of S.267 of 794 would not be out of place in view of
the lengthy Latin ones of the time of Cynewulf. The
long Old English ones of BCS.102 are clearly very
much later than the ostensible date of the document,
701. It has even been suggested that the very brief
bounds of BCS.3 may well be a point in its favour.
(Brooks, 'Anglo-Saxon Charters', p.217).

Anglo-Saxon Charter Boundaries

65. see T.R. Thomson, 'The Early Bounds of
Wanborough and Little Hinton', Wiltshire Archaeological Magazine, 57 (1958-1960), pp.201-211, and M.
Gelling, 'Recent Work on Anglo-Saxon Charters',
Local Historian, 13 (1978), pp.209-216.
66. BCS.752, 802, 1225.
67. see H.S.A. Fox, 'Approaches to the Adoption
of the Midland System', in T.R. Rowley,(ed.), The
Origins of Open Field Agriculture (1981), pp.64-111.
68. M. Gelling, (ed.), 'The Place-names of
Berkshire', Part III, English Place-name Society, 51
(1976).
69. D. Hooke, Anglo-Saxon Landscapes of the
West Midlands: The Charter Evidence, British Archaeological Reports, British Series 95, (1981).
70. M. Reed, 'Buckinghamshire Anglo-Saxon
Charter Boundaries', in M. Gelling, (ed.), Early
Charters of the Thames Valley (1979), p.172.
71. P.H. Sawyer, (ed.), Anglo-Saxon Charters
II, Charters of Burton Abbey (1979), pp.36. n.
72. M. Gelling, (ed.), 'The Place-names of
Berkshire', p.675. Similarly, Tunweorth, the name
for a part of Kingsbury, in Middlesex, has also
disappeared. see J.E.B. Gover, A. Mawer and F.M.
Stenton, (eds.), 'The Place-names of Middlesex',
English Place-name Society, 18 (1942), p.219.
73. BCS,254, 380, and J.K. Wallenberg, Kentish
Place-Names (Uppsala 1931), pp.73-4, 156-158. The
land of bishop Leuthere, of blessed memory, which
lay on the south of an estate at Fontmell, in Dorset (BCS.107) is perhaps an example of another
personal name that failed to establish itself as
a place-name.
74. M. Gelling,(ed.), Early Charters of the
Thames Valley (1979), p.134, H.P.R. Finberg, (ed.),
The Early Charters of Wessex (1964), p.155, and H.
P.R. Finberg, (ed.), The Early Charters of the West
Midlands (1972), p.87.
75. M. Gelling, (ed.), Early Charters of the
Thames Valley (1979), No.148 and Appendix, pp.178-
181.
76. P.H. Sawyer, (ed.), Anglo-Saxon Charters
II, Charters of Burton Abbey (1979), No.26. Similarly, the trendelmere, wyllepole and draegmere of
the Yaxley, Hunts., boundary of 956 appear on eigh-
teenth century maps, but disappear with the draining of Whittlesey Mere in the nineteenth century.
C.R. Hart, (ed.), The Early Charters of Eastern
England (1966), p.164.
77. Lincoln Record Office, Barrow upon Humber
Tithe Award.

304

78. BCS.820. see A.R. Rumble, 'The Merstham (Surrey) Charter Bounds, A.D. 947', Journal of the English Place-name Society, 3 (1970-1971), pp.6-31.
79. D.W. Rollason, 'The Date of the Parish boundary of Minster in Thanet', Archaeologia Cantiana, 95 (1979), pp.7-17.
80. cf.the disagreement over the location of the estate at Stantun granted by Edgar in 968. C.R. Hart, in his (ed.), The Early Charters of Northern England and the North Midlands (1975), p.179, suggests Stanton in the Peak, P.H. Sawyer, in his (ed.), Anglo-Saxon Charters II, Charters of Burton Abbey (1979), No.23, suggests Stanton by Newhall.
81. e.g. G.B. Grundy, 'The Saxon Land Charters of Wiltshire', Archaeological Journal, 76 (1919), pp.143-301, and his (ed.), 'Saxon Oxfordshire', Oxfordshire Record Series, 15 (1933).
82. see e.g., A.E. Brown, T.R. Key and C. Orr, 'Some Anglo-Saxon Estates and their Boundaries in Southwest Northamptonshire', Northamptonshire Archaeology, 12 (1977), pp.155-176.
83. see T.R. Thomson, 'The Early Bounds of Wanborough and Little Hinton', Wiltshire Archaeological Magazine, 57 (1958-1960), pp.201-211, and H.P.R. Finberg, West Country Historical Studies (1969), p.68.
84. see A.E. Brown and T.R. Key, 'The Badby and Newnham (Northamptonshire) Charters, Journal of the English Place-name Society, 10 (1977-1978), pp.1-7, and D. Hooke, 'Anglo-Saxon Landscapes of the West Midlands', Journal of the English Place-name Society, 11 (1978-1979), p.3
85. M. Gelling, (ed.), 'Place-names of Berkshire', Part III, p.621.
86. see M. Reed, 'Buckinghamshire Anglo-Saxon Charter Boundaries', in M. Gelling, (ed.), Early Charters of the Thames Valley (1979), pp.168-187.
87. see, eg. H.P.R. Finberg, 'Anglo-Saxon England to 1042', in his (ed.), The Agrarian History of England and Wales I, ii (1972), pp.385-525.
88. see refs. 68 and 69.
89. see M. Reed, 'Buckinghamshire Anglo-Saxon Charter Boundaries', in M. Gelling, (ed.), Early Charters of the Thames Valley (1979, pp.178-181.
90. M. Gelling, (ed.), 'Place-names of Berkshire', Part III, p.675.
91. see G.R.C. Davis, Medieval Cartularies of Great Britain (1958), Nos. 434 and 435.
92. This is the suggested first elementin Dauntsey put forward in J.E.B. Gover, A. Mawer and

F.M. Stenton, (eds.), 'The Place-names of Wiltshire', English Place-name Society, 16 (1939), p.68.
93. G.B. Grundy, 'The Saxon Land Charters of Wiltshire', Archaeological Journal, 76, (1919), pp.168-169.
94. J.Y. Akerman, 'Some Account of the Possessions of the Abbey of Malmesbury in North Wiltshire', Archaeologia, 37 (1857), pp.257-315.
95. D. Hooke, Anglo-Saxon Landscapes of the West Midlands (1981), p.107.
96. but see BCS.948, 1036, 1048, 1285 and 1315.
97. A. Cameron, 'The Dictionary of Old English and the Computer', in S. Lusignan and J.S. North, (eds.), Computing in the Humanities (Waterloo, Ontario, 1977), pp.101-106.

NOTES ON CONTRIBUTORS

J.T. Coppock has been Ogilvie Professor of Geography at Edinburgh University since 1965. He became interested in the agricultural census in the course of preparing his Ph.D. thesis on land use changes in the Chilterns and has made extensive use of it, as well as contributing to a monograph in the Reviews of United Kingdom Statistical Sources.

  Dr. R.J.P. Kain is a Senior Lecturer in Geography at the University of Exeter. His principal teaching and research interests are in English agrarian history and the architectural and urban planning history of France. He has published books on Planning for Conservation (1981), and, with J.M. Hooke, Historical Change in the Physical Environment (1982). He is currently compiling an Atlas of Agriculture in England and Wales, circa 1840, and, with H.C. Prince, he is writing a handbook to the Tithe Surveys for Cambridge University Press.

  Dr. Mark Overton lectures in geography at the University of Newcastle upon Tyne. He has published a number of articles on probate inventories and is at present writing a book on agricultural change in early modern England.

  Dr. Marilyn Palmer is a Senior Lecturer in History at Loughborough University. She has written the introduction to industrial archaeology in the new edition of Pevsner's Buildings of Leicestershire and Rutland and has just edited a book on the industrial archaeology of the county, to be published by Leicester Museums. She is a council member of both the Association for Industrial Archaeology and the Historical Metallurgy Society.

  Dr. Michael Reed is Senior Lecturer in Library Studies at Loughborough University. His publications include The Buckinghamshire Landscape (1979), 'The Ipswich Probate Inventories, 1583-1631',

<u>Suffolk Records Society</u>, 22 (1981), and 'Pre-
Parliamentary Enclosure in the East Midlands',
<u>Landscape History</u> 3, (1981).

Dr. B.K. Roberts is Senior Lecturer in Geography
at Durham University. He has published <u>Rural Sett-</u>
<u>lement in Britain</u> (1977) in addition to a number of
periodical articles concerned with village morphology
and settlement patterns.

Dr. C.F. Slade is Reader in Archaeology and
head of that Department in the University of Reading.
He contributed the article on Reading to Volume 1 of
<u>The Atlas of Historic Towns</u>. He has edited the Pipe
Roll for 12 John, (<u>Pipe Roll Society</u>, New Series
26 (1951)) and was joint general editor and contri-
butor to 'A Medieval Miscellany for Doris Mary
Stenton', <u>Pipe Roll Society</u> New Series 36 (1962 for
1960). He has also published a number of excavation
reports, and is currently editing the Lyell and
Chatsworth cartularies of Abingdon Abbey.

Dr. Michael Turner lectures in economic and
social history at Hull University. In addition to
a number of articles he has published <u>English Par-</u>
<u>liamentary Enclosure</u> (1980), and edited the life's
work of the late W.E. Tate, <u>A Domesday of English</u>
<u>Enclosure Acts and Awards</u> (1978).

INDEX

310

mountains and heathland
21-22, 65

Nant-y-Moch, reservoir
Cardiganshire 99
National Coal Board 88
110, 122
National Library of
Wales 100, 102
National Register of
Archives 125, 144
Newatun (Newton Cap,
Co. Durham) 226, 230
Newbold, Yorks. East
Riding 150-1
Newcastle upon Tyne 82,
108
Newcomen, Thomas 89
Newington, Kent 64
Newspapers 120-121, 207
Newton Cap, Co. Durham
230
Newton, Cumberland 65
Newton Harcourt, Leics.
148
Norfolk 60, 76, 138-9,
152, 171, 174-5, 182,
185-6, 245, 263
Archdeaconry 175
Earls of 233, 238
Norhamshire (Northumber-
land) 234
Normanton on the Wolds,
Notts. 67
Northamptonshire 60,
132-3, 138-9, 149,
157, 160
Northman, earl 226
Northumberland 67, 77,
226, 234, 247-8, 250
Northumbria, earldom
of 234
Norwich
Archdeaconry 175
Consistory Court 170,
174-6
Nottingham 218
Nottinghamshire 57, 60,
77, 105, 107, 161,
173
Nuffield, Oxon. 32-3

Oakham, Rutland 107
Oakthorpe, Leics. 91
Odstock, Wilts. 263
Offa, King of Mercia
274-5, 285
Ogilby, John, carto-
grapher 107-8
Old Warden, cistercian
abbey, Beds. 225
Olney, Bucks. 132
open fields 107, 138
152-6, 225, 251-2,
280
orchards 11, 24, 62-3
Ordnance Survey 20, 31,
38, 89, 94-5, 99,
104, 107, 113-117,
121, 127, 142, 145,
148, 150, 216-17,
239, 246-7, 282
Osberhting lond, Kent
281
Osberht, thegn 281
Osmund, minister 273
Overseal, Leics. 92
Owen, Aneurin, assistant
tithe commissioner
58
Oxford 20
Oxfordshire 10, 27, 30,
32-4, 36, 39, 51,
132-3, 139-41, 145,
147, 153, 160-1, 175,
270, 281

Padbury, Bucks. 135
Page, R. 75
paintings as sources
126, 199-200
parishes
boundaries 30-1, 34,
36, 39, 142, 148,
151, 156 and see
chapter 8
rate books 9-10, 18
size 28-9, 239
Parliament 107
Parliamentary Enclosure
Acts 57, 133, 138-9
Awards 142, 150, 283
chronology of 138-

317

Weedon, Bucks. 31, 153,
   155
Wells, minster, Somerset
   273
Welsh Development
   Agency 99
Welsh Potosi Company 104
Wendover, Bucks. 135
Wessex 273
West Grinstead, Sussex
   60
West Stow, Suffolk 66
Westmorland 22, 58
   Earls of 234
Wharram Percy, Yorks.
   East Riding 240
Wheldrake, Yorks.
   East Riding 247
Whitchurch, Bucks.
   148
Whixley, Yorks. East
   Riding 241
Whorlton, Co. Durham
   229, 231
Wight, Isle of 270
Williams & Eyton, mining
   company 102
Wiltshire 60, 81, 150,
   261-3, 269-70, 273,
   279-80, 287
Winchendon, Lower and
   Upper, Bucks. 300
Winchester, bishiops
   of 233
Windle, Lancs. 77
windmills 105, 107, 117,
   128
Winsford, Somerset 58
Wistow, Leics. 148
Wittan le Wear, Co.
   Durham 230
Wolds, Yorks. East
   Riding 132, 150-3,
   159
Wolland, Dorset 273
Wood, John, cartographer
   117
Woodchester, Gloucs.
   272, 276
Woodhouse, Jonathan,
   engineer 92

Woodhouse, Mr., agent 93
woodland 38, 63, 65,
   73, 76, 135, 156,
   170, 277
Wolley, Thomas Smith,
   local tithe agent
   and assistant tithe
   commissioner 60,
   66-8, 77
Woolstone, Berks. 281,
   286
Worcester 276, 297
   bishop of 273
Worcestershire 73, 142,
   184, 269-71, 273-4,
   280, 285
Wotton Underwood, Bucks.
   269, 273
Wreake, river 108
Wrotham, Kent 285
Wuduntun (Wittan le
   Wear, Co. Durham)
   226, 230
Wudetune 280
Wulfric, thegn 281

York, Prerogative Court
   of 175
Yorkshire 65, 77, 119,
   263
   East Riding 36, 132,
   138, 143-4, 148,
   150-3, 157-8, 161,
   240-1
   North Riding 74, 138,
   229-30
   West Riding 66, 138,
   143